D1175011

Literature in context

RENAISSANCE VIEWS OF MAN

Literature in context series

General editor
DOUGLAS BROOKS-DAVIES

Jonathan Swift:
the contemporary background
CLIVE T PROBYN

In preparation

Renaissance Latin poetry
IAN MACFARLANE

Petrarch and Petrarchism: the English
and French traditions
STEPHEN MINTA

English Romantic Hellenism,
1700-1824
TIMOTHY WEBB

RENAISSANCE VIEWS OF MAN

Stevie Davies

*Literature
in context*

BARNES & NOBLE BOOKS . NEW YORK
(a division of Harper & Row Publishers, Inc.)

Published in the U.S.A. 1979 by
HARPER & ROW PUBLISHERS, INC.
BARNES & NOBLE IMPORT DIVISION

ISBN 0-06-491621-9

Computerised Phototypesetting
by G C Typeset Ltd., Bolton, Greater Manchester

Printed in Great Britain
by The Pitman Press, Bath

Contents

General editor's preface

One of the basic problems in reading literature is that of establishing a context for it. In the end the context of any work is infinite and unknowable. But if we approach the problem more simple-mindedly (and ignore questions posed by biography) we can say that a work's context is to a large extent definable by the ideas – theological, philosophical, political, and so on – current in the period in which it was written, and by the literary forms and genres that a period fosters and prefers. It is the ultimate aim of this series to try to help the student of English literature place works of all periods in their various contexts by providing volumes containing annotated selections of important background texts on the assumption that it is through contact with original texts only that true understanding may develop. Some of the volumes will be wide-ranging within a given period, containing a variety of texts (some in full, some extracts) illustrating dominant ideas and themes or forms; others will be more specialised, offering background material to the ideas and forms embodied in individual works of a particular author or concentrating on one or two thematic obsessions of a period. Although the emphasis is on English literature, much of the background material adduced will be of European origin. This will be presented in translation and, in appropriate cases (usually verse), the original will be printed with a translation on the facing page. The series should thus be of use to students pursuing comparative literature courses as well as interdisciplinary courses involving literature. In each volume there will be a substantial introduction, explanatory headnotes to the texts, and a bibliography of suggested further reading.

Douglas Brooks-Davies

Preface

Because this collection is designed to be of help most particularly to students of English literature, in order that they shall be able to make their own assessment of the subtle relationship which existed between ideas and art in the period, I offer here no attempt at rigorous definition of the chronological limits of the Renaissance, nor seek the exact point where the Renaissance ends and other movements like the Reformation begin. This volume covers a range of ideas emerging approximately during the years from about 1400 to 1650. I chose the earlier date not as celebrating any real birthday but as having a dual convenience in denoting the opening of the *Quattrocento,* the grand period of Renaissance visual art in Italy, and then as being a date late enough to avoid making any incursion into a time which it still comes naturally to most people to think of as predominantly 'medieval'. The latter date was chosen because the Renaissance, arriving late in Britain (with the Tudors) had its most clear and beautiful effects on English literature only in the latter part of the sixteenth century, and stayed on rather late here too, with John Milton, whose greatest humanistic writings were achieved in the middle of the seventeenth century, as its last important representative.

Definition is also left deliberately loose because the Renaissance, by its very nature an eclectic and various movement requiring to be felt as much as analysed, had an effect on Spenser, Shakespeare, Jonson, which was diffuse and contradictory, and because I think that the richness of such authors' works is actually dependent on the complexity of their sources as they blended together in the poets' minds. There is no such thing as Renaissance Man. There are only many ideals and prototypes, made in the image of Socrates or Aristotle, Alexander the Great, Christ, Cicero or Calvin, or (and this I think of as being in some ways the most significant archetype of humanity included in this book because the most neglected by those who try to define the genus, Man) woman.

In my commentary, I use the philosopher Hobbes as a kind of symbolic representation of the death of the Renaissance in England, not because I hold him personally responsible, but because, in a way which any student of literature will feel from the touch of his style and manner, his writing belongs to another world—and, read alongside the echoing, Ciceronian rhythms which make us recognise his contemporary, John Milton, as being to the quick a Renaissance humanist still, Hobbes with Bacon is so obviously on the verge of a tradition which will lead outside the scope of this book.

I have quoted primary sources rather than secondary sources throughout my notes, in order to keep my readings and interpretations as uncluttered and pristine as possible. There is, of course, a great wealth of Renaissance scholarship available to the student. A very select bibliography of suggested further reading is included at the end of the book, and I use one cue title in my text: Cassirer refers to *The Renaissance Philosophy of Man*, ed. E. Cassirer et al. (University of Chicago Press, Chicago, Ill., 1948). All references to Hobbes' *Leviathan* are to the Pelican Classics edition, ed. C. B. MacPherson (Harmondsworth, 1968).

Finally, I must add that the selection of which works should be included was very much a personal one, and, while I have tried to cover as many current notions of man's nature as possible, it has been important to me that the excerpts I have included should be either finely written or strange or entertaining enough to sustain the interest of the student of literature. I have hoped that the book might be a starting point for the student to explore in his own manner the complex relationship between ideas and literature in the Renaissance: there is much room for originality and a very personal approach in such exploration.

I should like to thank Leon Yudkin for his kind help on Hebrew and Arabic aspects of my work. Conversations with Gordon Neal have increased my understanding of Greek philosophy. My deep gratitude is due to Professor John Davies Jump, whose too early death I bitterly regret. I should like to thank Lesley Kissell for typing the manuscript so beautifully. My greatest debt of all, too absolute either to express or repay, is to Douglas Brooks-Davies.

FOR ROSALIE, LOVE
FOR EMILY, WELCOME

Introduction

1 CLASSICAL ORIGINS

In the beginning were Plato and Aristotle, and the Greek culture which formed them and which they in return helped to shape. There is a sense in which we may date the Renaissance in Europe as having its origins in the Athens of the fourth century before Christ, for what was 'reborn' all over Europe in the fourteenth to the sixteenth centuries after Christ was that spirit of man's enquiring self-consciousness which Greek civilisation nourished and imparted to its neighbours and successors. Europe was reborn most especially in the image of Plato. In his dialogues he celebrates and expresses a philosophy evolved by his dead mentor, Socrates, whom he so dearly loved that he mythologised him in the most artistic philosophical disquisitions ever written. It is worth beginning by sketching Plato's most important ideas. First of all, his metaphysics were transcendental in nature, based on the concept of 'two worlds', the invisible 'real' world of perfect Forms and the imperfect, merely material one, a poor copy of the original. This led him to a kind of mysticism in the pursuit of ideal Beauty (*The Symposium, Phaedrus*) and an ethic which, equating knowledge and virtue, preached passive resistance to violence, selfish obedience to Reason, other-worldliness and the active pursuit of the Good (*Apology, Gorgias*). His religion held in contempt the too human rabble of gods who inhabited the Greek Pantheon (*Republic, Euthyphro*) and substituted for them the One God of the *Timaeus*, whose creation of perfect harmony Plato tenderly and with the utmost quaintness describes, both in terms of cosmology and the harmony of the inner soul of man. In his *Phaedo* he argues the case for the soul's immortality and in the final section of the *Republic* declares a belief in reincarnation. But the main aim of the *Republic* is to apply his transcendentalism to the problems of politics. Here he invents a meritocracy, where philosophic 'Guardians', or a philosopher-king, enact the justice which they have learnt through absorbing themselves in the reality of the Good, in a revolutionised State which recognises the potential equality of the sexes and the value of selective breeding in a human community.

Yet such summaries as this, even allowing for their over-simplicity, cannot begin to do justice to the richness and intricacy of what Plato created, nor why he appealed to such incompatible people at such varying moments in history. Firstly, perhaps it is something to do with the personality of his writing. Where Aristotle propounds his *Ethics,* austere, formal, dreamless, Plato's dialogues are as much works of art as treatises. Aristotle is interested in the biology and physics of the material world for the sake of its own patterns and forms, and because as he says in the *Metaphysics* the most valuable kind of experience is to know things in their causes. But Plato is continually slipping right through the appearances that surround him to contemplate the pure forms which lie on the other side of matter. His quest is always urgently moral and spiritual, so extreme in its need to elude the physical that it presses onwards past the point where even pure mathematics cannot cope with experience, and myth begins. It is undertaken not in his own person but in that of his teacher Socrates, whom the State of Athens had executed in 399 B.C., for alleged impiety and corruption of the young, but whom Plato presents as the victim of an institution terrified at the extent to which other-worldliness might subvert a State. It is in his peacefulness that the figure of Socrates must have appeared to later generations of Christians as a true symbol and precursor of Christ. 'I would rather suffer wrong than do wrong', says Socrates to the Sophist in the *Gorgias* (469C). And when Socrates is dead, Phaedo grieves, 'we felt just as though we were losing a father and should be orphans for the rest of our lives' (*Phaedo*, 115). For great mystics like Saint Augustine, the death of Socrates blended its emotion with the Crucifixion; later, in the fifteenth century, Marsilio Ficino's introduction to his translation of the *Crito* extended the analogy, and Erasmus asked, 'Saint Socrates, pray for us'.[1] With the Renaissance, Christian Platonism became an important and very Romantic movement; all the known texts were translated into Latin, and the Platonic Academy established in Florence sent out waves of emotional commentary on the dialogues which reached nearly all parts of Europe.

Yet the possibility of a Christian assimilation does not fully explain Plato's appeal. For Socrates is much more complex than Christ. He is enigma, not paradox. People are his victims – Meno calls him a 'sting-ray' (80A), objecting to the way the dialectical method (essentially an act of intellectual aggression) numbs people of merely common sense into stupidity. He is polite and sophisticated, untender in a rather gentle way, makes courtly fun of everyone and egoistically depreciates himself. If his audience do not respond at regular intervals with cries of 'Absolutely right, Socrates', they are, in the nicest possible way, annihilated. So in Christian terms he is hardly the model man, though to most Renaissance thinkers he seemed to be. And the variety within his character is matched by the variety of his techniques. The abstractly reasoning Socrates of the *Republic* with his sanctimonious attacks on poetry is liable at any time to soar off himself into myth and poetry. Still enigmatic, since he does not always claim to believe in the myth himself (in the *Meno* (86B), having shown that we existed before conception, he covers himself, 'I shouldn't like to take my oath upon the whole story, but . . .'), there is always the feeling that Socrates–Plato finds, as the Renaissance found in him, his greatest fulfilment in the mind's ecstasies and their symbolic representation. Past the mystic numbers he learnt from the Pythagorean school, he was aware of unconscious intuitions only expressible through the enchantments of the stories and poetry which he elsewhere deplored.

Through these myths, Renaissance thinkers derived much of their feeling for man's intellectual and spiritual possibilities, and their view of the relationship of the human mind and body to the universe around it and the divine principle informing it. The myth or Er in the *Republic,* possibly Orphic in origin (that is, deriving from the mystery cult based on Orpheus' descent to the Underworld), prefiguring Virgil and Dante, is a vision of the harmonious cosmos perceived after death and between incarnations. In the same book there is the famous myth of the cave in which men stand facing a wall upon which a fire casts the shadows of images held behind them. This is the world, and our perception of it. The fire itself is only a feeble image of the sun, by whose light mortal men can perceive only the shadows of the images of shadows. Stumbling out into the Sun (the Good) we should be dazzled into blindness: the soul has to train itself intellectually in order to encounter this light. And in a similar image in the *Phaedo* (109–110), Plato imagines us as living beneath the sea, or as living in a hollow of the earth containing all its slime. The people on the purer earth 'see the sun and moon and stars *as they really are*'. Everywhere in Plato you find the same hunger for vision and light, and it is a very personal thing. It is hardly any wonder that the blind humanist Milton, two thousand years later, found himself in such affinity with Plato. The search was the same – to pass beyond the decaying beauty of earth to an intellectual light filling and satisfying the mind. This involved a dual view of man – a dim view of his present state (of blindness); an enjoyable confidence in man as he *might* become. Just as in the *Republic* Plato's dweller in the cave, meeting the true Sun, found himself 'dazzled with excess of light' (XXV, 232), so God's creatures in Milton's *Paradise Lost* thought him 'Dark with excessive bright' (III, 380). Platonic and Christian blend in Renaissance poetry and prose because each tradition preaches renunciation *and* beatitude. It was the ecstasy which caught the imaginations of the Florentine Platonists, giving them a concept of man who could by pure contemplation pierce with his spirit out of the imprisoning, undignified body.

Plato also gave to Western civilisation something equally or more important than this: a way of thinking of man, society and the cosmos in structural terms. The *Timaeus* lies somewhere between myth and primitive science. It contains a beautiful creation myth (capable of being conflated by medieval Christians with Genesis) and might be thought of as a kind of inspirational celebration of the idea of proportion. The perfectly spherical world repeats its perfection by the circular rhythms within the mind of the well-proportioned man (90D). The four elements (earth, air, fire and water) which constitute the universe are mirrored in the four humours of man, who has to harmonise them to maintain his health (82A–B). But man is also a tripartite being. Located in his head is Reason; in his heart sits the spirited element; in the 'lowest' place of all, his belly, lodges Appetite (69–73). To be fully human, you control the spirit by the reason and make it direct the appetites, and, as the *Republic* explains, the State should operate according to the same method as the individual – rulers, warriors and populace function in terms of a descending hierarchy (433–434). The larger context for these patterns is of course the notion which is mainly referred to as the Chain or Scale of Being, which, beginning with God and moving downward through spiritual creatures, man, animals and plants to the inanimate world, offered a vision of conservative order and a secure frame of reference to both medieval and Renaissance thinkers and poets.

If Plato was the natural son of Socrates, then Aristotle was Plato's son, but in this case a rebellious, iconoclastic heir who left the Platonic Academy in Athens to found his own Lyceum, and gradually left off referring to 'we [Platonists]' (*Metaphysics*, 990B), in order to distinguish between 'us' and 'them'. Aristotle was not as fashionable as Plato during the Renaissance, but we might perhaps regard him as having been an unpalatable necessity. He provided answers to many questions which Plato did not seem to think worth asking, and, starting from a much more scientific bias, thought hypothetical 'Forms' silly. On one occasion in the *Metaphysics* (A9) he was able to list an unsmiling total of twenty-three objections to the Ideal Forms. Abandoning such notions meant that he could put a higher value on the actual world than Plato did, so that he became the originator of most of the scientific 'knowledge' (of biology and physics) which the Middle Ages and Renaissance felt it reasonable to take on trust, till the earth changed places with the sun as centre of the universe (Copernicus and Galileo); his doctrine of circular motion[2] started elongating into ellipses (Kepler); Baconian experiment began substituting proofs for folklore in biology, and the world began to change radically in colour and dimension. It was, in its way, as frightening as Darwinian evolution was to a generation of Victorians, and as challenging to the customary view of man.

But the Renaissance reaction against Aristotle is not simply a matter of disproving his aged scientific dogmas. For in an age of discovery, Aristotle was too old and familiar. While only a small proportion of Plato's works had been available during the Middle Ages to European scholars and Greek was not well known, most of the corpus of Aristotle's works were not only accessible (in Latin translation) but obligatory. Education was Aristotelean and so was theology: the scholastic Aquinas had in his *Summa Theologica* rationalised Faith by applying Aristotle to St Paul so as to mould each to the shape of the other. The humanists struggled to get free from these misshapen images. It could be done by abuse, so from Petrarch right through to Hobbes, 'the Vain Philosophy of Aristotle' (*Leviathan,* IV.46.691) is rudely assaulted, an attack whose ferocity over such a period is an index of the sturdiness of the institution Aristotle had become. For some of the earlier humanists the attack is synonymous with an attack on Reason itself as a proud thing (Aristotle's *Ethics* celebrates pride); an inadequate thing (the *Metaphysics* calls the reasoning process divine) and, most importantly, a sour thing.[3] Anti-Aristotelean humanists all show distaste because of temperamental lack of affinity with a dry thinker whose God is not much more than a 'supreme intellect', unconcerned to grant immortality to the individual, and whose ethical system appears to be a horrible arithmetical table for calculating virtue. Petrarch protested in 1368 that Aristotle knew about as much about true Happiness 'as the night owl does of the sun, namely, its light and rays and not the sun itself' (*On his Own Ignorance,* Cassirer, 74–5). In this unconsciously Platonic simile, Petrarch embodies the characteristic humanist preference for love over reason, and symbolism over classification and syllogisms.

Yet the Renaissance tortures the student with its paradoxes, for, whilst Aristotle does undergo eclipse, he is always very much a presence throughout the period. Lacking in the symbolic emotiveness which Plato bequeathed to art and literature, he even more than Plato was able to offer a complex structural framework on which the individual could base his own visions. First of all, he extended Plato's Chain of Being. His biological researches proved to him that there was a principle of continuity in Nature, whereby each species contains and transcends its inferior, and all shades in a marvellous pattern into one whole. This interconnection is stressed in the *Metaphysics*. But perhaps the most influential work on Renaissance authors was his *Nicomachean Ethics,* for it was here that, proceeding from his belief that each entity is created for its own appropriate and definable end, Aristotle enquires into man's behaviour with a view to fulfilling the purpose for which he is constructed. Since Reason differentiates man from the animal species, man's aim for Aristotle must be to fulfil its promptings, which turn out, not surprisingly, to be virtuous action through the maintenance of proportion within the self. Such a notion is of course consistent with the Platonic view (although Aristotle disputed Socrates' favourite assertion that knowledge must bring virtue) but the way in which Aristotle works it out bears little resemblance to methods characteristic of Plato.

To a person approaching his work for the first time, Aristotle will perhaps seem to display a curious, and at times almost pathological, addiction to the number three. Everything in his world is threefold. In the *Politics* (1279A – 1279B) he discerns three possible political constitutions, and three deviations from these norms. In the *Nicomachean Ethics* (I) he shows that we have three souls, the rational, the appetitive and the vegetable, and that the second must be controlled by the first. Further, the way to virtue turns out to involve another division into three and the choice of 'the intermediate'. 'Virtue, then, is a state of character concerned with choice, lying in a mean ... between two vices, that which depends on excess and that which depends upon defect...' (1107A), deducible by 'right rule'. Aristotle toils through a catalogue of virtues pointing out where they lie with regard to their excess and defect. (Pride, for instance, is a mean between vanity and false humility.) It is an unlovely book, but essential to the structure of a good deal of the moral thinking of Renaissance artists. Spenser's epic could not have been written without it; the theory of the golden mean activates Book II of *The Faerie Queene*[4] and underlies the superficially anarchic surface of the plays of Ben Jonson.

However, it would be very wrong to suggest that Renaissance scholars and artists simply leapt the gap back to the Golden Age of Greek philosophy without taking any notice of what lay between. The works of Aristotle permeated medieval theology; dominated the Universities, and travelled to Arabia, where they formed the foundation of a very fruitful tradition of science and scholarship, of whom Averroës (A.D. 1129–1198) and Avicenna (A.D. 980–1036) were the chief protagonists. From Plato, a meandering and constantly dividing river of thoughts ran through history into Renaissance Europe and beyond. Cicero, writing in Italy during the first century B.C., in an age of deep anxiety and bewilderment about the human identity, introduced Plato systematically to Rome, adding nothing materially to the philosophy but his own voice and culture, and a little of the Stoic philosophy, but giving to literature something new in his enduring awareness of what constituted '*humanitas*', a concept which would endlessly recur in Renaissance thought. However, in the writings of the Neoplatonists and Christian Platonists, Plato's image became always stranger and more obscure. Disciples like Plotinus (*c.* A.D. 203–262) and Porphyry (A.D. 233–*c.* 301) begat disciples of disciples, and Commentators were themselves subsumed into a following generation's Commentaries. Christian Platonism, represented, for instance, by the fifth-century Dionysius the Areopagite, stressed the ecstatic elements of Plato, and, assimilating the One God of Plato's *Parmenides* to the Christian God, felt free to dissect Christian experience into Platonic categories undreamt of by the great Pagan himself and baffling to merely common sense. By the time Marsilio Ficino and Pico della Mirandola received the tradition in the fifteenth century, it had multiplied in all directions, and drawn into itself all kinds of other cultures and theologies, giving a perfect place for the random, learned and eclectic mind of fifteenth-century Florence to fulfil itself. The Florentine Platonists were interested in discovering and synthesising Ancient Religions, especially those which had in common elements of magic, rites of purification, esoteric doctrine and a myth of rebirth. So Ficino and Pico embellished Platonism with the mysteries of the ancient Hebrew Cabbalistic teachings, the *Chaldean Oracles* (attributed to the Persian Zoroaster), the Greek Orphic cult, even Islam. Plato's image was reborn strange and transformed in a world he would not have recognised.

2   HUMANISM

Between the palaver of medieval Aristotle-based theology and the complications of modern Baconian science, it was as if the process of European thought paused, to allow a new and very welcome simple-mindedness to emerge. Aristotle receding, Plato advancing, brought the foundation of the Florentine Platonic Academy of the fifteenth century, reawakening especially the sweet-natured, mythologising Plato of the *Symposium* on which Ficino with breathless enthusiasm commented volumes and sent them around

Europe where they bore fruit in the extreme, unearthly passion of Renaissance love poetry, both secular and religious.

But there was also a new kind of Aristoteleanism among some of the humanists. Pomponazzi in *On the Immortality of the Soul* (1516), celebrating the *mortality* of the soul and the possibility of harmonious diversity producing an optimistic social morality, does not dwell upon too subtle distinctions: 'I who feel am the same as I who think.' And in this finding of intellectual peace in the representation of individual experience itself, Pomponazzi adds to the eclectic jumble of differing views which makes the Renaissance at once so odd and so endearing, something that is characteristic of nearly everyone we can classify as humanist. This is a deep regard for what is meant by the verb 'to be' and especially 'I am'. Petrarch, Pico, Vives, Gelli, Bruno, all in their individual ways are caught by the light of history in the act of creating metaphors, symbolisms, myths, to represent the nature of individual being. But their method is not that which Erasmus laughed at in his *Praise of Folly* – the deduction of abstraction from abstraction till rarefied thoughts in chains fly out of the grasp of anyone in his right mind. The method may *look* traditional, as in Ficino's *Five Questions Concerning the Mind*, but really it is an act of the exploring imagination. The humanist is interested in everything because he wants to compare himself with it. Therefore the stars light his orations and disquisitions; the animals and plants are there too. Gelli's Ulysses spends his time in discussion with oysters and elephants to see if man's position is more desirable than theirs, and we are aware that, if the pain of intelligence distinguishes us from them, so does a singular combination of dignity and silliness. Ficino's Man, pathetically fallen out of the condition of Nature, still has superiority to the animal kingdom and can take comfort from having 'a kind of eye turned toward the intelligible light'. Animals, he seriously notes, are not generally credited with religious tendencies.[5] But all these non-human entities which fill the humanists' meditations are not there simply to differentiate man by fixing him on the middle rung of the Ladder of Being, to hang there for ever in mid-air between stars and stones. New, dangerous hopes began to dance round the humanist mind: Pico's *Oration* of 1486 showed man to be an incredible chameleon, tumbling through air, mimicking the planets or earth-bound as he chose. This image of the chameleon is a platitude of the new, risky view of the colossally free will. Gelli picks it up and admires it in the dedicatory epistle to his *Circe,* and he repeats too the fashionable identification of man's nature as 'Protean', charging up and down the Chain of Being at will. (See Introduction to Pico's *Oration,* pp.63–4, on the image of Proteus.) A similar egoistic and theatrical view is found in Vives' *Fable About Man* (1518) where man, through miming all creation, including 'that multiform Proteus' (Cassirer, 389), demonstrates an acting ability which causes the gods to deify him.

Such speculations might easily shift from the whimsical to the blasphemous, and the humanists themselves recognised and tried to temper the liberating, egocentric tendencies of their philosophy. Grave warnings issued from humanists like Lorenzo Valla. Looks of shock came from an increasingly hostile Catholic clergy. Such repercussions were on the whole averted by early deaths (Pico) or recantations before ecclesiastical tribunals (Gelli). But humanism inevitably led to a good deal of heresy, because its excitements touched not only the emotions but the mind. Its implications seemed to many to invite one to a freedom to be sceptical of old, worn-out cosmologies, obsolescent physics, and while Copernicus was able shyly to accept orthodox superstitions *and* the heliocentric theory at the same time, thereby ensuring his safety from persecution, a later generation could not. Giordano Bruno, having dispensed a remarkable number of heresies, scientific and otherwise, was chased all round Europe till the Inquisition had the satisfaction of burning him in Venice in 1591. He labelled the universe Copernican, Aristotle's cosmology incredible, dogma silly, truth pre-Socratic, fornication tolerable, God nature, and Oxford University (a profoundly Aristotelean institution) 'a constellation of the most pedantic, obstinate ignorance and presumption'.[6]

Galileo fixing his telescope on the moon and Kepler computing the deviations of Mars represent the scientific mind of the later Renaissance discovering how elderly Aristotle had become and how young their science was. Science, like humanism itself, here looks up, away from earth, and in that absorption with what is beyond common experience seems to be testing its individuality against space, custom and the past. And yet it would be wrong to suggest that humanism may simply be equated with novelty. For even the idea of the heliocentric universe was in reality venerable –

Aristarchus, born in 310 B.C., is a faint and lonely voice from Greek civilisation telling that the sun and not the earth is the centre of the universe. And neither the modern philosophers nor scientists felt secure in their freedom: it was too extreme. Kepler, in a Faustian mood, wrote his own epitaph:

> I measured the skies, now the shadows I measure.
> Skybound was the mind, earthbound the body rests.

Each thinker seems to look in two directions at once. The humanists take shelter in *Christian* humanism, or rather it is their natural home, from which they let loose the grand gestures of their speculations only to have them correct their course and end placidly in orthodox Catholocism. For instance, Pomponazzi, having proved that the soul is mortal, not immortal, escaped from the implications of this by including a passage at the end of his *On the Immortality of the Soul* to the effect that because the *im*mortality of the soul is an article of faith, it must necessarily be believed in (Cassirer, 377–81). Man swings dizzily between earth and sky, at the very mean of creation for Pomponazzi, dignified but dying, yet there remains for him the old, tried route to salvation through a faith which confounds all his most sensible conclusions. Reason and faith fight each other in many humanist works, and while reason convinces, faith wins. Pomponazzi's blasphemous denunciation of fictions like hell and possession by demons as explicable by natural causes such as politics, black bile or insanity, prefigure Marlowe's Faustus with his sophisticated contempt for the authority of Christian orthodoxy: 'I thinke Hel's a fable'. But in Pomponazzi's tract faith admits the truth of fables in accordance with a supernatural view of things; and Mephistopheles replies to Faustus' taunt with reasonless simplicity: 'I, thinke so still, till experience change thy mind' (II.i).

Yet it was natural that with time the kind of naturalistic thinking which informs *On the Immortality of the Soul* should ultimately lead past the fear of the dark engendered by the Church and embodied in *Dr Faustus,* and into a new kind of almost wholly unsuperstitious consciousness. Hobbes is of this generation. He regarded possession by spirits as a primitive fantasy (*Leviathan,* IV.45); Satan as a metaphor, not a person (IV.45.662), and (in a

11

pleasant mood not habitual to him) the idea of eternal damnation as unkind, and consequently unlikely in a good God (IV.44.646). Authority and superstition do not at this stage in the growth of philosophy have the old power to terrify, so that where Pomponazzi was forced into his graceful capitulation to the Church, Hobbes remains calm. With perfect equanimity he worked his way through hundreds of tedious pages of Biblical exegesis, using Reason on Scripture to maintain his purely metaphorical interpretation of the forces of good and evil. Where the humanists looked back, Hobbes did not, and while his independence of the past is a positive gain in purely scientific terms, it is a diminution emotionally.

For the humanists welcomed and embraced all available mythologies into their vision, feeling that there could be no absolute monopoly of the truth about man's nature and place in the universe. As a result, Proteus, Circe, Prometheus give their Christianity colour and passion. Bruno, in *The Expulsion of the Triumphant Beast,* looked back as far as ancient Egypt in order to retrieve for the modern imagination its pantheistic beast-gods. His God is 'the nature of Nature . . . the soul of the Soul of the world', and he asks that we link all beauty emblematically together in order to achieve contact with this informing principle. Bruno enchants himself and his reader with symbolisms drawn from many sources: 'Think thus, of the Sun in the Crocus, in the narcissus, in the heliotrope, in the rooster, in the Lion . . . one ascends to Divinity through Nature.'[7] Faith here asks to be expressed in a moving-out of the mind into perception through patterns of likeness, to reach a final Platonic *ekstasis*. But it was not just the heretics like Bruno who sought to engage the heart through myth and mystery, pagan and Christian. Humanism, tolerating many kinds of truth, passed the pagan myths round like wine, and achieved for them Christian force and respectability by providing allegorical interpretations.

To illustrate this we need only compare two treatments of the same myth – the Prometheus of Marsilio Ficino's *Five Questions* of 1450 and the Prometheus of Hobbes' *Leviathan* (1651). The humanist Ficino *experiences* the myth at the same time as he explicates it. He is speaking of the great sorrow endured by the immortal soul tragically linked (for it is itself outside nature) to the mortal body. Pallas (God) gave the heavenly fire of reason to

Prometheus (man), but on the highest mountain of all (contemplation) Prometheus found himself hanging to be gnawed by vultures (representing the famishing human spirit of enquiry and curiosity) and he cannot be made whole until he returns to the source of light itself (God) in death (Cassirer, 208). Ficino's regret at being a merely corporeal being, allied with his sense of man's frustrated energy painfully searching upwards towards perfection, finds an emotional and natural expression in his Christian—Platonist interpretation of the myth. But, turning to Hobbes, to whom human beings are only at the best of times machines, and inclined to be miserable, Prometheus has become a rather small, thin and thoroughly ordinary man. The cosmic proportions of the myth (along with the humanist dream) have gone, and Prometheus is, like most of us, 'the prudent man'; the vultures are his fear of the future and their nightly disappearance is the escape into sleep:

For as *Prometheus,* (which interpreted, is, *The prudent man*) was bound to the hill *Caucasus,* a place of large prospect, where, an Eagle feeding on his liver, devoured in the day, as much as was repayred in the night: So that man, which looks too far before him, in the care of future time, hath his heart all the day long, gnawed on by feare of death, poverty, or other calamity; and has no repose, nor pause of his anxiety, but in sleep. (I.12.169)

Prometheus here is an *exemplum,* not a symbol. Hobbes, with that fascinating apparatus for systematically draining myth of its passion which he applies to all phenomena including Christianity, has reduced ideas by discarding their emotiveness, and with Bacon helped found the area of discourse which we recognise as truly modern philosophy. But with that innovation, man as the humanists had pictured him is dying.

3 FREEDOM AND DETERMINISM

On the ceiling of the Sistine Chapel in Rome, Michelangelo's Adam is seen at the moment of his creation, an image so mighty and dignified that he seems to be made very exactly in the image of the fathering God who contemplates him. In St Peter's his *Pietà* treats, of course, the conventional theme of the mother of God with the corpse of her Son: but the observer experiences a slight shock in looking at her face, for it is younger than her Son's and seems rather to belong to the Virgin we would expect in a Madonna and Child – serene, beyond pain and, for all its tenderness, remote. Incarnation and crucifixion, past and present, become identical, reminding the person who watches of the Gospel's enormous optimism. Mary is an image of Christian transcendence of mortal agonies, and yet, looking from her face to the body of Christ, its lines flowing across and into the drapery of her gown, there is also a contrary feeling, for while Christ is here very beautiful, he is at the same time very dead. In Michelangelo, God's humanity is vivid, while conversely man is divine, or at least potentially so. And to say this of Michelangelo is not to describe an eccentricity but to define a characteristic of much of the art of the High Renaissance in Italy (c.1400–1550). Botticelli, Raphael, Leonardo and Titian embody aspects of humanism, and especially its Platonist tendency, not only in their insistence on classical proportion, perspective and anatomical reality, but also in their ability to present in visionary form ideal states of being. The heroic postures and physiques of their sculptures, modelled often on the public statuary of ancient Rome, are tempered by inwardness, a new God-reflecting intelligence and, most importantly, the human power to choose. Their art in many cases seems to incarnate a state of freedom for the soul, and a Christianity which, far from inhibiting the ego, liberates it. The concept of the temperamental genius began to be current in Italy: the artist was a creator whose inspiration was, in Leonardo da Vinci's words, a divine power, for 'In Art we may be said to be grandsons unto God'.[8]

But it would be dangerous to confuse Italy with the world, or to suggest that the humanist scholarship which it generated throughout Europe in all cases acted to multiply the same images, or that such images were necessarily successful in capturing European minds. It is worth remembering that the patron who caused Michelangelo to produce many of his humanist masterpieces was Pope Julius II, daemonic, warlike, and belonging to a tainted and worldly Catholicism, a man rather resembling Tamburlaine than St Peter, and of whom his own protégé Michelangelo could write:

> Heaven, it appears, itself is made impure
> When worldliness has power. I live to take
> Fruit from a tree too dry to bear or break.[9]

If such a man was a repository of the sublimely energetic free will, there were nations in northern Europe who concluded that free will was something that could be dispensed with.

In the early sixteenth century, the Protestant Reformation began in Germany to annihilate the image of human nobility, pride in learning and the expansion of individual possibilities, and to replace it with an alternative model of man, based on the doctrine of St Paul and St Augustine. This model was of a low, ignorant being, of insect status and insect morality, whose function was not to choose but to be chosen. The Lutheran and Calvinist imagination was possessed not by Michelangelesque figures of towering dignity but rather by a Gothic grotesque in whom the human structure of flesh and muscle has something intrinsically hideous about it. Consciousness of his own sin blackened the heart of the Austin friar Luther, until he became aware through prolonged meditation on the text 'the just shall live by faith' (Romans, 1: 17) that there may be a certainty of salvation, even though we are of ourselves so low, not through our own actions but through the undeserved grace of God. He also saw and was disgusted by the unspiritual nature of the Catholic Church, whose Popes fought bankruptcy by selling pardons, producing mechanical miracles and condoning the habitual breaking of all three vows by the priesthood. The day on which Luther nailed his 'Ninety-five theses on Indulgences' to the door of the castle church of Wittenberg in October 1517 has become for Protestants a great symbolic day of beginning. It was also the source of Europe's fracture, not only into old Romanism and new Protestantism, but also within Protestantism itself, twisting and breaking into more sects within the next two hundred years than it is possible to enumerate — there were, for instance, the austere, disciplinarian Calvinists; communistic Hutterites; pacific Quakers; anti-social Anabaptists; anti-Trinitarian Socinians, and the high and mighty Anglicans. To mention these examples of conflicting sects is at once to suggest the intensity of the individualism which characterises Protestantism, for if you claim the right to protest against the orthodox, you isolate yourself, and may generate a new kind of orthodoxy against which other sceptical persons may feel called upon to protest in their turn. The rise of the vernacular Bible, opening God's arcane mysteries to all the literate, combined with Protestant emphasis on Scripture as the ultimate criterion of truth, may also be interpreted as contributing to a new individualism and freedom from the Church's pontifications.

And yet, especially at first, Protestant thought did not appear to be tending in the direction of a greater libertarianism. Martin Luther had a very great heart but he saw his schism as a movement towards greater control by God and away from an institution which was libertine and impure. Calvin in Geneva went even further. A deeply unlovable man, he reformed the Swiss Church into groups of small tyrannies, where beady-eyed consistories of elders and pastors scrutinised each aspect of their congregations' lives, cultivated the uncharitable doctrine that Christ died only for a few, the 'elect', and encouraged the idea of predestination, with the duty of the soul's unqualified surrender of its depraved will to God. It became suspect to sing or dance, and, with the suppression of the ego, personality itself seemed threatened. This, of course, is the point where humanism and Protestantism cannot meet, for where humanism places great value on the liberal arts and especially the classics, on moderate eclecticism and tolerance based on respect for man's possibilities, the zealous reformer is bound to feel that such idealism has elements both of the unregenerate pagan and the Faustian.

This, in simple form, represents a conflict between what was new in philosophy and what was new in theology. But there are, of course, areas where Renaissance and Reformation blend, the same spirit informing each. Philistinism was an undeniable consequence of Protestant zealotry, yet it does not define Protestantism: Luther himself had had humanist aspirations, loved music and in youth assumed the humanist name of 'Eleutherius', while his milder disciple, the gentle Melanchthon (also a Greek coinage) remained when all was said and done a person who revered knowledge.[10] But more importantly, in essence many northern humanists (whose learning was in general more devotional in application than that of the Italians) sought similar ends to those of the Lutherans. Sixteenth-century people said: 'Erasmus laid the egg that Luther hatched', so frequently that it became an aphorism, and Erasmus was both a Catholic and a humanist scholar of international reputation. He had the gift of laughter, and in an exquisitely turned Latin prose ridiculed Catholic obscurantism, the deviation of the Church from an original simplicity, and fraud and vice amongst a priesthood which had come to be the scorn of every village. He expressed this view in many, many thousands of pages, of which the English people have most loved his *Praise of Folly* (1511), a book which deeply influenced later Renaissance satire and drama, and was written for his friend Sir Thomas More. Partly this is social satire: contemporary man is a silly or a wicked fool, and each profession has perfected its own particular kind of silliness, especially the ecclesiastics. But the book rises to a nobler idealism, connected with the archetype of the 'wise fool', the nature and place of Christ-like people on a worldly planet. Nearly one hundred years later, towards the end of *King Lear,* Shakespeare has Lear lament, 'And my poor fool is hang'd' (V.iii). We do not know if he means his clown, whose cap and bells are the index of his function as the reminder to human beings that their status in the universe is little higher than that of a joke, or whether he means the greatest fool of them all, Cordelia, the image of a perfection too simple for long survival in mortal form. Both meanings are Erasmian, and the confusion is even more so.[11] Erasmus' humanism, witty and confident in its attack on pretension, allows man the freedom to choose and perhaps approach, the most difficult kinds of goodness.

It is easy to see how he and Luther could in some things have been so close, and in others worlds apart. Erasmus applauded when Luther began attacking Papal abuses of power, dogma and money; he went quiet when Luther moved into the phase of rejecting the Papacy itself, and ended by attacking Luther himself as, with deepening unease, he saw the effects of the Lutheran movement as enacting, not a radical reform of the existing Church, but a revolution directed against it, with a ferocity that was not merely verbal. Theologically, Erasmus was most offended at the elements of determinism within Protestantism, and its insistence on man's abject, fallen nature; emotionally, he reacted against its lack of moderation. The debate on the freedom of the will printed here between Luther and Erasmus is intended as representative of the quarrel between humanist and Protestant, which was not outgrown for 150 years. In Renaissance English literature both tendencies –

the emphasis on human degeneracy, helpless of itself and, without grace, damnable; and delight in the variety and specialness of the human mind – are everywhere present, often running counter to one another within the same work of art and producing the excitement of an unresolved tension. In Marlowe's *Dr Faustus,* humanist aspirations are crushed within a morality play framework by a God for whom man's desire for widening knowledge is evidence of his depravity, yet the humanist element of the play (Faustus' aspiration) demands sympathy; in Shakespeare's *Hamlet* each contradictory view is expressed without either choice or synthesis being attempted.

What a piece of work is man! How noble in reason! how infinite in faculty! in form, in moving, how express and admirable! in action how like an angel! In apprehension how like a god! the beauty of the world! the paragon of animals! And yet, to me, what is this quintessence of dust? (II.ii)

Only in Milton's *Paradise Lost,* with the Renaissance at every moment trembling on the edge of the past, could an epic synthesis finally be reached by a poet in whom fanatical Protestantism and temperate humanism existed in equal balance.

4   MAN AND THE STATE

Most of the Renaissance thinkers I have spoken of so far spent their main energies philosophising with a view to exploring the nature of the human soul. Such freedoms as they found for it could not remain confined to the purely theoretical: it was natural that they should spill over into political speculation, in order to declare themselves in practice by stamping their image on the structure of the State.

But many factors besides that of the search for political truth enter here and, in thinking of man's place in society, we remember that even the authors of Utopias like More, advisers to politicians like Machiavelli, and revolutionary theoreticians such as John Milton, belonged to particular nations to whose history they were responding with the allegiances which their personalities combined with the particular circumstances seemed to demand. It cannot be forgotten, for instance, that Niccolò Machiavelli (1469–1527) was an estranged Florentine in a period when Florence was bleeding under the Medicis. Though he was 'Old Nick' to the English, he wrote according to the perspective offered by the kind of world to which he belonged. In the same way, Hooker's patient *Laws of Ecclesiastical Polity* (1593), with his important elucidation of the application of 'natural law' and 'right reason' to society, ought to be read in the light of our knowledge that he was driving the mighty ship of Anglicanism and the English establishment through the narrowest possible straits, with different kinds of subversion (revolutionary Catholicism and revolutionary Puritanism) on either side. The political writings of the period especially require a particular measure of forgiveness from the reader of another age – Machiavelli's cynicism, Hooker's conservatism, are equally the products of anxiety in an endlessly metamorphosing world.

It is because of this changefulness that truly representative political writings are hard to find: in a Europe where religious wars stretched from end to end for two centuries, the political philosopher nourished on humanism might easily come to any number of conclusions. But certain patterns can be made out, not only patterns of left and right, Republican and Royalist, but also ties with the past (or lack of them) which do not necessarily correspond with modern views of 'left' and 'right'. Mainly, as one would expect, traditional views and not their absence predominate, for more than anything political analysis, and the civil laws and constitutions which are proposed on the basis of such analysis, seem to require a solid foundation of precedent and authoritative experience to secure them. Even revolutionary social thinkers like Machiavelli seemed to travel forward with their eyes cast resolutely back into the past. And again, Plato and Aristotle were the key authors of antiquity, providing authority for the timid and fathers for the disinherited; and, of all their writings, the *Republic* and the *Politics* are the most influential. But just as definitive in establishing precedents for political systems was that huge record of kings, patriarchs, judges, tyrants and even revolutionaries provided by the Old and New Testaments, regarded by Christian theorists as containing not only divine law applicable to individuals but also a body of civil laws sanctioned by God, which the patient enquirer had to sift in order to discover the correct social plan.

Milton's revolutionary republican tracts, *The Tenure of Kings and Magistrates, Eikonoklastes* and *A Defence of the People of England*, justifying the execution of Charles I, are clotted with discussions of King David's activities, and the political implications of Pauline doctrine, with the conclusions to be drawn as regards the present situation. But so is Hobbes' Royalist *Leviathan*. The identity of method used by these two late Renaissance thinkers reminds one that Biblical exegesis was not just something invented by Puritans to justify the ways of Parliaments, but a common procedure implying a certain common view of man. Much more of *Leviathan* is actually devoted to discussions of King Ahab and the Book of Kings in this connection than to logical reasoning in favour of absolute monarchy. So although these two massive figures, Puritan and Royalist, stand in baleful confrontation of one another, each recognises that the eye of God which never closes is equally observing both of them. Man exists, argues and especially rules only under the Kingship of Christ. I know of no other Renaissance thinker who would have thought fit to disagree. Machiavelli in *The Prince* (1513) found it convenient to omit discussion of Christ's Kingship, and in his *Discourses* deplored the feeble and effeminate Christian ethic by comparison with Roman vigour, but even he, having a mind saturated with Biblical stories, introduced as a matter of course analogies between the state of contemporary Italy and the vicissitudes of the ancient Hebrews in captivity.[12]

In this fashion, Renaissance political thought did not question that man could only establish a just and viable commonwealth under God and in obedience to him. Allied with this, it is worth emphasising the fact that for all its flights of imagination humanist individualism did not really tend toward a radiantly optimistic attitude to the human race *as a whole*. Most Renaissance thinkers tended to take a dim view of most men, and all women. Great wariness is to be exercised in interpreting what such a writer means when he extols 'man' or 'the nation' or 'the commonwealth'. He may be talking of an oligarchy, plutocracy or aristocracy under the denomination of 'the nation', and his statements will scarcely ever be as inclusive as they appear. We may trace a theory of true democracy only to certain rare spirits who appear late in European history. I am thinking of Huguenots such as the anonymous author of the sixteenth-century *Defence of Liberty against Tyrants*, and revolutionary thinkers like the Levellers Walwyn, Lilburne, and the sweet-natured 'Digger' Winstanley – and even here it was scarcely humanism which produced the new compassionate view of who comprises 'the nation', for all that Athens had handed down its democratic ideology and Plato his meritocracy. For humanism was on the whole aristocratic, not allowing its individualism to pass in practice beyond academies of remarkable individuals. The seventeenth-century English Leveller movement was based not on humanism but on Puritanism and common sense. Lilburne handed to every honest and rational man the rights appertaining to the individual; Winstanley led his little group of sturdy Diggers to St George's Hill to work the land on communistic principles not because either of them was a bookworm feeding on the heritage of Greek liberalising ethics and oratory but because they were English Puritans, burning with outrage against what the old economic and governing regime had done to ordinary people. Their ideas on the worth of the ordinary human being were founded on Puritan revolutionary ethics and, looking back only so far as a folk-memory of lost Anglo-Saxon freedoms, looked forward to the building of a new Paradise on earth. These were the real believers in the natural dignity of man, who counted each man as neither more nor less than one, and in their researches into natural and civil law, their attempts at establishing Utopia in England, they were the true originators of the trinity of modern political virtues, liberty, equality and fraternity.[13]

Therefore, when humanists wrote approvingly of man's infinite possibilities with a view to constructing a perfect society, they did not necessarily mean that *every*one was equally perfectible. Athenian democracy itself, as any scholar knew, had established itself on a foundation of slave-labour, and the slave class was universally regarded as sub-human, defined by Aristotle in the *Politics* as the 'natural' property of its superiors, bearing a relationship to them analogous to that which the body bears the soul (1255A–1255B). One step above slaves were women, ruled by men as a statesman his subjects, and then the class of mechanics and artisans, too menial to be counted as citizens (1278A). All these classes were habitually seen by Athenians as rightly unfranchised and ineligible for public office, not to be counted as equals, because 'the naughtiness of men is a cup that can never be filled' (1267B), a sentiment which accorded conveniently with the assumptions of aristocratic Christians born two thousand years later. Humanists and scholars therefore inherited a gradated class system from antiquity, its rules enshrined in Aristotle and not really disturbed by the novelties dreamed up by Plato for his *Republic*, for even Plato relied on a threefold system of Guardians, Warriors and Populace for his ideal State, a benevolent despotism in which the excellent intelligentsia were to direct the ignorant for their own good. Again, the soul of society 'naturally' rules the body. And so Milton's seventeenth-century enthusiasm for killing kings may be balanced by a contempt for the people hallowed by antiquity; his 'nation' consisted only of the wise, who ought to be wary of 'an inconstant, irrational, and Image-doting rabble . . . a credulous and hapless herd, begotten to servility'.[14] The majority of men according to this view are not much more than overgrown animals.

In this Platonic and Aristotelean equation of the populace with the body and the rulers with the soul I have touched upon one of the most important of the images of society which the Renaissance had received from antiquity – the body politic. Man, the microcosm, mirrors in little but exactly the structure of the universe as a whole, and that intermediate organism, the State, ought also to be constructed in this image. This notion of order is, at its most primitive, quaint and easy. There is *one* sun in the sky; there is *one* head on the human body; the State would therefore have only *one* 'head' or ruler. As the head should govern the body's appetites, so the ruler should govern the restless, greedy populace, co-ordinating all the members and organs of the 'body' so as to create an orderly, integrated and 'natural' entity. This myth, basically a conservative one, was fashionable in England under the Tudors, and is the ethical basis of (for instance) all Shakespeare's history plays, Roman plays and tragedies.[15]

Such a myth could work to expand the image of the king to almost godlike proportions, for a relegation of the status of the populace to that of the hands and feet of the body politic may involve a corresponding access of power and glory to the 'soul', the sovereign. The individualism which we have defined as a primary element in the European reawakening becomes in this case attached to the single figure of the nearly absolute monarch. Yet this need not necessarily imply a servility on the part of the admiring subjects: a beneficent and politic sovereign, in exploiting a kind of quasi-divinity, might confer on the nation itself a value and glamour of which the monarchy could be seen as the embodiment. This is what happened in Elizabethan England, where a happy coincidence of the birth of a long-lived 'prince' who was herself a humanist scholar (educated under Ascham in the Ancients and humane studies) with an expanding country longing for peace, made possible an emotional new idealism about the monarchy. The Renaissance came with a kind of fortunate belatedness to England, for its coincidence with the rise of the Tudor family was a deeply fruitful marriage. Elizabeth I crafted and fostered a mystique around her person, offering to her contemporaries an image beyond the merely life-size, magical because its begetter was 'only' a woman, and a kind of allegory of perfection in the ordering of the State. Her speeches are distinctly humanist in their temper and eloquence: they bear the imprint of the Ciceronian oration (she had read almost all his works) and their flavour is directly comparable with the kind of enthusiasm about man's dignity which inspired Pico's *Oration*. In the soaring periods of her speech to the troops at Tilbury before the Armada in 1588, nationalism and humanist idealism take fire from one another:

Let tyrants fear! I have always so behaved myself that under God I have placed my chief strength and safeguard in the loyal hearts and good will of my subjects. And therefore I am come amongst you, as you see, at this time, not for my recreation and disport; but being resolved in the midst of the heart of the battle to live or die amongst you all; to lay down for my God and for my people my honour and my blood even in the dust.[16]

To a generation of English poets she was the 'sun' of her world, 'Astraea' or Justice lately returned to earth after long absence, 'Gloriana', a golden virgin being who had given to order in the State the attribute of joy.[17]

As long as such a myth could be sustained (and in reality Elizabeth I was often as Machiavellian as the next man) the old order in the body politic could still be celebrated as fruitful and dynamic. Her successors, James I and Charles I, having her individualism without her grace, and living in a world of growing capitalism, religious faction and class change to which they seemed able to respond only by waving around their prerogatives in a challenging fashion, tried to be sun-kings with a deliberateness both sad and absurd. The Renaissance was over, and the last real representative of Renaissance humanism in England, John Milton, was to regard kings in *Eikonoklastes* as the enemies of order and proportion in the State, and 'a peaceful Reformation [as] our true Sun light, and not he [Charles I], though he would be tak'n for our sun itself' *(Complete Prose Works,* III, 455). Though Royalists continued to idolise the 'royal Martyr', the events of 1649 demonstrated that the kingship was in the end as perishable as the head of a man axed abruptly from his shoulders.

5   WOMAN

This half of the human race was not in general considered very highly by the Renaissance. Most authors had always thought of her as, at her best, useful rather than edifying. According to that faculty which men arrogated to themselves and quaintly defined as 'Reason', it followed that woman's inferior biology dictated a corresponding limitation as a human being. The small size of her skull showed that not much in the way of mind could be expected of her; her adaptation to child-bearing demonstrated that this was the specific reason for her creation, and the Greek belief (to be found, for example, in Plato's *Timaeus,* 91D) that woman contributed nothing to the formation of the child except to act as temporary receptacle for it, was still in the mid nineteenth century accepted as scientific; her lesser stature and muscle-power, unfitting for the noble arts (like war) justified paternalism and made it sensible to view her as a species of property — here Aristotle's *Politics* provided authority (1264B); and finally the beauty of her face and the completeness of her body, combined with perturbed male consciousness of desire for her and his sense of his own lumbering inadequacy by comparison, issued in the nearly universal belief that there must be something wrong with her. The Old Testament myth of Eve's responsibility for the Fall of Man allowed modern Protestants, as it had medieval Catholics fearful of their own sensuality and needing somewhere to deposit their guilt at being so far fallen, to see in woman something Satanic, without the existence of whom it was possible to imagine that man might still be walking with God in the cool of the evening, in Eden. Renaissance Europe had epidemics of witch-hunts and burnings; paintings and engravings still often showed illustrations of the temptation of Eve in which the Serpent appears (to the confusion of the archetypal symbolic meaning of the myth) with a leering, female face.

And yet an opposite belief also prevailed during this period, and was one of the most important features of both the Renaissance humanist movement and the Catholic Counter-Reformation. In humanism, the most obvious emergence of an idealising vision of woman as representing not the lowest but the very highest reaches of the human spirit comes in Italian art of the fifteenth century. It is easy to see how revival of Greek and Latin culture could have brought an awakening of the value of the feminine, for whereas in the Jewish and Christian religions a thunderously male God dominates, and qualities which are traditionally seen as feminine (charity, peacefulness, the courage of endurance and not resistance) are centred in Christ, the Son, the Greek and Roman deity was split off into an interesting multitude of divinities, both male and female. The female gods are often as powerful as the male in their intervention in human affairs, and the qualities they symbolise have dignity and value: Venus is love, Diana chastity, Minerva wisdom, Astraea justice and Juno, the Queen of Heaven, is marriage. Fifteenth-century Christian humanists, without feeling any urge or temptation to regard these figments of the classical imagination as real, nevertheless found them compelling, and conflated them with the only significant feminine element in Christian mythology, the Virgin Mary, who, sharing the attributes of chastity, love, justice, wisdom and queenliness, was seen as having been prefigured in these goddesses, who hinted at her greater truth and were in due time transcended in her.

Perhaps ordinary people had always felt a greater natural affinity with Mary than with her mightier Son, for her humanity as *Madonna* and *Mater dolorosa* made her more immediately acceptable than the Godhead and she might intercede with the Intercessor on your behalf. In the Renaissance she became elevated (soaring above the human race in innumerable portrayals of the Assumption into areas of blinding light) so as to symbolise the human soul itself, in its wisdom and harmony with the Creator. Again, there is nothing new here, except the emphasis. In Plato's

Symposium, one of the most dearly loved of his works during the Renaissance, Socrates explains that mystical apprehension of the nature of love is given him not by his own perspicacity but by someone far above him, Diotima (201D). Diotima seems to be the soul itself in a state of knowledge, the *anima* which has traditionally been regarded as feminine in nature. Two thousand years later, following this tradition, Giordano Bruno introduces as the source of all the knowledge available to human beings in his dialogue, *The Expulsion of the Triumphant Beast,* Sophia, the personification of wisdom, and feminine.

A radical, nearly insoluble split begins to emerge here, between what woman is felt to be in the ordinary world (stupid), and what it is felt she symbolically represents in the ideal, and Platonically more real, world (intelligence itself). In this latter vision, her very flesh, naked, becomes the substance of the soul, so that in Titian's *Sacred and Profane Love,* where a clothed and a naked figure confront one another, it is the nude Venus who represents Christian charity. And in Botticelli's *Primavera* of 1477 the Three Graces and Flora, and in his *Birth of Venus* and *Venus and Mars* Venus herself, all apparently including studies of the same model, share a beauty which is both of form and of an expressiveness much more elusive, as though in each picture Botticelli were trying through new emblems and attitudes to enact with paint the soul in a state of achieved Platonic contemplation. Equally, English literature, both the greatest and the least, became distracted by this Platonist image of woman, from Spenser in the *Amoretti* (1595) to Drummond of Hawthornden, and his Platonist vision of the beloved:

> That learned *Graecian* (who did so excell
> In Knowledge passing Sense, that hee is nam'd
> Of all the after-Worlds *Divine*) doth tell,
> That at the Time when first our Soules are fram'd,
> Ere in these Mansions blinde they come to dwell,
> They live bright Rayes of that *Eternall Light,*
> And others see, know, love, in Heavens great Hight,
> Not toylde with ought to *Reason* doth rebell:
> Most true it is, for straight at the first Sight
> My Minde mee told, that in some other Place
> It elsewhere saw the *Idea* of that Face,
> And lov'd a Love of heavenly pure Delight.
>   No Wonder now I feele so faire a Flame,
>   Sith I Her lov'd ere on this *Earth* shee came.[18]

Such ecstatic dreaming seems wholly to alienate the artistic world from the real world, yet there was a way in which the two could be made to connect emotionally, a method contingent upon a combination of the particular events of history and the existence of individuals grand enough to fill an idealised role in a state or Church. The idealisation of women in the Renaissance was not confined to Christian cults, Florentine Platonising, to Petrarchan love poetry or any other unlived world, for the myth was so strong that it clung around certain individuals, or could be exploited by them. Should the accidents of history vacate a heroic or powerful role (such as happened, for instance, when the male heirs to a throne died or were not provided in the first place) a woman might ably fill it. Teresa of Avila (1515–82), taking advantage of the devotional feeling of the Counter Reformation and the emotiveness of the cult of the Virgin Mary, reformed and extended the Carmelite order in Spain, and offended the Inquisition through the abandoned ardour of her religious autobiography. In England the cult of the Virgin, abandoned by Protestantism, gave way to the cult of the Virgin Queen, and Elizabeth I was able to capitalise expertly on her femininity in order to stabilise the monarchy, using the idealising symbolism (Christian, Platonic, chivalric and pagan) which could be manipulated to make her person into a living myth and her court an embodied allegory.[19] Spenser in his April eclogue of *The Shepheardes Calender* was more eloquent than most but entirely characteristic of court poets in making Elizabeth the restorer of the classical Golden Age; by implication Flora, symbolic of spring and its renewed fertility; offspring of Pan and Syrinx (music, and thus the concord of the State), and finally a Fourth Grace with the suggestion that the image of the Three Graces has been an incomplete one before her advent.

Such extravagance had some basis in the real: it is a platitude to call the Elizabethan period the most fruitful in the history of English culture, not so platitudinous perhaps to add that its greatness depended to some extent on the rise of a feminine-based culture. With a woman as sovereign, the status of aristocratic women did to some extent rise – some were educated in liberal studies and many were influential property-holders. But most significantly Renaissance English literature has overwhelmingly as its preoccupation woman, and loving her. Sonneteers praised her inaccessible charms in appalling multitudes of sonnet–sequences; epithalamia celebrated her initiation through the sacred marriage night into the ripeness of her being; and in the drama she (and not the male character) could often be the true hero. This is especially true of Shakespearean comedy and tragi-comedy. The convention of male disguise which Shakespeare employs in, for instance, *The Merchant of Venice* (Portia), *As You Like It* (Rosalind) and *Twelfth Night* (Viola), allows the transcendence by the heroine of normal social limitations, so that these characters are at liberty. In this state of liberty, the feminine is seen as an active principle, with its own kind of absolute intelligence and strength. Such individuals have a great wholeness of being. They bring laughter (Viola: 'A little thing would make me tell them how much I lack of a man', III.iv), but more profoundly the wisdom to discriminate rightly (Portia as judge is like a Christian Astraea returned to restore justice and harmony to the damaged world) and finally reconciliation. In *King Lear* and the tragi-comedies, which are his final and most perfect spiritual statement, a series of fathers and daughters lose and find one another, and the feminine characters - with perhaps less personality but greater symbolic value than their earlier counterparts - are the agents of harmony within plays which, like some great archetypal dream, restore to man in old age his lost integrity. The child here is the beloved *anima,* arresting man's movement towards death and salvaging for him some meaning from the futility of the process:

> Falseness cannot come from thee, for thou look'st
> Modest as justice, and thou seem'st a palace
> For the crown'd truth to dwell in. I believe thee,
> And make my senses credit thy relation
> To points that seem impossible; for thou lookest
> Like one I lov'd indeed.
>
> (*Pericles,* V.i)

NOTES

1   Erasmus, *Colloquies*: 'What a wonderful elevation of Mind was this in a man that only Acted by the light of Nature! I can hardly read the story of this Worthy without a *Sancte Socrates Ora Pro Nobis*' (*Twenty Select Colloquies of Erasmus,* tr. R. L'Estrange, 1680; Abbey Classics reprint, London and Dublin, n.d.).

2   *On the Heavens*, 296B; *Physics*, 265A. See also Ptolemy's second-century *Almagest*; Copernicus, *Book of the Revolutions of the Heavenly Spheres* (1543); Kepler, *New Astronomy* (1609); Galileo, *Star Messenger* (1610).

3   *Nicomachean Ethics*, 1123A–1125A: 'Pride . . . seems to be a sort of crown of the virtues; for it makes them greater, and it is not found without them' (1123B); *Metaphysics*, 983A.

4   See, for instance, *Faerie Queene*, II.i.58.

5   *Five Questions Concerning the Mind*, Cassirer, 207; 206.

6   *Opere italiene*, ed. G. Gentile and V. Spampanato (Bari, Gius. Laterza & Figli, 1925–7), I, 101.

7   *The Expulsion of the Triumphant Beast*, 1584, tr. D. Imerti (Rutgers University Press, New Brunswick, 1964), 236; 240.

8   *The Notebooks of Leonardo da Vinci*, ed. E. MacCurdy (Cape, London, 1938), II, 228.

9   *The Sonnets of Michelangelo*, III, tr. E. Jennings in her *Collected Poems 1967* (Macmillan, London, 1967). See also Erasmus' satire against the Pope, *Julius Excluded* (1517), tr. P. Pascal (Indiana University Press, Bloomington, Indiana, 1968).

10 See the revised *Loci communes* of 1555, tr. and ed. C. L. Manschreck (Oxford University Press, New York, 1965), where denunciation of the virtuous pagans is more in sorrow than in anger (5–6).

11 See Erasmus' *Praise of Folly*, tr. B. Radice (Penguin Classics, Harmondsworth, 1971), 196–208, where Erasmus celebrates so movingly 'the folly of the cross' (199) and the sweet stupidity of those who are gentle and innocent.

12 *The Prince*, tr. G. Bull (Penguin Classics, Harmondsworth, 1961), 132.

13 For Puritan accounts of political liberty, see *The Leveller Tracts 1647–53*, ed. W. Haller and G. Davies (Columbia University Press, New York, 1944); *Leveller Manifestoes of the Puritan Revolution*, ed. D. M. Wolfe (Humanities Press, New York, 1967).

14 *Eikonoklastes* (1649), *Complete Prose Works*, III, 601.

15 For example, *Coriolanus* (*c.* 1608), I.i. This symbolism was not, of course, invariably or necessarily conservative: Milton's use of the 'huge and monstrous Wen' competing with the head in his *Of Reformation in England* (1641) has revolutionary implications (*Complete Prose Works*, I, 581).

16 *The Public Speaking of Queen Elizabeth*, ed. G. P. Rice (Columbia University Press, New York, 1951), 96.

17 For example, George Peele, *Descensus Astraeae* (1591); Sir John Davies, *Hymnes ot Astraea* (1599); Spenser, *Faerie Queene*, I.vii.46, V.9–10.

18 Sonnet vii, *Poems* (1616).
19 For Samuel Daniel, eulogising in his *Civile Wares* (1609), ed. L.
    Michel (Yale University Press, New Haven, Conn., 1958), the
    'tumultuous Broyles' of the past were all justified in the emergence of
    Elizabeth I:

> Yet now what reason have we to complaine?
> Since hereby came the calme we did injoy;
> The blisse of thee *Eliza*; happie gaine
> For all our losse . . . .

MARSILIO FICINO

Commentary
on Plato's 'Symposium'
1484 (1574 edition)

Translated by Gordon Neal

It would not be possible to exaggerate the influence of Plato's *Symposium* (along with his later *Phaedrus*) on the thought, poetry and drama of the English Renaissance: on the other hand, it is equally impossible to satisfy the scholarly desire to locate that influence exactly. There are two reasons for this. The first is that the influence of the *Symposium* was endlessly diffusive, to a considerable extent through Ficino's *Commentary,* with the result that it became part of the common fabric of consciousness amongst educated people in Europe, so that even those who had not read it seem saturated in the Platonist way of thinking about the nature of Love. The second reason is that English poetry simultaneously inherited a complex of different love traditions, all exciting to the mind and none absolutely incapable of assimilation to Platonist modes of thought – medieval chivalric love, the *Caritas* of the New Testament, the 'Petrarchan' love ideal with its own conventions. This coincidence of different traditions, combined with the individualism of the particular author and the curious haziness of Platonist thought itself, means that no English love poet can justly be spoken of as specifically 'Platonist', and yet nearly all English poets *must* be thought of as Platonist in general terms.

The passage which follows is Ficino's Commentary on that part of the *Symposium* (208B–212B) which represents Diotima of Mantinea's instructions to an uncharacteristically passive and unironical Socrates on the nature of love, which, contradicting or transcending most of the speeches which have already been made by other characters in the dialogue, is the climactic vision of the *Symposium* and the most impressive statement of Plato's identification of Beauty with the Good. The soul is shown as able to ascend through a love which widens the perspective of the lover's vision, past a preliminary centring of attention on the physical attractions of an individual, to a perception of his spirit's beauty, and thence through a widening vista of greater partial beauties to a final, inclusive and abstract knowledge of the Idea of Beauty. The passage contains an implicit image of the Ladder of Contemplation (which Ficino makes explicit) and an optimism about man's capacity to attain to immortality in a variety of ways – perpetuation of the species; renown; creation of immortal verse; and finally vision of and union with the Immortal itself. All these possibilities are called upon by Renaissance love poets to counteract the distressed awareness which they shared with Plato of the mutable state of Nature in which man is grounded, and the crumbling, unsteady nature of the self.

Plato's idea of beauty is, finally, inhuman in its visionariness, remote in leading to the love of something even more abstract than thought itself (211E):

What may we suppose to be the felicity of the man who sees absolute beauty in its essence, pure and unalloyed, who, instead of a beauty tainted by human flesh and colour and a mass of perishable rubbish, is able to apprehend divine beauty where it exists apart and alone?

Ficino and his fellow Platonists tended to express this remoteness by dwelling on and extending the symbolism of Light which Plato presented as the experience of true knowledge. English Renaissance love poetry expressed it by emphasising that Beauty was unseeable by mortal eyes, and then returning to concentrate on what *was* seeable as an image of it. Sidney in *Astrophel and Stella* (1591), V, recites orthodox Platonic doctrine to the effect that earthly beauty 'can be but a shade' of 'true beauty', but circles back with relief away from the demanding 'inward light' to the comforting human figure of his earthly lover – 'True, and yet true it is that I must Stella love'. Sir John Davies in *Orchestra or a Poem of Dancing* (1596) moved, without loss of sweetness or eloquence, further toward the kind of joy in abstract love (celebrated in terms of the relationship between loving beings rather than in the beings themselves) characteristic of Plato; and Spenser, in his *Hymne in Honour of Beautie* (*Fowre Hymnes,* 1596), described Beauty in authentically Platonist terms as a 'wondrous Paterne', according to which the Divine Architect created the universe, and which 'mortal sence' cannot perceive. Of all English poets, Spenser is the most learnedly and dedicatedly Platonist.

However, there is no author more satisfactory as an index of the unique intensity of the response made by the Renaissance to Plato's dialogues than Ficino, whose fifteenth-century translations made him for the first time fully accessible to the Latin-speaking world, and whose commentary on the *Symposium* (itself in dialogue form) shaped European patterns of thinking on the nature of love for at least one hundred and fifty years. The extract quoted here is a substantial part of that speech in the *Commentary,* spoken by Tommaso Benci, fifteenth-century merchant, love-poet and dabbler in philosophy, whose task it is to interpret Plato's Socrates–Diotima speech. I reluctantly omit the following speech, which describes Socrates as a person, and, alarmingly, as a Cupid, or a type of the Platonic lover. Socrates himself would have been much amused, no doubt, at the thought of qualifying as a Cupid, and also at the deadly earnestness with which Ficino treats every word of Plato, oblivious of jokes, whimsy, contradictions between the opinions of different speakers, and the poetic licence enjoyed by Plato in the original. He would have been bewildered at the way this idolatrous frame of mind could smilingly lie down with a simultaneous willingness to take liberties with the Master's meanings, so that what in Plato is clear and crisp is smudged by the Platonist's dreamy imaginings, while his genuine poetry is analysed down into classifications and categories which make monstrous assaults on the credulity of the reader (see chapter 16 and the carefully made distinction between 'God, the Angelic Mind, Soul, and Body'). Such curiosities are in the tradition of Plotinus and his

Enneads rather than in an original reading of the text itself. So is the commentator's love of wandering in his thoughts far from the original, visiting the *Republic* and the *Meno* briefly in his ramblings, and occasionally just glancing off the surface of the *Symposium* again as if to show willing: this free treatment of the original text makes it impossible and probably irrelevant to state exact correspondences between text and commentary. Where they do occur, some indication is made in the notes.

And yet this combined literality of view and passion for creating precious distinctions which makes the Renaissance version of Plato's thought so unlike Plato's own is balanced by an emotional affinity with him which issues in passages like Ficino's interpretation of the myth of Narcissus (chapter 16), and his treatment of the imagery of the Light of Knowledge, which come as close to the *spirit* of Plato in its absorption in the idea of *ekstasis* as any Platonist ever has. It was in their apprehension of the passion of Plato and their interpretation of his view of the beatific vision and how man may achieve it by breaking, through love, out of the material world and into the reality beyond, that Renaissance Platonists and poets showed an unmatched fidelity to one of the most important moods of Plato.

The passage below begins after Ficino's explanation of Diotima's definition of Love as a daemon, son of Contrivance and Poverty (201D–204C).

TRANSLATOR'S NOTE: FICINO'S LATIN STYLE

Ficino may rank as a verbose author in the sense that he elaborates his arguments to put his point beyond ambiguity to a degree repellent to modern taste. But his verbal style is in fact remarkably taut and terse: it relies heavily on carefully balanced antitheses, relieved by a considerable amount of studied variation. His sentences are often short, sometimes longer and periodic in structure, but in that case the train of thought within the period is usually very clearly and carefully marked by some of the many logical indicators which Latin boasts, or by verbal repetition and antithesis. I have tried to preserve as much of Ficino's style as possible. What has suffered most, I think, is on the one hand the terse economy of the Latin (which English will not reproduce) and on the other the occasional periodic sentence (sacrificed in the interests of clarity).

The rhetoric is usually subordinated to the overriding aim of logical exposition, but there are passages where it takes momentary flight and breaks through to a higher emotive level, most noticeably here in chapter 19.

Repetition is a particular stylistic trait of Ficino's. At times it gives to his Latin a slightly naive feel. An especial favourite is the device (with a pedigree going back to early Greek historical writers such as Herodotus) of beginning a sentence by repeating one or more words drawn from the close of the previous sentence, usually in a slightly different grammatical form. But the naivety is deliberate. It is a sophisticated device to achieve the maximum blend of terseness and clarity. And the repetition is frequently tempered with gratuitous variation. For example, the first paragraph of chapter 19 closes with the variation of 'shadow', 'likeness', and 'image'. Or notice the omission of 'beauty' in the last sentence of the opening paragraph of chapter 17.

Chapter 11
THE BENEFITS OF LOVE
ACCORDING TO ITS DEFINITION

After Diotima has expounded the origin and the nature of Love in itself, she then explains the goal at which he aims and the purpose for which he is of benefit to mankind.

We all want to have the good things of life, and not simply to have them, but to have them continuously. But the individual good things which mortal men enjoy change and wear out, and they would all soon vanish, if as they go their place was not daily taken by new blessings. In order, therefore, to ensure by whatever means it may be a continuous succession of blessings, we wish to replace those we lose. Replacement is achieved by procreation. This is why the urge to procreate is native to us all.

But since procreation makes mortal things similar to divine through the continuity it bestows, it must be a gift of God. Of the divine, as being beautiful, the ugly is the opposite; the beautiful is the counterpart and the ally. For that reason procreation, a gift of God, is perfectly and easily achieved in the case of that which is beautiful, but in the case of the opposite the opposite is true. That is why the effort to procreate demands the beautiful and shuns the opposite.

You ask what human love is? What purpose it serves? The desire to procreate in the beautiful[1] for the sake of preserving the continuity of life in mortal things, this is the love of the people who dwell on the earth, this is the end and aim of our love. For even within the period during which any individual creature is said to live and maintain its identity, for example from childhood to old age, it never in fact retains the same constituent parts, although it is called the same creature. It is, as Plato says,[2] continually being renewed and casting off the old material in respect of hair, flesh, bones, blood, and indeed every part of the body without exception. And that happens not only in the body, but in the soul as well. Traits, habits, opinions, desires, pleasures, aversions, and apprehensions change continually; none of them remains identical or alike; the old wither away and are succeeded by new which grow to maturity.

In addition, and even more remarkably, not only do some items of knowledge fade away and others arise, so that we are not always the same in respect of knowledge, but virtually the same thing happens to every single item of knowledge. For reflection and recollection is a kind of retrieval of lost knowledge. Forgetting appears to be the escape of knowledge. But reflection, continually supplying a new memory to replace that which has gone, preserves the item of knowledge in a way that makes it appear to retain its identity.

This is the manner in which everything that is subject to change in our souls or our bodies is preserved — not because each thing is always completely identical (that is a prerogative of the divine), but since what decays and is lost leaves behind something not only new but also like itself. And indeed by this means the mortal gains some likeness to the immortal.

In both parts of the soul, therefore, both in that which concerns cognition and in that by which the body is governed, there is an innate love of procreation in order to preserve the continuity of life. Love in this latter part which is adapted to governing the body motivates us from the moment of birth to take food and drink in order that these nutrients may produce the Humours needed to replace what continuously drains away from the body. The procreation by which the body is fed and grows, stimulates the actual seed when the body has come to maturity and instigates a desire to produce offspring in order that what cannot in itself continue for ever may be preserved in progeny very similar to itself and so continue in perpetuity.

But there is also the love of procreation allocated to the cognitive part of the soul which causes the soul to desire truth, which is its proper nutriment and by which in its own way it needs to be fed and to grow. Whatever is lost to the soul through forgetfulness or is blunted through laziness and apathy, this love as it were regenerates by its keenness to remember and reflect, and it calls back to mind what had been lost through forgetfulness or blunted through indolence. Eventually, when the soul has come to maturity, it now inspires it with a burning desire to teach and to write, in order that, by means of the knowledge produced either in his writings or in his pupil's mind by the teacher's own understanding, truth may continue among men to eternity.

And so it is thanks to love that in human life continuous survival, of body as well as of soul, may be thought of as possible for every individual.

Both kinds of love pursue beauty. Indeed the love which governs and controls the body desires the meals on which it nourishes its own body to be as tasty, delicious and beautiful as they can be, and it desires to produce beautiful offspring with the help of an attractive woman.[3] And the love which belongs to the soul is keen to imbue it with the most distinguished and important disciplines, and to disseminate knowledge as like its own as possible by writing in a polished and beautiful style, and to reproduce it, by teaching, in some very beautiful soul – in a soul, I stress, that is pure, sharp, and of the highest excellence.

The soul itself we cannot of course see: so we cannot observe its beauty either. But we can see the body, which is a shadow and image of the soul: and so surmising from its image, we conjecture that in a handsome body there is an attractive soul. That is why we prefer handsome pupils.[4]

Chapter 12
ON THE TWO LOVES,
AND THE FACT THAT THE SOUL IS BORN
ENDOWED WITH TRUTH

We have dealt adequately with the definition of love: we must now explain the distinction drawn by Plato on the subject of love between productivity of soul and of body. Every human being, he states, is fertile and pregnant in body, fertile also in soul. The seeds of all the characteristics of the body are implanted in it at the very beginning of its development. They are the source from which, at predetermined intervals of time, the teeth come through, the hair grows, the beard develops, and the reproductive seed is released.

If the body is productive and pregnant with seeds, the soul, which is a more excellent thing than the body, will much more certainly be highly fertile and possess from the start the seeds of all its characteristics. So the soul has earlier on been given its allocation of the principles of morals, skills, and disciplines, and from this store it brings into the light of day its own offspring at predetermined times, if it is properly tended. The evidence for the fact that the soul has innate principles of all its characteristics comes from its choices, its investigations, its findings, its judgements, and the comparisons which it draws.

Who would deny that the soul from a very tender age chooses what is true, good, virtuous, and useful? But nobody wants what is unknown to him. Therefore some kind of notion[5] of those things exists in the soul even before it chooses them. It is through such notions, which are like the forms or principles of the things themselves, that it judges them to be choiceworthy.

The same point is proved by the fact of inquiry and discovery. If Socrates were to look for Alcibiades in a crowd of people and were to have any chance of finding him, there must be some kind of picture of Alcibiades in Socrates' mind: otherwise he will not know who in particular it is that he is looking for, or be able to distinguish Alcibiades from others in the dense throng when he finds him. Similarly the soul could neither pursue those four objects nor ever find them, if it did not have some kind of notion of them (i.e. of Truth, Goodness, Virtue and Usefulness). It is this that enables it to search with some chance of finding them, recognise them whenever it finds what it has been seeking, and to distinguish them from their opposites.

We can prove our point not only from the fact of choice, pursuit, and discovery but from judgement as well. For anyone who judges someone to be friendly or hostile towards him, cannot be unaware what friendship and malice are. By what possible means, therefore, could we make the many judgements that we do customarily make every day about what is true or false, good or bad, and make them correctly, if truth and goodness were not in some way known to us beforehand? Again how could so many people, even those not versed in the arts concerned, so often correctly approve and disapprove the products of architecture, music, painting, and the other arts, if they had not been endowed by nature with some awareness of the Idea and principle of those things?

The same thing is shown by the fact of comparison. For anyone who compares honey with wine and pronounces one sweeter than the other knows what constitutes sweet taste. And anyone who compares Speusippus and Xenocrates with Plato and decides that Xenocrates is more like Plato than is Speusippus, obviously has an image of Plato in his mind.[6] In the same way when we correctly evaluate one among a number of good things as being better than another, and when because of its greater or smaller participation in goodness one is seen to be better or worse than another, it cannot be that we do not have some knowledge of goodness. In addition, we often judge very adroitly among a number of conflicting opinions offered by philosophers, or even others, which is more like the truth and more probable; so we must possess some insight into truth or how could we have any idea what was like it and what was not?

It is for this reason that some people of adolescent years, a few even without any instruction but most after a very limited demonstration by instructors of the rudiments of the subject, are said to have emerged with the highest knowledge. This could never have happened except, as we have said, with considerable assistance from nature. This was more than adequately demonstrated by Socrates to Phaedo, Theaetetus, and Meno when they were boys; he showed that in every subject boys could give correct answers if they were questioned intelligently, precisely because they were endowed by nature with the principles of all the skills and disciplines.

Chapter 13
THE LIGHT OF TRUTH IN THE SOUL

Plato seems to be ambiguous about the way in which principles of this kind exist in the soul. Anyone who scans the works which Plato wrote earlier in his life, the *Phaedrus*, *Meno*, and *Phaedo*,[7] will probably conclude that they are painted on the substance of the soul in something like the way that pictures are painted on a wall. This is a point which you and I have both touched on several times earlier in our conversation, for this seems to be his meaning at that stage.

But in the sixth book of the *Republic*[8] that divine genius makes the whole matter plain and says that that light of the mind which enables it to understand all things is the very same God by whom all things were made. For he compares the sun and God to each other, making the point that what the sun is to our eyes, God is to our minds. The sun creates our eyes and gives them the power of sight. But this would be useless and buried in eternal darkness, if the sun's light were not there to convey the colours and shapes of physical objects. It is in the light of the sun that the eye sees the colours of physical objects and their shapes. The eye does not perceive anything except light. It appears to perceive many different things, because the light which streams into it is ornamented with the many subtle differences that exist in external objects. The eye can observe this light as it is reflected from physical objects: but direct sunlight from its source it cannot bear.

In the same way God creates the soul and endows it with intelligence, the power of understanding. But this would be empty and dark, if the light of God were not present in it, in which it can perceive the principles of everything. And so it is through the light of God: and the actual object of its cognition is nothing but the divine light.

It appears to be aware of a variety of objects, because it perceives that light under the varied Ideas and principles of things. When anyone catches sight of a human being and forms in his mind the image of man and lets his mind work for some considerable time on reflecting on and assessing it, he lifts his intellectual gaze to look at the principle of man which exists in the divine light: then suddenly a point of light flashes in his mind, and the very nature of man is truly understood. And the same is true with every other example you could take. So we understand everything through the light of God: but that pure light itself and its source we cannot see in this life.

It is evident that productivity of soul consists solely in the fact that the eternal light of God shines in its inner being, charged with the principles and Ideas of all things, and that the soul can turn to this light whenever it wishes by purity of life and intense concentration of attention, and that when it has so turned it is illuminated with flashes of the Ideas.

Chapter 14
THE SOURCE OF LOVE FOR MEN
AND OF LOVE FOR WOMEN

It is in these senses, as Plato has it, that the human body is fertile and that the human soul is fertile, and both are motivated to produce by the stimulus of love. But some people, either by nature or by education, are better fitted to produce offspring of the soul than of the body; others, and indeed the majority, the opposite. The former follow the heavenly love, the latter the common love. The former accordingly naturally love males, and indeed males who are just reaching maturity, rather than women or children; the reason is that in such people there is a more complete flowering of that keenness of intellect which is particularly suited, because of its own more outstanding beauty, to the learning which they aim to produce.

The opposite is true, however, of the other group because of the pleasure of sexual intercourse and because of the constraints of physical production. But the sexual drive of our soul is completely irrational and makes no distinction of gender, but is stimulated to produce by its own nature whenever we judge any body beautiful. And so it often happens that those who associate with males have intimate relations with them to satisfy the urges of the sexual part of the soul. This is most frequent in the case of those at whose birth Venus was in a masculine sign and either in conjunction with Saturn, in the terms of Saturn,[9] or in opposition to Saturn. They should have noticed that the end and aim of the promptings of the sexual part is not this fruitless effort of emission but the function of fertilisation and reproduction, and they should have redirected them towards females instead of males.

We believe it to be by some error of this sort that that outrageous crime arose which Plato in his *Laws*[10] most strongly outlaws as a form of homicide. Anyone who denies life to a human being yet to be born must indeed be considered no less guilty of homicide than the man who gets rid of one who has been born. It may be more brazen to cut life short when it is already present, but it is crueller to deny the light of day to one still to be born and to murder one's own as yet unborn children.

Chapter 15
THE SOUL IS HIGHER THAN THE BODY, ANGELIC MIND THAN THE SOUL, AND GOD THAN ANGELIC MIND[11]

So much then on the twin fertility of the soul and the twin loves. We must next discuss the steps by which Diotima takes Socrates from the lowest level to the highest. She guides him back from body to soul, from soul to Angelic Mind, and from Angelic Mind to God.

We may offer the following proof that these four levels of things must exist in nature.

Every physical body is moved by something else. It cannot by its own nature move itself, since it is not able to do anything by its own agency. It is because of the presence of soul that it appears to move by itself, and because of the presence of soul that it appears to be alive. And when soul is present, it does move itself in a kind of way; but when it is absent, physical body can only move through the agency of something else. This is not surprising because it is something which does not have this natural ability of itself, unlike soul which does possess the property of being able to move itself. For soul imparts the power to move itself to anything in which it is present; and what it imparts to other things by its very presence, it must much more certainly first possess itself.

Therefore soul is above physical bodies. It is indeed something which can move itself according to its essential nature. And for that reason it must be above things which attain self-motion not of themselves but through the presence of something else.

When we say that soul moves by itself, we do not use the verb in what we may call a transitive sense, as Aristotle wanted it to be understood in Plato,[12] but intransitively, as when we assert that God stands by himself, the sun shines by itself, or fire is hot. For it is not the case that one part of the soul causes motion and another is set into motion; but the whole of it moves by itself, i.e. by its own nature – that is, it progresses in reasoning from one point to another and performs the tasks of feeding, growing, and reproducing at different periods of time.

The reason why temporal progression of this kind belongs to soul through its own agency is that what is above soul does not reach understanding of different things at different moments, but understands everything simultaneously at the single point of eternity. Therefore Plato was right to attribute to soul the first movement and the first interval of time; from it movement and time both pass to physical bodies.

Since rest must be prior to motion, for rest is logically more perfect, it is necessary to discover above the changeable reasoning of soul some stable intelligence which is intelligence in its own total nature, and which is indeed always intelligence in actuality. Soul does not have understanding with its total being or continuously, but with one part of itself and on some occasions, and it does not possess a certain, but an uncertain ability to understand. Therefore, in order that what is more perfect may have precedence over that which is less perfect, we must posit above the intelligence of soul, which is changeable, only a part, intermittent, and uncertain, an intelligence of Angelic Mind, which is stable, whole, continuous, and of the greatest certainty. In this way, just as the self-moving soul has precedence over the body that is set in motion by another's agency, so the intellect that is of itself stable will have precedence over the soul that is of itself subject to motion.

And just as body has the power to move itself through the agency of soul, and hence it is not all physical bodies, but only animate bodies that seem to move of their own accord, so it is through the agency of Intelligence that the soul has its ability to understand on any occasion. If the soul possessed intellect through its own nature, intellect would belong to the souls of all animals, as does the power of setting themselves in motion. So intellect does not belong to the soul by its own nature and in the first place. And for this reason it is right that what does possess intelligence through itself and in the first place should have precedence over it. Angelic Mind is of this kind, of higher quality than souls.

But the intelligence of Angelic Mind is necessarily far surpassed by that first principle of things and supreme good, which Plato in the *Parmenides* calls the One itself.[13] For the One itself is simple and so must by nature be completely above the plurality of composite things; for number comes from one, and a whole compound is an amalgamation of simple elements. But that intelligence, although it is unchangeable, nevertheless does not exist as itself a pure and simple one. For it understands itself. And in such a case there seem to be the following three elements, all in some way or other different from each other; the understanding *subject*, the

45

content of understanding, and the act of understanding. For its own reasoning, the essence of intelligence, is one thing in as far as it is the content of understanding, another thing in as far as it is the object of understanding, and another again in as far as it is the act of understanding.

In addition it has the potentiality of cognition, and this is absolutely formless of its own nature before the act of cognition; it is given form in cognition, and in understanding it desires and receives the light of truth, which it seems to have been without before it understood.

It also possesses in itself the plurality of the range of Ideas.

You see how great and how varied is the plurality and compositeness of Angelic Mind. It is for this reason that we are forced to give the pure and simple One precedence over it. We cannot give anything preference over the one God himself, because the true One has no trace of plurality or compositeness. If it had anything above it, it would undoubtedly be made by that thing; and therefore, being derived from it it would by that very fact have a nature inferior to its source, as does every effect compared to its cause. For that reason it would no longer be one and simple, but a composite of at least two ingredients, namely the contribution received from its cause and its own inferiority.

Hence, the One itself, as Plato believes and Dionysius the Areopagite confirms, far surpasses everything. They both judge the most excellent name for God to be 'the One itself'.[14]

The pre-eminence of the One is also demonstrated to us by the principle that the most outstanding cause should have the largest influence, and through the superiority of its powers should extend its effects to cover everything there is. The influence of the One does spread itself over everything in the universe. For not only is Intelligence one, the individual soul one, and the individual physical body one, but even the unformed matter and negation of form itself is said to be one in a certain sense. For we say that silence is one, darkness is one, and death is one.

The influence of Intelligence and soul, however, does not extend as far as matter. For Intelligence supplies creative form and order; soul provides life and movement. But the unformed prime matter and negation of form of the universe is devoid of form and life. Hence the One itself has precedence over Intelligence and soul, since its influence is more widespread.

On the same principle Intelligence is clearly superior to soul, since life, the contribution of soul, is not given to all physical bodies. But Intelligence does bestow shape and order on them all.

Chapter 16
THE COMPARISON BETWEEN GOD, ANGELIC MIND, SOUL AND BODY

We have then ascended from body to soul, from this to Angelic Mind, and from this to God. [15] God is above eternity: Angelic Mind is totally within eternity. Indeed its activity remains as stable as its essential nature. And stability is the characteristic property of eternity.

Soul is partly in eternity, partly in time. Its substance persists always the same and without any alteration by way either of increase or diminution. But its activity, as we indicated just now, is progressive over different periods of time.

Physical body is entirely subjected to time. Not only does its substance change, but its entire activity requires the lapse of time.

Hence the One itself exists above stability or motion. Angelic Mind is located in stability, soul equally in stability and motion, physical body in motion alone.

Again the One remains above number, motion, and position. Angelic Mind is placed in number above motion and position. Soul is placed in number and motion, but above position. Physical body is subject to number, motion, and position.

Indeed, if the One itself neither has any number or a nature composite of parts nor changes in any way from that which it is, and is not confined by any position, Angelic Mind certainly has number in respect of its parts (the Ideas) but is free from motion and position, and soul has number in respect of its parts and conditions and is subject to change in the processes of reasoning and the variety of its disturbances but is exempt from the confines of position, while physical body, however, is subject to all these things.

Chapter 17
THE COMPARISON BETWEEN THE BEAUTY OF GOD, ANGELIC MIND, SOUL AND BODY

As these four grades of being compare with each other, so do their forms of beauty. Indeed the beauty of physical body consists in the composition of its many parts, is circumscribed by position, and is subject to the lapse of time. The beauty of the soul certainly suffers the vicissitudes of time and contains a plurality of parts, but is exempted from the bounds of position. The beauty of Angelic Mind, however, only has number, and exists free from the two other factors. But God's suffers none of these limitations at all.

The beauty of physical body you can see without difficulty. But you want to see the soul's beauty as well? Subtract from physical beauty the weight of nature itself and the confines of position, but leave the other factors. You now have the soul's beauty. You want also to see that of Angelic Mind? Take away, I pray you, not only position and extension, but also temporal progression, but retain the plurality of composite nature, and you have it thereby. You also wish to see God's beauty? Please remove as well the plurality that comes from being a composite of Ideas: leave absolutely simple beauty, you will have instantly reached God's beauty.

But when I have subtracted these things, what on earth am I going to have left? Do you think that beauty is anything but light? Moreover, the beauty of all physical bodies is the light of the sun, which you see infected by these three factors, plurality of forms (for you see it decorated with a plurality of shapes and colours), extension, and temporal change. Take away its base in matter, but let it retain the other two apart from position. Beauty of mind is precisely of this kind.

Take away from that, if you will, temporal change, and leave the remaining factor. There remains light in its brightest form, without motion, but engraved with all the principles of everything. That is Angelic Mind, that is the beauty of Angelic Mind.

Take away finally the plurality of different Ideas, and leave one simple and pure light analogous to the light which stays within the sun's own circumference and is not radiated through the air. Now you are grasping to an extent the beauty of God, which surpasses the other forms of beauty at least as far as that sunlight, pure, single, and uncontaminated in itself, excels the brightness of the sun that is radiated through the cloudy air, divided, infected, darkened. And so the source of all beauty is God, the source of all love is God.

Further, the sun's light in water is a kind of shadow compared with its brighter light in the air. Similarly, its brightness in air is a shadow compared to its radiance in fire. Its radiance in fire is a shadow compared to its light as it shines within the sun itself.

The same comparison can be drawn between those four kinds of beauty, that of physical body, that of soul, that of Angelic Mind, and that of God. God is never so mistaken as to love the shadow of his own beauty in Angelic Mind, and neglect his own true beauty. Nor is Angelic Mind ever so captivated by the beauty of soul, which is a shadow of itself, as to be diverted by its shadow and desert its own proper beauty. But our soul, most regrettably, for this is the origin of all our unhappiness, [16] our soul alone, I say, is so fascinated by the blandishments of physical beauty that it puts its own beauty last and forgetting itself pursues the beauty of physical body, which is its own shadow.

That is the reason for the tragic fate of Narcissus that we are told of by Orpheus. That is the reason for the pitiable plight of humanity. The young Narcissus, that is the soul of rash and inexperienced man, does not look at his own face, does not notice his own proper substance and qualities, but pursues his shadow in water and tries to embrace it, that is he admires beauty in a fragile body and in running water, which is a shadow of the mind itself, and turns his back on his own beauty.

He never catches hold of his shadow, because the soul neglects itself by pursuing physical body and cannot be satisfied by enjoyment of the body. For the true object of its striving is not the body itself but its own beauty, although it is attracted by the physical beauty which is an image of its own beauty, just as Narcissus was in his fascination. And since he fails to notice the error, so long as he wants one thing and pursues another, he cannot fulfil his desire. And so he dissolves into tears and is destroyed, that is since the soul is in this way located outside itself and has slipped down to the level of physical body, it is tormented with disastrous disturbances, infected by the filth of the body, and as it were, dies, since it seems now to be more body than soul. It was in order that Socrates might by some means avoid this death, that Diotima led him back from body to soul, from there to Angelic Mind, and from that to God.

Chapter 18
HOW THE SOUL CAN BE RAISED
FROM THE BEAUTY OF PHYSICAL BODY
TO THE BEAUTY OF GOD

Just think, my dear friends. Imagine Diotima putting it to Socrates in these terms.

'No physical body is beautiful in every respect, Socrates. Either it is beautiful in one part, ugly in another; or it is beautiful today, but at another time anything but; or it is thought beautiful by one man, but ugly by another. Hence physical beauty, contaminated as it is with the pollution of ugliness, cannot possibly be pure, true, and basic beauty. Also, nobody ever regards beauty as being ugly, just as nobody regards wisdom as being stupid either. But we do consider the construction of physical bodies now beautiful, now ugly, and at any one time different people have different views about it. So basic and true beauty does not exist in bodies.

'Take into account too the fact that a plurality of bodies is described by the single predicate beauty. This implies a single common quality of beauty in a plurality of bodies to explain why they are all similarly called beautiful. But a single quality of this sort, since it is in something other than itself, that is, matter, must also be regarded as derived from something other than itself. For that which does not possess in itself the power to maintain its existence can much less be derived from itself. But surely it will never be derived from matter? No, indeed. Nothing that is formless and incomplete can make itself attractive or complete. Now, what is one must originate from one source. Therefore the one beauty shared by a plurality of bodies derives from some one incorporeal maker. And the one maker of all things is God, who through the agency of angels and souls daily gives all the matter in the universe its beauty. For these reasons you must accept that the true principle of beauty is to be found in God and in his ministers rather than in the body of the universe.

'To this beauty, Socrates, you will, I believe, find it easy to ascend by these steps. If nature had given you the eyes of a lynx, my dear Socrates, to enable you to penetrate to the heart of anything that came into your sight, the great external beauty of your favourite Alcibiades would look to you like extreme ugliness. What does the object of your love for him actually amount to, Socrates? It is the external appearance and no more, or rather the colour that captivates you: or rather a kind of reflected light and a most insubstantial shadow. Or what if it is an empty fantasy that deceives you? In that case you are in love with what you are dreaming rather than what you can see.

'But I do not want you to think I am totally prejudiced against you: let us accept that Alcibiades is in fact attractive. But now let us ask in detail where his attractiveness lies. In all parts of his body, certainly, except for his snub nose and eyebrows that are rather higher than suits him. But in Phaedrus these particular features are shapely. In him, though, the stockiness of his legs jars. Charmides has well-proportioned legs, but his thin neck might offend you.

'If you examine people individually in this way, there will be nobody whom you will approve of in every respect. You will end up with a list of any features that were right wherever you found them: and so you will construct your own complete figure drawn from your observations of everybody. The result will be that the ideal beauty of the human race, which is found scattered among many physical bodies, will be collected together in your soul by your mental construction of a single image.

'You will put little value on the beauty of each individual human being, Socrates, if you compare it to that image. It is thanks not so much to physical bodies as to your soul that you possess that image. You should therefore love that image of beauty which your soul has constructed, and the soul itself that constructed it, much more than that external, deformed, and scattered beauty. [17]

'But what is it that I am telling you to love in the soul? The soul's beauty. The beauty of physical body is light: the beauty of the soul is light, and the light of the soul is truth. This alone is what your friend Plato seems to request from God in his prayers. "Grant me, O God," he prays, "that my soul may be made beautiful; that the things that pertain to the body may not mar the beauty of the soul; and that I may consider the wise man alone to be rich." [18] In these petitions Plato declares that beauty of soul consists in truth and wisdom, and that it is a gift of God to men.

'Truth is one, and it is the gift of God to us. But in its different aspects it acquires the names of different qualities. It is called wisdom' – that which Plato requested from God above all other things – 'in as far as it reveals things divine, science in as far as it reveals things natural, prudence in as far as it reveals things human, justice when it makes men fair-minded, courage when it makes them invincible, and temperance when it gives them tranquility of mind.

'In this list two kinds of virtues are included: the moral virtues, I mean, and the intellectual, which are superior to the former. The intellectual virtues are wisdom, science, prudence: the moral virtues justice, courage, temperance.

'The moral virtues are better known because of their practical applications and their public functions: the intellectual are more concealed because of the complexities of the truth they reveal.

'Moreover, the man who is brought up with virtuous morals, can easily be lifted up to the intellectual virtues, in as much as he is purer than other people. That is why I recommend you to attach first importance to the beauty of soul which consists in morality, in order that you may understand that the principle of all morality is one (it is through this that all actions are alike called virtuous), that it is in fact the one truth of the pure life, which through the actions of justice, courage, and temperance, brings us to true happiness. So give first place in your affections to this one truth of morality, and the most beautiful light of the soul. Recognise moreover that you will ascend further above morality to the extreme brilliance of the truth of wisdom, science, and prudence, if you will regard these virtues as open to the soul that is brought up with the best morals and accept that the most correct rule of the moral life is contained in them.

'But even if you get insight into the many different doctrines of wisdom, science, and prudence, nevertheless remember that the one, single light of truth is behind them all. It is through this that they are all alike called beautiful. It is this that I urge you to love most ardently as the supreme beauty of the soul.

'Nevertheless, this one truth in so many different doctrines cannot be the basic truth of all things for the reason that it exists in something other than itself, since it is shared among a plurality of doctrines. But whatever depends on something other than itself clearly is derived from something other than itself. Nor indeed is the one truth produced from the plurality of doctrines. For what is one must originate from one source. And on these grounds there must be some one wisdom above the soul of man which is not distributed between many different doctrines but is one wisdom, and from whose single truth the multiple truth of human beings arises.[19]

'And remember, Socrates, that the single light of the single wisdom is the beauty of Angelic Mind: you must pay honour to it above beauty of soul. As we have shown earlier in our discussion, it excels the beauty of physical bodies because it is not restricted by position or distributed over the parts of matter, and it cannot be corrupted. It also excels the beauty of soul because it is eternal and does not move in any temporal progression.

'But since the light of Angelic Mind sparkles with the numerous range of forms, and since unity, which is the source of all number, must be above all plurality, this light necessarily emanates from the one principle of all things which we call the One itself. The utterly simple light of the One itself, therefore, is infinite beauty, because it is not contaminated by the pollution of matter like the beauty of physical body, it is not subject to change by temporal progression like the beauty of the mind, and it is not, like the beauty of Angelic Mind, dissipated by plurality.

'Any quality is called infinite in natural philosophy when it is abstracted from any external additions. Whenever heat exists by itself, unimpeded by cold or by wetness and unburdened by the weight of matter, it is called infinite heat because its force is free and not restricted by any limitations arising from the addition of other factors. Similarly, light is infinite when it is free of all physical body, for it shines without measure or bound in the way that its own nature dictates when it is not bounded at all by body. And so the light and beauty of God, which is pure, is completely free from all other things and is beyond all doubt called infinite beauty.

'But infinite beauty requires a correspondingly boundless love. Wherefore I beg you, Socrates, to love other things with a definite measure and limit, but to love God with an infinite love. Let there be no bounds to your love for God.'

Chapter 19
HOW GOD IS TO BE LOVED

Such is Diotima's exhortation to Socrates. But, my distinguished friends, we will not only love God without limit, as Diotima is depicted as urging, but we will love God alone. For Intelligence is to God as eyesight is to the Sun. The eyes do not only desire light above all other things; they desire light alone. If we do love physical bodies, if we do love souls, if we do love angels, we shall be loving God in them — the shadow of God in physical bodies, the likeness of God in souls, his image in Angels.

So for the present let us love God in all things in order that eventually we may love all things in God. For if we live in this way we shall progress to the goal of seeing God, and all things in God, and of loving both God in his very self and all things which are in him.Everyone who in this life surrenders himself in love to God, will in the end find himself again in God. Indeed he will return to his proper Idea, the Idea through which he was created; and there anything in him that has been damaged will be repaired again, and he will for ever be in harmony with his own Idea.

But the true man and the Idea of man are the same. Hence because we are all separated from God on earth, none of us is a true man; each one of us is divided from his own Idea and nature. To that Idea love and devotion towards God will guide us, even though we are here mangled and mutilated. But on that day, united with our proper Idea, we shall emerge as whole people. From this perspective it is clear that we have first worshipped God in things in order afterwards to be able to worship things in God, and that the reason for revering things in God is so that we may embrace ourselves above all other things, and it is clear that in loving God we have loved ourselves.

NOTES

1 *desire to procreate in the beautiful*: see *Symposium*, 209B. The belief that procreation is a divine function was common in Renaissance England. The Anglican Church encouraged it within marriage (*The Form of Solemnization of Marriage*); the Erasmian doctrine of increase was also influential, through his *Praise of Marriage* (tr. in Wilson's *Arte of Rhetorique*, 1553; 1560 edn., ed. G. H. Mair (Oxford, 1909)). Through Erasmus, it seems to have filtered into the thinking of, for instance, Shakespeare, who in *Sonnets* I–XIII duplicates many Platonic and Erasmian arguments for procreation, and, following the pattern of the *Symposium*, goes on to contemplate the higher function of 'spiritual procreation'. See also Spenser's *Hymne in Honour of Love*

(1596), which distinguishes the libidinous instinct to multiply which impels the animal species from the higher human urge to reproduce:

> But man, that breathes a more immortall mynd,
> Not for lusts sake, but for eternitie,
> Seekes to enlarge his lasting progenie.   (103–5)

This is very close to Plato, Ficino and Erasmus: 'For what is more blessefull then to live ever? Now, where as nature hath denied this, Matrimonie doeth give it by a certaine sleight, so much as may be' (*Arte of Rhetorique*, 45).

2   See *Symposium*, 204–208B for these arguments, which Ficino at this point does little more than restate. This questioning of the validity of human identity lies at the heart of much of the greatest English art of the period. The doubts aroused in anyone by thinking of the fact that the human being himself is a constant process of change, that we cannot be said (even in physical terms) to be the same person this year as we were last year, in that the human organism is in constant process of decay and self-renewal, destroys the certainties in which the self is accustomed to find its security. See Shakespeare, *Sonnets*, LXII, LXIII, with the solving factor of the Platonist 'marriage of true *minds*' in Sonnet CXVI; Spenser's *Amoretti*, LXI–LXIII; Samuel Daniel, *Delia* (1592), XXXIII; Michael Drayton, *Idea* (1619), VIII. Immortalisation of Beauty by Art is, it is felt, the classic and only feasible remedy.

3   *Symposium*, 209C–209E. We should bear in mind, in considering Plato's and Ficino's valuing of love between men above love for a woman, that it had been customary for at least two thousand years to think of women as vehicles rather than as contributors to human life: in the *Timaeus*, the woman's womb is only 'ploughland' to the man's 'seed', which all by itself becomes a complete living creature (91D). Plato, however, did not subscribe to the 'moronic' theory of the nature of women, and the *Republic* accepts them as being of potentially equal intelligence and authority (445B–457B). It is broadly fair to say that the structure of Plato's political philosophy requires the idea of the possible equality of the sexes; while his philosophy of love relies solely on the ideal of a noble homosexual union. Ficino moderates the homosexual content of the idea radically, in accordance with Renaissance taboos.

4   The relationship between beauty of mind and beauty of body is a complex one, in both Greek and Renaissance European thought. Plato presents an ideal correspondence between internal and external beauty (209B), but later shows that such concord is not a necessary one, and that a lover in a higher state of spiritual development will recognise in an ugly body a transcendingly beautiful soul (210B–210C). Ficino stresses the ugliness of flesh. Spenser, also, in his *Hymne in Honour of Beautie* accepts that 'oft it falles that many a gentle mynd / Dwels in deformed tabernacle drownd' (141–2). The main force of the Platonist

influence, however, seems to have expressed itself in the symbolic identification of outer and inner beauty, particularly feminine beauty. This was especially true of works conceived according to an allegorical or symbolist frame of reference, for obvious reasons. Thus Spenser's Una (Truth) in *The Faerie Queene*, I, is represented as pure, shining beauty, 'as brightest skye' (I.vi.4); in *King Lear*, Cordelia's 'heavenly eyes' (IV.iii) reflect both her own physical beauty and the divine perfection of which she is a nearly unflawed mirror; Ben Jonson's pious and beautiful Celia is 'Coelia' (Heaven) and, to emphasise her status, cries at intervals, 'O Heaven!' However, this system of analogies between earthly and heavenly beauty was complicated in the Renaissance mind by Christian recognition of the existence of counterfeit beauty, allegorised in *The Faerie Queene* in the Una/Duessa pair. The difficulty of distinguishing between true and false beauty provided much of the tension in Elizabethan drama: e.g. *Much Ado About Nothing*, IV.i; *The Winter's Tale*, II.i, etc.

5   In his account of the existence of innate ideas within the human mind, Ficino partially forsakes the *Symposium* itself, in favour of a little general Platonising, founded especially on the doctrine of knowledge as recognition of pre-conscious experience as set out in the *Meno*, and on the *Phaedrus*. Socrates proves to Meno that we were alive and in a state of knowledge before birth; that with entrance into the mortal world we forgot what we had known beforehand; but that our life may be a process of recovery of knowledge (81C–81D). Ficino identifies this prior knowledge with contact with the Ideas or Forms themselves.

6   *Speusippus* and *Xenocrates*: two followers of Plato who were, however, in disagreement with him on various issues.

7   i.e. in the dialogues which bear their names.

8   *Republic*, VI.508A. The beautiful imagery of light irradiating the human mind, representing the God-given intelligence which is the source of uniquely human dignity, is a mainstream Neoplatonist tradition which gathered strength from Plotinus (see *Enneads*, V.3.12; V.5.7) down through the centuries to the Renaissance. Its importance in English poetry can hardly be overestimated. See for example the blind Milton, recognising inner light as the source of all that is divine and valuable in human life (*Paradise Lost*, III, 51–5):

> So much the rather thou celestial Light
> Shine inward, and the mind through all her powers
> Irradiate, there plant eyes, all mist from thence
> Purge and disperse, that I may see and tell
> Of things invisible to mortal sight.

Milton's use of this symbolism in the epic may be more fully understood when it is thought of in terms of the Christian Platonism of Ficino's statement that 'productivity of soul consists solely in the fact that the eternal light of God shines in its inner being', and can be more fully experienced through 'purity of life' (p. 42).

9   *terms*: degrees of a zodiacal sign supposed to increase the influence of a planet entering them. Ficino's passion for astrological explanation of behaviour would have struck Plato as distinctly quaint: however, it remained an important quirk in the Renaissance mind through to the seventeenth century, despite campaigns by the Church and science to discredit it.

10   *Laws*, VIII.836ff., etc. Ficino does not admit that the late *Laws* to some extent represent a recantation by their author on the subject of homosexual love: his earlier attitude (e.g. *Phaedrus*, 256; *Symposium*, 209B–209C) seems to have been more temperate in accordance with the current Greek theories of the essential nobility of love between men, who were potential equals intellectually and spiritually. Although Renaissance taboos against homosexuality were much stronger (and Ficino's antipathy reflects this), the Greek tradition also managed to be reborn. See Spenser's *Shepheardes Calender* (1579): 'For who that hath red Plato his dialogue called Alcybiades, Xenophon and Maximus Tyrius and Socrates opinions, may easily perceive, that such love is much to be allowed and liked of, especially so meant, as Socrates used it: who sayth, that in deede he loved Alcybiades extremely, yet not Alcybiades person, but hys soule, which is Alcybiades owne selfe. And so is paederastice much to be preffered before gynerastice, that is the love which enflameth men with lust toward woman kind' ('Ianuarie', Glosse, 423). Compare also Shakespeare, *Sonnets*; *The Two Gentlemen of Verona*, V.iv, where Valentine values his friend above his mistress; *Twelfth Night*, II.i, Antonio to Sebastian: 'come what may, I do adore thee'; Christopher Marlowe, *Edward II*, *passim*, for treatment of intimate relationships between men.

11   See Pico, *Oration*, pp. 71–2 below, for clarification.

12   i.e. in Aristotle's *On the Soul*, I.2, commenting upon the *Timaeus*, 34.

13   Plato, *Parmenides*, 130B–130C. Ficino's derivation of the Many from the One, and his preference for the latter, is staple Neoplatonist and Pythagorean teaching. See Spenser's Una, *Faerie Queene*, I, representing divine simplicity in a fragmented universe.

14   See Plato, *Parmenides*, *passim*. Dionysius the Areopagite professed to be St Paul's Athenian convert, Dionysius, but was probably a fifth-century Syrian monk. See his *Divine Names*, XIII.184: 'the Divine Science attributes all qualities to the Creator of all things and attributes them all together, and speaks of Him as One', *On the Divine Names and The Mystical Theology*, tr. C. E. Rolt (Macmillan, London and New York, 1966). Both Ficino and Pico were heavily influenced by Dionysius.

15 A concise statement of Ficino's version of the Platonic Chain of Being, each link definitively and lovingly described in its proper place. Compare *Symposium*, 210E–212A; Pico, *Oration*, pp. 67–8 below; Gelli, *Circe*, p. 142 below; Milton, *Paradise Lost*, V.461–512; Shakespeare, *Troilus and Cressida*, I.iii. The nature of the Chain and its ascent was infinitely variable according to the imagination and philosophy of the particular author.

16 *all our unhappiness*. The Narcissus story is not in the original. However, this beautiful passage gives a very deeply felt account of the grieved awareness which Ficino shared with many of his contemporaries of the fact that, for all the wonderful possibilities of man, he was in some obscure way at odds with the rest of Creation and unable to find a happy place upon the Chain of Being with his fellow creatures. In his *Five Questions Concerning the Mind* (Cassirer, 209), Ficino lamented the result of the Fall by which 'we have been placed outside the order of the first nature, and – O sorrow! – live and suffer contrary to the order of nature', the prey of spiritual desires incommensurate with our mortal nature. Here, Ficino expresses this tragic sense of man's fatal flaw in being perversely drawn by desire downwards along the Chain of Being, so that his soul is enthralled by his body, in the myth of Narcissus. This myth may be found in Ovid's *Metamorphoses*, iii.341ff. The image of man as a uniquely tragic figure haunted the imaginations both of the artists of the Italian High Renaissance, and the dramatists of the English Renaissance, who polarised the contrary attributes of man, his sublime soul and his pathetic status as 'poor, bare, forked animal' (*King Lear*, III.iv) in a tragic art unparalleled since the Greek theatre. In a sense, this awareness of man's homeless condition may be understood as a converse of the humanist absorption in his freedom from fixed order which was celebrated and explored by, for instance, Pico, but which could at any moment turn to nightmare.

17 *Symposium*, 212A. Compare the imagery of Shakespeare's Sonnet CXLVI, 'Poor soul, the centre of my sinful earth'; Sidney, 'Leave me, O Love which reachest but to dust'.

18 See *Phaedo*, 66A–67D.

19 Ficino here reveals, and also 'places' the humanist eclecticism which he shares with Pico and Gelli (see Pico's *Oration*, Introductory Note), allowing that truth may take different forms without ceasing to be truth, but reminding the reader not to confuse these scattered elements of reality with the one final reality, the Divine, which inspires them all but has an existence separate from the diversity of the material world. This fundamentally Platonist and humanist doctrine was re-imagined by Milton in his emotional defence of freedom of thought, *Areopagitica* (1644): 'Truth indeed came once into the world with her divine Master, and was a perfect shape most glorious to look on: but when he

ascended, and his Apostles after him were laid asleep, then strait arose a wicked race of deceivers, who ... took the virgin Truth, hewd her lovely form into a thousand peeces, and scatter'd them to the four winds ... We have not yet found them all, Lords and Commons, nor ever shall doe, till her Masters second comming' (*Complete Prose Works*, II, 549).

GIOVANNI PICO DELLA MIRANDOLA

Oration: on
the Dignity of Man

1486 (1572 edition)

Translated by
Douglas Brooks-Davies and Stevie Davies

This is the first half of the rhetorical introduction which Pico
provided for the nine hundred theses which he published in 1486,
meaning to defend them in a public disputation to be held in Rome
the following year. Papal condemnation of a number of these theses
as heretical meant that the disputation never occurred, and the
Oration was not printed until Pico's painfully early death, to
become celebrated and plagiarised all over Europe. Pico's vast
learning, both in the Platonic studies he undertook under the
influence of Ficino; in the Ancients; in Cabbalistic literature and
the medieval Arabian and Jewish schools, was brought together in
the nine hundred theses to produce a philosophy that was
essentially syncretistic. For Pico's feeling that truth was scattered
throughout every serious theology and philosophy, Islam as well as
Christianity, sent him rifling through philosophies of every age,
place and language he could find (which meant that there had to be
rather a lot of theses). The *Oration* is established upon a basis of
this conviction of the essential unity of truth, and it pours out the
philosopher's delight in his conclusion that man is free as air to be

whatever he likes, making him potentially not just the equal but the superior of any other single created being, angels included. The Fall might as well have been just a bad dream.

The dominating image in the *Oration* is of man as Proteus, the sea-god, of whom Ovid had said in the *Metamorphoses:*

People have seen him at one time in the shape of a young man, at another transformed into a lion; sometimes he used to appear to them as a raging wild boar, or again as a snake, which they shrank from touching; or else horns transformed him into a bull. Often he could be seen as a stone, or a tree . . . (*Metamorphoses,* VIII.7)

Proteus had therefore come to be associated with all that is changeful, shapeless and partaking of flux: and he had come to have an ambiguous moral identity, both in ancient Greek, Roman and Renaissance thought and art. Plato, searching towards a God of changeless unity and morally deploring the Greek Pantheon of amoral, fickle gods, ridiculed and repudiated 'false tales of Proteus and Thetis transforming themselves' (*Republic*, II.381D). But Pico, along with many Renaissance humanists, was restlessly excited by the idea of change, and trustful enough not to think it a frightening prospect that man could be free and indefinable in every aspect of his being. The humanists Vives and Gelli followed Pico exactly in their admiration of the protean nature. In Vives' myth, *A Fable About Man* (1518), man, an acting genius able to imitate all life-forms, is called by the admiring gods 'that multiform Proteus, the son of the Ocean' (Cassirer, 389), and this theatrical ability in man, at once fascinating and dangerous, prefigures in Vives' account the Shakespearean preoccupation with the world as a stage. Gelli's prologue to his *Circe* also calls man a new Proteus, closely following Pico, and the image spread, as the Renaissance reached England, into both drama and poetry, where, however, it was both celebrated and distrusted. Spenser's Archimago, the evil magician of *The Faerie Queene* (1590) is explicitly identified with Proteus (I.ii.10), but here the capacity to metamorphose is associated with duplicity and the Satanic nature; in Ben Jonson's *Volpone* (1605), the hero and his tool, Mosca, flourish in a variety of evil disguises, and Volpone himself praises the protean nature (III.vii.150–153); while in Milton's *Paradise Lost*, Satan himself is early established as a master of change (III.630–740). All these protean figures generate exactly the same excitement in the reader as Pico's, but such pleasure as is felt is accompanied by a sense of moral disturbance because these authors *include* awareness of the existence of evil in man's very fallen nature where Pico chooses, in the earlier part of the *Oration*, to ignore it, and later to lay little stress upon it.

That part of the *Oration* which links Pico most significantly with Ficino is his definition of the techniques by which the transformation towards a condition of divinity may be effected, and these are specifically Platonist, including use of the dialectic as an instrument of moral and spiritual purging, and the embracing of a 'love' which unites the New Testament *Caritas* with the visionary elements of Plato's *Symposium* and *Phaedrus*. Pico's notion of the love through which transcendence of the flesh is possible is reminiscent of the possibilities offered in the *Phaedrus* for the lover of rediscovering the absolute beauty which the soul knew before its incarnation:

beauty was once ours to see in all its brightness, when in the company of the blessed we followed Zeus ... to enjoy the beatific vision and to be initiated into that mystery which, we may say with reverence, brings supreme felicity ... Pure was the light and pure were we from the pollution of the walking sepulchre which we call the body, to which we are bound like an oyster to its shell. (250B–C)

Socrates' sense of the spirit's pain at being buried in the gross and dying body is at its most intense in the *Phaedrus*; Pico knows but neglects the pain, in his conviction that the light had not receded too far to be recaptured, with not too much difficulty. It is not a humble vision: it poured into Renaissance culture an egoism which, though it was often tempered by Christian awareness, contrary evidence, or a sense of *hubris*, characterised in some degree the self-consciousness of most artists. As Donne put it in a sermon of 1625:

For, man is not onely a contributary Creature, but a totall Creature; He does not onely make one, but he is all; He is not a piece of the world, but the world itselfe; and next to the glory of God, the reason why there is a world.[1]

The text, we discovered, is (like so much Renaissance philosophic writing) a web of allusions and near-quotations from various sources, but particularly the first section of Hermes Trismegistus' dialogue, *Asclepius* (see n. 4), especially paragraph 6Aff., which Pico nearly paraphrases. Pico's Latin is full of buried images of rebirth and creation, which our translation attempts to render: these images confirm our impression of the over-riding significance for Pico, as for other Neoplatonists, of the idea of the transmigration of souls. Wherever this occurs in religions known to him (see n. 23) he includes a reference, to the point where one suspects that his theory of spiritual rebirth rests on an actual (rather than merely metaphorical) heretical belief in reincarnation. This sheds interesting light on the frequent occurrence of the idea in Renaissance English literature – invoked, for instance, in Faustus' desperation at his impending death (*Dr Faustus*, V.ii), and satirised by Jonson in the skit on the soul of Pythagoras in *Volpone* (I.ii). The idea seems to have had a more than merely academic appeal.

For ease of reading, we have introduced paragraphing, which does not exist in the original.

PICO DELLA MIRANDOLA
ORATION: ON THE DIGNITY OF MAN

Most Reverend Fathers,[2] I have read in the records of the Arabians that Abdala the Saracen,[3] when he was asked what there was to see in this, so to speak, theatre of the world most deserving of admiration, answered: 'There is nothing more wonderful than man to be seen.' This opinion accords with the saying of Hermes Trismegistus:[4] 'Man is a great miracle, Asclepius.' But when I pondered the reasoning behind these statements, those many arguments[5] brought forward by so many for the pre-eminence of human nature were not enough to satisfy me: that man is the mediator between created things, the familiar of the gods above, king of those below, and the interpreter of nature by the acuteness of his senses, the searching and all-embracing power of his reason, the brightness of his understanding; the interstice between enduring eternity and the ebb and flow of time; and (as the Persians[6] say) the one who holds the world together, or rather its wedding song, on David's authority,[7] little removed from the angels. It is true that these are great reasons but they are not the main ones, I mean those which may assume their unquestioned right to the highest admiration. After all, why should we not rather admire the angels themselves and the singing of the most blessed heavenly spheres? At last I seem to perceive why man is the most favoured being and so deserving of all admiration, and what exactly his allotted place is in the universal chain – one to be envied not only by the brute beasts but also by the stars and the intellects far beyond this world. It is beyond belief wonderful. And why not? It is for that very reason that man is justly said to be a great miracle and truly esteemed a most admirable creature.

But hear what this rank is, Fathers, with favourable ears and through your human-kindness be open to this fable of mine. Now [8] the Supreme Father, God the Architect, had just constructed by the laws of His mysterious wisdom this earthly abode of His divinity that we see, this most august temple. He had adorned the supercelestial region with Intelligences, He had animated the heavenly spheres with eternal souls, He had filled the parts of this excremental dungheap of a lower world with a host of creatures of every possible kind. But when the work was completed, the Creator wished that there was someone to consider the design of such a work, to cherish its beauty, and to wonder at its magnitude. And so, when everything was completed (as Moses and the *Timaeus* testify),[9] He finally thought about begetting man. But among His original patterns there was not one from which He could form a new race, nor in His treasuries was there an inheritance to bestow on His new son, neither in the benches of the whole world was there anywhere for him to sit as the contemplator of the universe. Everything was just fulfilled, all things had been distributed amongst the highest, middle, and lowest orders.

But the Father's power did not fade as though worn out by the struggles of his labour, at this greatest moment of the Creation. His was not the wisdom to hesitate in an inevitable and necessary matter through resourceless lack of ideas. It was not in the nature of His generous love that he who was to praise the divine liberality to other creatures should consider it harmful in so far as it concerned himself. At last the best of artists determined that he to whom He had not been able to give anything uniquely his own was to share whatever had been peculiar to the separate species. Therefore He took man as a creation with an unspecified image, and, placing him in the middle of the world, spoke to him as follows: 'Neither a determined dwelling place, nor a unique shape, nor a role that is peculiarly your own have we given you, O Adam, so that you may have and possess what habitation, shape and roles you yourself may wish for according to your desire and as you decide. The nature of all the rest is defined and encompassed by laws prescribed by us; you, restrained by no limitations, of your own free will in whose hand I have placed you, shall appoint your own nature. I have placed you in the middle of the world so that you may from there the more conveniently consider whatever is in the world. We have made you neither celestial nor earthly, neither mortal nor immortal, so that, freely choosing and for your own honour, as it were the moulder and maker of yourself, you may form yourself in what pattern you choose. You will be able to degenerate into the lowest ranks, which are those of the brutes. Through the judgment of your soul you will be able to be reborn into the highest ranks, those of the divine.'

O highest liberality of God the Father, greatest and most wonderful happiness of man, to whom is given whatever he chooses to have, to be what he wills. Brutes, as soon as they are born, bring with them from what Lucilius[10] humorously calls their mother's basket whatever they are to possess. The spiritual ones above either from the beginning or very shortly afterwards were what they are to be for the whole of eternity. On man when he was born the Father bestowed the seeds of all kinds of things and, in embryo, every species of life. Whichever of these he cultivates[11] shall come to maturity and bear fruit in him. If [12] they are vegetative, he will be a plant. If sensitive, he will become a brute. If rational, he will rise to the level of a heavenly being. If intellectual, he will be an angel and the son of God. And if, content with the lot of none of the other creatures, he withdraws into the centre of his unity, his spirit, made one with God, in the darkness of the Father who is established to be above all things, will stand above everything. Who would not admire this chameleon[13] of ours? Or who could more greatly admire anything else whatever? It is he who Asclepius the Athenian[14] not unjustly argued was signified by Proteus in the mysteries because of his self-transforming qualities and the changeability of his nature. Hence those metamorphoses[15] celebrated amongst the Hebrews and Pythagoreans. Thus the cabbalistic theology of the Hebrews sometimes transforms the Holy Enoch into a divine angel whom they call *Mal'akh Shekhinah* and sometimes gives others other names. And the Pythagoreans deform evil men into brutes. And, if Empedocles is to be believed, even into plants. Mahommed, imitating the notion, often gave voice to this: 'Those who fall away from the divine law become animals in the end'; and this is indeed true.

For the bark does not define the tree,[16] but its senseless and insentient nature; nor does the hide define the pack-horse, but rather its brutish and sensitive soul; neither does the circular frame define the heavens, but rather their rational plan; nor is it separation from the body but spiritual intelligence that makes an angel. For if you see someone given over to his belly and grovelling on the ground, it is a senseless tree and not a man that you see; if you see one blinded by the vain illusions of the fantasy, as of Calypso,[17] and aroused by its specious allurements, delivered over to his senses, it is a beast and not a man that you see. If you see a philosopher distinguishing the qualities of things with right reason, you will revere him as a heavenly, not an earthly, being. If you see a person who has withdrawn into deepest contemplation,[18] unaware of the body, absorbed into the innermost reaches of the mind, he is neither a celestial nor an earthly being but rather deserves to be called a sacred creature clothed in human flesh.

Is there anyone who would not admire mankind? Not without justice is he sometimes designated in the sacred writings of Moses and the Christians 'all flesh', and sometimes 'every creature',[19] because he himself fashions, forms, and transforms himself into the shape of all flesh and into the essence of every creature. Therefore Euanthes the Persian,[20] explaining the Chaldean theology, writes: 'There is not anything of man's own nor any innate pattern but many that are external and develop after birth' – hence the Chaldean saying: '*Enosh hu shoni vechamah tebaoth beolme.*'[21] (Man is a various and multiform being of an inconstant nature.) But to what end do I emphasise this? So that we may understand that after we have been born into this condition we become what we will ourselves to be. And so we should take the greatest care that it should not ever be said against us that, being in an honourable position, we did not acknowledge it and turned instead into the images of brutes and foolish beasts of burden, but rather that we should live out the saying of Asaph the Prophet: 'You are all gods and sons of the Highest';[22] not abusing the most tender generosity of the Father and making that free choice which He has given, into something harmful from what was beneficial. A certain sacred striving should seize the soul so that, not content with the indifferent and middling, we may pant after the highest and so (for we can if we want to) force our way up to it with all our might. Let us despise the terrestrial, be unafraid of the heavenly, and then, neglecting the things of the world, fly towards that court [23] beyond the world nearest to God the Most High. There, as the sacred mysteries recount, the Seraphim, Cherubim and Thrones possess the first rank. [24] Let us, feeling ourselves incapable of giving them precedence and impatient of an inferior position, emulate their dignity and glory. If we have truly willed it, we shall be second to them in nothing.

But how do we go about doing this? Let us see what they do and what life they lead. If we come to live like that (for we can) our lot will equal theirs. The Seraph burns with the fire of love. The Cherub blazes with the brilliant light of intelligence. The Throne stands in the firmness of judgement. Therefore if, given over to the active life, we undertake the care of lower creatures after duly pondering the matter, we will be established in the enduring stability of the Thrones. If, disengaged from the active life, we spend our time in contemplative calm, meditating on the Creator in the created, the created in the Creator, we shall blaze all over with Cherubic light. If we burn with love for the Creator Himself alone, we shall flame suddenly with His devouring fire into the likeness of a Seraph. Above the Throne, that is, above the just Judge, sits God, the eternal Judge. Above the Cherub, that is, the contemplator, He hovers, warmly brooding over him as a bird over its nest. For the Spirit of the Lord[25] moves upon the waters, the waters which, I say, are above the heavens and which, according to Job, praise the Lord with hymns before morning light. He who is a Seraph, that is, a lover, is in God and God in him, or rather, he and God are one. Great is the power of Thrones which we possess in judging, highest is the sublimity of the Seraphs, which we attain in loving.

But how far can one agree upon judging or loving the unknown? Moses loved the God whom he saw, and administered as judge amongst his people what he had previously seen as a contemplator on the mountain.[26] Therefore, the Cherub acts as an intermediary with his light and prepares us for the Seraphic fire, and at the same time illuminates the judgement of the Thrones. The Cherub is the mediator between the first rank of Minds, representing the order of Pallas,[27] the guardian deity of contemplative philosophy; this is the one for us to emulate first and to grasp and apprehend, whence we may be ravished to the extreme heights of love and descend, well instructed and prepared, for the duties of the active life. But truly if our life is to be formed after the example of the Cherubic life we must have in front of our eyes its nature and quality, what actions and what numberless works it performs. Because it is not permitted to us, who are flesh and know only those things which are of the earth, to pursue it by ourselves, let us go to the ancient Fathers who, because they were familiar and thoroughly acquainted with these matters, can give us an enriched and certain assurance. Let us consult the Apostle Paul,[28] the chosen vessel, as to what he saw the multitude of Cherubim doing when he himself was exalted to the third heaven. He will reply, at any rate according to Dionysius' reading, that he saw them being purged and illuminated, and finally perfected.

Therefore, imitating the Cherubic life on earth, and restraining the assault of our base desires through moral science,[29] scattering the darkness through the dialectic of reason,[30] purifying the, as it were, filth of ignorance and the vices, let us purge our soul so that its passions may not rage furiously and at random or its reason from lack of foresight deviate from rectitude. Then let us bathe the well-composed and purified soul in the light of natural philosophy[31] so that we may at last perfect her in the knowledge of divine matters and in case the testimony of those of our own circle is not enough, let us consult the Patriarch Jacob[32] whose image blazes forth carved on the throne of glory. Sleeping in the lower world, watching in the upper world, this wisest of Fathers will remind us. But he will advise us through a figure (in this way all knowledge reached the Fathers), that of a ladder extending from the lowest depths of earth to the height of heaven, consisting of a series of many separate steps, with God seated at the very top and contemplative angels in constant succession ascending and descending. If this is what is to be practised in our striving for the angelic life, I ask you, who will reach for the ladder of God with unclean foot or wicked and worldly hands? The mysteries tell us that it is unlawful for the defiled to touch the pure. But what do we mean by these feet and hands?[33] Surely, by the 'foot' of the soul one means that most lowly part whereby the soul is connected to the body, that earthly part of us, that is the power of sustaining and nourishing, the kindling-wood of lust and mistress of the weaknesses of pleasure. Why should we not say that the hands of the soul are its irascible power which fights as the champion of the soul's appetite and, as a plunderer, grabs openly in the glare of day, what the appetite will devour drowsing in the shade. These hands and feet symbolise the specious, sensual power of the body over the soul, which keeps the soul in check, holding it by the scruff of the neck. So that we may not be thrown down from the ladder as being profane and defiled, let us cleanse ourselves in the living river of moral philosophy.

But this will not be enough if we want to be partakers with the angels in the ascent and descent of Jacob's ladder, because first we have to have been well fitted and prepared to be advanced from rung to rung in due order and in no way to err from the ladder, and to participate in the alternate ascents and descents. When we have acquired this through the art of disputation or reasoning, then, brought into the correct frame of mind by Cherubic inspiration, we shall pass along, in our philosophising, the steps of the ladder, that is, nature – penetrating to the central meaning of all things. Sometimes we shall descend, and, as in the myth of Osiris,[34] unity will be scattered into multiplicity with titanic strength, and sometimes we shall ascend, with the force of Phoebus, turning multiplicity into unity as when the limbs of Osiris were collected together; until, reposing at last in the bosom of the

Father who is above the ladder, we are made perfect in the beatitude given by theology.

Let us particularly inquire from just Job,[35] who entered into a compact for life with God before he himself was brought into life, what God the Most High longs for most of all in those tens of hundreds of thousands who attend on Him. He will reply without a doubt that it is peace. This accords with what we read in him, of 'Him who makes peace in high places'; and since the middle order explains to the lowest the counsel of the highest order, let the philosopher Empedocles[36] explain to us the words of the theologian Job: he explains to us that there is a double nature present in our souls, through one of which we are carried up to the celestial regions and through the other we are thrust down to the infernal regions, through Strife and Friendship, or War and Peace, as he bears witness in his verses, in which he laments that he is being hurled into the depths of the sea, behaving like a madman, a fugitive from the gods, through strife and discord.

Surely, Fathers, there is much greater discord in us. We have around us grievous internal wars, wars more than civil [37] which, if we do not want them, and if we strive for that peace which can carry us up on high so that we may stand among the elevated ones of the Lord, philosophy alone will truly curb and calm in us. First of all, if our man will only seek a truce with his enemies, moral philosophy will destroy those unbridled sallies of that hydra-headed beast and the leonine passions of quarrelling and wrath.[38] If then, consulting within ourselves as we need to, we desire eternal, untroubled peace, it will come to us and abundantly fulfil our prayers. Certainly after both beasts have been killed like a stabbed sacrificial pig, moral philosophy will establish an inviolable covenant of most holy peace between flesh and spirit. Dialectic will subdue the turmoils of reason which has been made distressed and confused through contradictions of language and the sophistries of the syllogism.[39] Natural philosophy will soothe the disagreements of opinion which agitate, perplex, and rend in pieces the unquiet soul from all sides. But she will calm them in such a way as to make us remember that nature, according to Heraclitus,[40] was born from Strife and was on this account called 'Contention' by Homer.[41] Therefore it is not in her power to give us true quiet and the stability of peace, for that is the responsibility of her mistress, that is, it is the duty and prerogative of holiest theology. She will direct us to the way and as a companion will lead us to her, who, seeing us in the distance hastening towards her, will cry out: 'Come to me, you who have laboured; come and I will restore you; come to me and I will give you the peace which the world and nature cannot give you.'[42]

Thus gently called and courteously invited, with winged feet, like earthly Mercuries[43] flying up to the loving embraces of our most blessed mother, we shall fully enjoy that longed-for, that most holy peace, indivisible bond, unanimous friendship, through which all souls will not only harmonise in the One Mind which is above all mind, but, in some measure and in a way unutterable, ascend to become most deeply one. This is that friendship which the Pythagoreans say is the end of all philosophy.[44] This is that peace which God creates in His highest heaven, which the angels descending to earth announced to men of goodwill so that through it men themselves, ascending to heaven, might be made angels. Let us wish this peace for our friends, for our age. . . .

NOTES

1 *A Sermon Preached at S. Pauls, May 8. 1625* (*Selected Prose*, ed. H. Gardner and T. Healy (Clarendon Press, Oxford, 1967), p. 263).
2 *Most Reverend Fathers*. Pico addresses himself to the company of distinguished scholars who are to dispute with him. The *Oration* is structured on the form of the customary speech which might open an academic year at medieval and Renaissance schools and universities.

3 *Abdala*, representing Arabian scholarship, is probably 'Abdulláh b.–'Abbás, Mohammed's cousin and the founder of Koranic exegesis. Since his actual works had perished, Pico is no doubt quoting one of the innumerable traditional sayings of Islam.

4 *Hermes Trismegistus.* Neoplatonists conflated the Egyptian god Thoth with the Grecian Hermes, father of wisdom (Cicero, *On the Nature of the Gods*, III.56). From the third century A.D., a group of Neoplatonic writings were attributed to the fabulous Hermes Trismegistus. The work cited here is the *Asclepius*, I.6A, which purports to be a dialogue between Hermes and his equally legendary disciple, Asclepius, and would be known to Pico through Ficino's Latin translation. In Hermes' *Poemander* (I.12), it is asserted that 'God begat a man equal to himself '.

5 *those many arguments.* The list that follows has no identifiable source in a single culture: it is deliberately miscellaneous, combining Greek, Roman, Christian, Moslem, Jewish Cabbalistic and Persian allusions. For Classical sources on similar lines, see Plato, *Republic*, 613E–620D; Aristotle, *Nicomachean Ethics*, 1168B–1169A; *Metaphysics*, 983A; Cicero, *On the Nature of the Gods*, II. Compare also Gelli, *Circe*, pp. 142–5 and n. 20 below.

6 *the Persians.* This is probably a reference to the dualism engendered by the Zoroastrian religion in Persia: the *Chaldean Oracles*, mysterious Greek verses ascribed to Zoroaster, and fascinating to the Platonists, gave directions on the magic by which man might confer with the supernatural.

7 *on David's authority.* The reference here is to Psalm 8:5, which answers the question 'what is man, that thou art mindful of him?' (8:4) with 'For thou hast made him a little lower than the angels, and hast crowned him with glory and honour'. The psalm goes on to celebrate man's kingship over creation.

It is revealing that Pico does not include in his list of differentiating factors man's capacity for virtue, which is traditionally one of the most common apologies for human nature (e.g. Plato, *Protagoras*, 323A–C; Cicero, *On the Nature of the Gods*, I.96). Presumably this is not forgetfulness but avoidance on Pico's part, for to introduce this defence would be to lay himself open to the irrefutable reply that man's capacity for evil is equally abundant.

8 This is a Creation myth, combining Christian, Classical and Oriental elements, but which is more after the quaint and human manner of Plato's *Timaeus* than the austere grandeur of Genesis. The Intelligences were, according to the Platonic doctrine, the cause of motion in the stars (see *Timaeus*, 33B, 34B, 40B); and it was widely accepted in pre-Copernican times that the dregs of the universe fell towards the centre, which was of course our unfortunate planet, where it collected as matter. (See Macrobius, *Commentary on the Dream of Scipio*, tr. W. H.

Stahl, Columbia University Press, New York, 1952, I.xxii.6: 'that vast, impenetrable solid, the dregs and off-scourings ... settled to the bottom'. For 'this earth is ... the very muck-hill on which the sublunary orbs cast their excrements'; John Webster, *The Duchess of Malfi*, IV.ii.)

9 Pico's is a very human God. Though he cites the *Timaeus* (taking the opportunity to associate the supposed author of the Pentateuch — Moses — with Plato's narrator, Timaeus) Plato's lonely deity is not really the same as Pico's. Pietro Crinito in his *On Honest Discipline* (Basel, 1532, 80–1) quoted Pico as saying: 'There have existed in every era a few pre-eminent thinkers, supreme in both understanding and knowledge, for instance Moses, Pythagoras, Hermes Trismegistus, Zoroaster and Solon, all in total agreement, and not only possessing an identical faith but also suasively proclaiming it. For if we are to abide by the ancients, we must accept that the whole corpus of ancient theology asserts exactly the same idea' (my translation).

However, the world-god of the *Timaeus* is self-sufficient, because perfect, whereas Pico's God in the *Oration* is capable of 'wishing' for the presence of someone to offer friendly congratulation on His great work; He is momentarily at a loss to know how to satisfy His need (and, in this, reveals Himself as being subject to necessity, for the plenitude he has created does not, by its very nature, allow of any addition), and, like a human father, He is obligingly anxious to do well by His much desired youngest son. This God with a human face recurs in even the most sophisticated of English literature: in Henry Vaughan's 'Easter-Hymn', 'Graves are beds now for the weary, / Death a nap, to wake more merry', and George Herbert's God is in frequent fatherly conversation with him ('The Collar', 'Love'). Compare Erasmus, *On the Freedom of the Will*, pp. 99–100 and n. 14 below.

10 *Lucilius*, second or first century B.C., a Roman satirist, whose use of the term *bulga* (bag) to signify the womb (*Satires*, xxvi.623; *Carmina*, ed. F. Marx, 1904) is the only known instance of such usage.

11 This theory of the external formation of man, who, upon emerging from the womb is nothing but the sum of his infinite potentialities, was a popular one in the Renaissance, though not always linked to a notion of the supremely free will. There is a contrast between the grammatical structure of Pico's statement that each man 'cultivates' his own nature, and the more general assumption that man is 'cultivable'. Plato's emphasis in the *Republic* on the necessity for rigorous education in creating individual and State along the right lines is constantly echoed by humanists. Erasmus, for instance, in *On Educating Children*, echoes Pico's distinction between vegetable, animal and human life, to slightly different purpose: 'Whereas trees are born either barren or producing wild fruit; and horses are born useless (unbroken), human beings, believe me, are not born at all but fashioned' (*Opera Omnia*, I–2, ed. J.-C. Margolin (North-Holland Publishing Company, Amsterdam, 1971),

p. 31). See also Roger Ascham, *The Scholemaster*, 1570, ed. J. E. B. Mayor (London, 1863), pp. 40–1. Pico, however, is uninterested in anything so banal as education, and does not really allow for the role of external conditioning in the fashioning of the human spirit.

12   The threefold distinction of man into vegetable, sensitive and rational souls derives (ultimately) from Aristotle's *On the Soul* (II and III); the 'intellectual' and 'spiritual' distinctions are the products of Platonism, deriving originally from the *Republic* (VI.511) and representing two further steps up the Christian ladder of contemplation.

13   The image of man as chameleon, with that animal's mysterious powers of instant adaptation, is constant in this period to the point of platitude: compare Vives, *Fable About Man* (*c.* 1518), who follows Pico in showing man as 'changing like a polypus and a chameleon' (Cassirer, 390); in Gelli's *Circe*, he has a flexibility more remarkable than the chameleon's adaptation to the colour of its environment (Dedication to H. Layng's translation, 1744), p. xxii.

14   *Asclepius*. Untraced by me.

15   *metamorphoses*. Pico conflates accounts of metempsychosis from Hermetic, Orphic, Hebrew Cabbalistic, Pythagorean, Pre-Socratic and Islamic sources, in accordance with the generally believed notion which is implicit in the syncretism of the *Oration*, that all these different mystical and magical theologies had an actual and not just a theoretical meeting point, for 'Orpheus and Homer, and Solon . . . and Pythagoras and Plato and several others . . . visited Egypt and profited by Moses' writings' (Pseudo-Justin, *Exhortation to the Gentiles*, *c.* A.D. 14–15, *Patrologiae Graecae*, T. 6, col. 268). Pico draws on the following sources:

   i. *the mysteries*, the Greek Orphic Eleusinian mysteries, a religious cult, with purification and rebirth rites which provoked Renaissance admiration as a spiritual precursor of Christianity.

   ii. *The cabbalistic theology of the Hebrews*. Pico was well versed in the esoteric Cabbala. See for this reference the Book of Enoch, XL.8 – XLI. Enoch was translated by faith into Heaven without having to die first. The Hebrew tag, *Mal'akh Shekhinah*, represents the editor's emendation of the faulty Hebrew of the original text, to give the possible reading, 'angel in the divine presence'.

   iii. *the Pythagoreans*. Pythagoras of Samos was the great Greek philosopher of the sixth century B.C. who united the study of mathematics and music in a way that was simultaneously religious and scientific. His doctrine of the transmigration of souls involved successive incarnations, the status of a particular incarnation being dictated by one's behaviour in a previous life. See Plato, *Republic*, X.613E–620D; *Phaedo*, 81C–83A. The latter stresses the release of the wise soul from this painful cycle, into unity with its Creator.

   iv. *Empedocles*, a fifth-century B.C. Sicilian philosopher. His belief in metempsychosis is most forcefully expressed in his poem, the *Purifications*, in which he recounts his own transmigrations as one of those who have been condemned to wander for thirty thousand years through different mortal forms, in expiation (Diels, 21B. 115). His philosophy owes much to Orphism and Pythagoreanism.

v. *Mohammed*. This may be a 'Hadith', or false tradition, for Mohammed's faith concentrates on punishment and reward in Hell and Heaven, and there is no room in Islam for the doctrine of transmigration (see Koran, Sura LXXXII, CI). It is possible either that the saying represents a Persian (Zoroastrian) corruption of Islam, or that Mohammed was speaking purely metaphorically.

16   In this section, Pico is quietly turning a simile (man may be 'like' an animal), to a metaphor (man, the brute), and finally to a literal identification (man may *become* an animal), on the grounds that the actual can only be defined by reference to the inner essence of a thing. See Cicero, *On Duties* (The Loeb *Cicero*, III, VI.32), who speaks of tyrants as 'fierce and savage monsters in human form' who should be 'cut off from what one might call the common body of humanity'. This concept of *humanitas* recurs in much Renaissance writing, uniting with the traditions described in n. 13 to produce a way of thinking about man's potentially 'animal' nature which in a sense transcends the merely metaphorical—for, when Othello at the height of his jealous passion cries 'Exchange me for a goat . . . ' (*Othello*, III.iii) he really is about to discard his human nature in favour of that of an animal, and in *King Lear*, Goneril and Regan in their lack of humanity to their father truly *are*, in a way that leaves metaphor far behind, 'tigers, not daughters' (IV.ii).

17   *Calypso*. Continuing the theme of man's transformation into the animal, Pico follows the Renaissance tradition of conflating the myths of Calypso and Circe. See Homer's *Odyssey*, V, for the story of Calypso's attempted seduction of Odysseus, and X, for Circe's attempt on his manly virtue and her success in reducing his sailors to the condition of beasts. The two figures were often taken to represent the enchantments of the flesh, 'the delights of sensation' (Plotinus, *Enneads*, I.6.8). In Spenser's *Faerie Queene* (II.xii), the Bower of Bliss episode is an allegory of sensuality based on a conflation of the Circe and Calypso stories, and the 'fantasie' (that part of the mind which is irrational, inventive and wish-fulfilling) is, as in Pico, the means to sensuality (II.xii.42). See also Roger Ascham, *The Scholemaster*, and his denunciation of 'wanton and dallying Dame Calypso' (I.72).

18   *contemplation*. Plato puts 'intelligence' above 'thinking' (*Republic*, 511), and Pico's 'contemplator' and 'philosopher' correspond to similar categories. Pico's attribution of divine qualities to each also agrees with Plato's description of the philosopher as 'godlike' (409–500). Aristotle in the *Politics* (1325B) also regards the activity of the mind at its

highest as being like the activity of God. Pico's contemplator, who sheds awareness of earthly things like so many unnecessary clothes is close to the mystical Socrates of the *Symposium* (210E–212A), and finds perhaps his most perfect embodiment in Renaissance English literature in Milton's 'Melancholy' in *Il Penseroso* (37–44).

19 *all flesh, every creature.* See, for instance, Job, 12:10, Ezekiel, 21:4, Colossians, 1:15, etc.

20 *Euanthes,* possibly the Euanthes mentioned by Pliny in his *Natural History,* (viii.22), but the exact source is not known to me.

21 *Enosh hu shoni.* This Aramaic sentence is translated in the following sentence of the text.

22 *Asaph.* This is from one of the Psalms of Asaph (Psalm 82), a great cry for God's too long delayed judgement on the wicked, and for His mercy upon His afflicted people. 82:6: 'I have said, Ye are gods; and all of you are children of the most High.' 82:3: 'But ye shall die like men ...' The context of this quotation, with its awareness of an Israel threatened with subjection and annihilation as a nation with its own identity, is appropriate to what seems to be a very emphatic shift in the direction of Pico's argument at this point. Whereas earlier passages have been broadly speaking more humanist in feeling than specifically Christian humanist, from this point a more Christian Platonism predominates. Just as the wandering temperament of the Jewish nation had brought repeated black looks and reprisals from Jahweh, so Pico seems to feel (if he does not specifically admit) that unlimited celebration of man's roving nature may bring corresponding dangers. Multiple choice is now discarded in favour of one single obligatory choice, involving difficulty and 'striving', although success is more or less guaranteed to the strenuous. This is the choice of the aspiration of the contemplative soul through a number of specified stages, to final union with the deity.

23 *that court.* See, for instance, Ezekiel, 10:4 and Revelation, *passim.*

24 *Seraphim, Cherubim, Thrones.* Biblical sources are Isaiah, 6:1–7; Ezekiel, 10:1–22; Colossians, 1:16. But Pico here draws on the *Celestial Hierarchy* of Dionysius the Areopagite (pseudo-Dionysius) who was given a credence beyond his deserts because he was wrongly taken for a disciple of Paul, though his writings in fact date from the fifth century A.D. Dionysius recognised nine orders of angels arranged in three groups of three: Seraphim, Cherubim and Thrones; Dominations, Virtues and Powers; Princedoms, Archangels and Angels. See the *Celestial Hierarchy,* VII, for Dionysius' description of the first group of three, which is Pico's main source.

25 *the Spirit of the Lord.* Translators' note: we have rendered *quasi incubando fovet* in terms of the imagery of a bird brooding above its nest so as to try to capture Pico's double allusion, first to Genesis, 1:2 ('the spirit of God moved upon the face of the waters') – patristic

writers translated the Hebrew verb which appears in the Authorised Version as 'moved' as 'incubabat' (to incubate) – and, secondly, to John, 1:32 ('I saw the Spirit descending from heaven like a dove, and it abode upon him'). Compare Milton's exquisite image of the Holy Spirit in *Paradise Lost*: 'thou from the first / Wast present, and with mighty wings outspread / Dove-like sat'st brooding on the vast abyss / And mad'st it pregnant . . .' (I.19–22). The Job reference is to the apocryphal Greek Testament of Job.

26   Exodus, 19–32.

27   *the order of Pallas*. In Conclusion X of his *Cabbalistic Conclusions*, Pico identifies Pallas (the goddess of wisdom) with Zoroaster's divine mind, and Hermes Trismegistus' Son of God.

28   *the apostle Paul* is spoken of in Acts, 9:15 as 'a chosen vessel unto me'. See also II Corinthians, 12:2–4. A fuller account of the third heaven can be found in the apocryphal Book of the Secrets of Enoch, VIII–X.

29   *moral science*. In the *Republic*, Plato sketched an ideal moral education, designed to help the aspirant pierce through 'unreal' matter to the real, which is knowledge of the Good (526C–527C). This course of moral education was meant to establish inner harmony and the capacity to restrain the emotions: for Christian Platonists, like Pico, moral science could only be a preliminary discipline, not a final one, which must be theological.

30   *dialectic of reason*. This mode of discovering truth through analytic and sceptical discussion between different minds is the basic method employed by Socrates in nearly all Plato's dialogues. But it became for him much more than a purely logical technique. In the *Republic*, large claims are made for its possibilities by Socrates, who calls the dialectic the only 'method of inquiry which systematically attempts in every case to grasp the nature of each thing as it is in itself' (533B); 'doing away with assumptions and travelling up to the first principle of all' (533D); distinguishing 'the essential nature of Goodness' (534B–C). See also *Phaedrus*, 264–266. For Pico also, the dialectic is the supreme moral tool, which will hone down the soul into a state capable of responding rightly to the next phase of knowledge.

31   *natural philosophy*. The Platonic cosmology, which derives all things (the Many) from an immaterial, changeless and perfect God (the One of Plato's *Parmenides*) had been for centuries acceptable to Christian thinkers, as far as it went. (See Augustine, *City of God*, VIII, 6:6, *The Platonist conception of natural philosophy*.) The study of natural philosophy leads of itself to God, since, being the study of first causes, it ends in contemplation of the immaterial First Cause of all, God himself, as, for instance, Faustus finds (too late) in Act II, Scene ii of Marlowe's *Dr Faustus*: 'Thinke *Faustus* upon God, that made the world' (625).

32   *Jacob*. In Genesis (28: 11–15) Jacob dreams of angels ascending and

descending 'a ladder set up on the earth, and the top of it reached to heaven' (12), after which God promises him that he shall father a huge race of people and that God shall always be with him. Jacob's ladder became a traditional Christian emblem, signifying, for instance, in Ambrose's *Commentary on Genesis* (28:11), the union of mortal and immortal in Christ, or, in Benedict's *On Humility*, the means of reaching celestial exaltation through humility. For Pico, the ladder is a useful figure because it coincides with his own vision of man as the interim between mortal and immortal, and includes the image of mobility between states of being. The associations of Jacob's ladder with the Platonic Chain of Being were also traditional. See Milton's *Paradise Lost* (III, 500–25) for a poetic representation of the image: Satan could not get his footing on it because the ladder is the ladder of humility, inaccessible to pride.

33 *hands and feet*. This eccentric passage may, perhaps, be better understood by reference to Plato's *Timaeus* (69–71), and his *Republic* (434D–441C), where he makes a threefold distinction between parts of the soul. The lowest is the irrational appetite; the intermediate is the 'spirited' or 'irascible' element; the highest is reason, which can make use of the spirited to control the appetite.

34 *the myth of Osiris*. This convoluted and (in the original) highly elliptical passage celebrates the dialectic as a means of purging and elevating the soul. The 'descent' of the ladder symbolises the dialectic's analytic function of breaking down experience into parts; the 'ascent' is the synthesis of these parts into total knowledge. (Compare Plato, *Phaedrus*, 266, where the dialectical method is seen as 'division and collection', 'the ability to discuss unity and plurality as they exist in the nature of things'.) The classical embellishments relate as follows: *Phoebus*, the sun-god, goes up the heavens each morning, and may therefore be associated with the ascent; *Osiris* is the Egyptian god who, having been murdered, dismembered and scattered by his brother, was sought and put back together by his wife Isis (dissection and synthesis). Osiris is commonly linked with Phoebus because of his identification with the sun; and the sun is also the great Platonic symbol of God. For a very beautiful use of the Isis and Osiris myth in relation to the quest for Truth, see Milton, *Areopagitica* (*Complete Prose Works*, II, 549).

35 *the just Job*. See Job, 25:2.

36 *Empedocles*. See his poem, *Purifications*. His dualism posited two moving causes in the universe, Love or Friendship, and Strife (attraction and repulsion).

37 *wars more than civil*. See Plato, *Gorgias*, 441C; *Republic*, 443–444B, for the image of 'civil war' within the soul mirrored in that in the State, and the need for geometric proportion to exist between all the elements of the cosmos, State and individual. Philosophy, according

to Pico as to Plato, is a way to harmonise the self, so as to attain harmonious agreement between thinking minds.

38 *that hydra-headed beast*, literally, 'many-sided', but we wished to evoke the image of the 'hydra-headed' populace which lies at the basis of the image of civil war within the self and the community. The beast's 'unbridled' nature suggests the horse of passion in Plato's *Phaedrus*, which always threatens to get out of control (246–256). The 'beast' is that which in us is beneath the human, that is, the irrational. It is many-sided because it has no cohesion or unity. Wrath and violence are 'leonine' because of their predatory strength.

39 *sophistries of the syllogism.* Humanism commonly attacked the absurdity and obscurantism of the fossilised 'Aristotelean' scholastic traditions in philosophy. Compare Petrarch's earlier attack, *On Dialectic* (1335), where he quotes the foolish syllogism proposed by a debater to Diogenes, as being typical: 1. What I am you are not. 2. But I am a man. 3. Thus you are not a man. (Cassirer, 136–7.) A later attack may be found in Erasmus' *Praise of Folly* (1511), pp. 151, 160 etc. (Penguin edn.).

40 *Heraclitus* of Ephesus took an estranged view of life, seeing war as 'the father of all things' (fragment 53), and change as being the only certainty. Soul and body, for him, were alien and mutually hostile, so that it is appropriate for Pico to remember him when thinking of the insecurity of the mortal world. But Heraclitus contained a secret optimism: man transcends the animal wholly ('Oxen are happy when they have peas to eat' – fragment 4), and after death the soul is released from the corpse ('man kindles a light in the night when he is dead' – fragment 26). The soul, as in Empedocles, having descended into flesh, ascends. In the most faint of allusions, Pico has consequently reiterated his theme.

41 Homer, *Iliad, passim.*

42 See Christ's words in Matthew, 11:28 and John, 14:27.

43 *Mercuries.* Mercury, who used to bring the gods' messages to and fro from Heaven to earth is an appropriate emblem of the free condition.

44 The Pythagorean Brotherhood was renowned for devoted and enduring friendship; and it was an article of faith with them that there was a bond of likeness between all living things which necessitated respect for all kinds of being. Their ethical aim was to approach and become more like the Divine. See Plutarch, *On Brotherly Love*, 488C, *Moralia*, VI, tr. W. C. Helmbold (Loeb, London, 1939).

DESIDERIUS ERASMUS

On the Freedom of the Will

1524

MARTIN LUTHER

On the Bondage of the Will

1525

For northern Europeans, Erasmus was the core of Renaissance humanism. He brought from the Italian movement a devotion to accurate scholarship in the pursuit of truth; a reverence for the classical values of temperance, tolerance and the civilising virtues of the liberal arts; and he introduced all these values into northern theology. The Erasmian theology is based on confidence in the possible co-operation between a friendly God and a well-intentioned humanity. The voice which defends these twin concepts in *On the Freedom of the Will* is urbane, composed and well-modulated: it is answered by Luther in the much longer *On the Bondage of the Will* in a rasping tone which claims no more than a peasant's eloquence, and, rejecting reason as anathema to faith, speaks of an incomprehensible, violent and (to the eye of common sense) arbitrary God, dictating to a humanity which has been universally created vile and impotent. In this exchange, then, it is possible to see the confrontation between humanist and Protestant images of man simply and clearly, and this contrast is further crystallised by the policy pursued by each theologian of crisply summarising the basis of his position in an introductory passage (part of which is printed here) and, in the case of Erasmus, in an Epilogue (also printed).

Erasmus, without embracing the excesses of the optimism about human liberty asserted by some of his Italian predecessors like Pico, expresses confidence in the survival in fallen man of a limited ability to choose the good, which can make frail though positive response to the grace bestowed by God on all who really want Him: Luther sees everyone as damnable and most as already damned in advance since the beginning of time. Erasmus' God has a kind and human face. He is good in the same way as we would expect a human being to be good: Luther's is explicitly *not* good in this way. Luther is not afraid to allow that a God who created you bad and then punished you for being so would be justly considered obscene if he were a human being. But for Luther this is exactly the point, for, since God is not a human being, he cannot be judged by human standards. The very absurdity of the God Luther worships, and his failure to fulfil the expectations of human reason and human charity, are what make him superhuman. It is the grand test of the elect that they should be able to bring themselves to believe in and love a divinity which reason deplores as a monster. Consequently, where Erasmus urges the quiet claims of reason, Luther demands a complete submission to the irrational. Where Luther condemns all authority but Scripture and the Holy Spirit, and all merely human virtue as disguised vainglory, Erasmus calls attention to the great human authorities of the past (the Church Fathers and the virtuous pagans) who taught or seemed to demonstrate the action of free will. For Luther, the virtuous pagans merited only hellfire; the classical philosophers, for whom he cannot prevent himself from feeling a lingering affection, taught nonsense; and the Church Fathers were of no importance. Luther in this document presents himself as the solitary revolutionary, willing to countenance violence and destruction if called upon, while Erasmus appears with the same gravity and finesse as are realised in the delicate features of his face as Holbein saw it in the famous portrait.

It would not be sensible to try to ascribe to the one view precedence over the other as an influence on Renaissance thought and literature. Indeed, some of the greatness of English literature in this period seems to depend on the irreconcilable conflict of the two opposite positions, continually grinding against one another. In Marlowe's *Dr Faustus,* there is an awareness of a friendly God on whom the sinner might freely call: 'Yet *Faustus* looke up to heaven, and remember Gods mercy is infinite'. But the Lutheran answer is relentless, for *'Faustus* offence can nere be pardoned, the Serpent that tempted *Eve* may be saved, but not *Faustus'* (V.ii). And in Shakespeare's *King Lear,* Donne's *Holy Sonnets,* Milton's *Paradise Regained,* the archetypal conflict between freedom and bondage, authority and inspiration, mercy and justice, is endlessly reiterated.

The text reproduced here, by kind permission of The Westminster Press, is from *Luther and Erasmus: Free Will and Salvation* (Erasmus, *De Libero Arbitrio,* tr. E. Gordon Rupp and A. N. Marlow; Luther, *De Servo Arbitrio,* tr. P. S. Watson and B. Drewery), The Library of Christian Classics (SCM Press, London, 1969), pp. 35–42; 85–96; 124–33.

DESIDERIUS ERASMUS
ON THE FREEDOM OF THE WILL

Prefatory observations: Erasmus acknowledges his limitations and states his point of view

In the Name of Jesus.

Among the difficulties, of which not a few crop up in Holy Scripture, there is hardly a more tangled labyrinth than that of 'free choice', for it is a subject that has long exercised the minds of philosophers, and also of theologians old and new, in a striking degree, though in my opinion with more labour than fruit.

More recently, however, it has been revived by Carlstadt and Eck,[1] in a fairly moderate debate, and now it has been more violently stirred up by Martin Luther, who has put an *Assertion*[2] about 'free choice' and although he has already been answered by more than one writer, it seemed good to my friends that I should try my hand and see whether, as a result of our little set-to, the truth might be made more plain.

Here I know there will be those who will forthwith stop their ears, crying out, 'The rivers run backward'[3] —dare Erasmus attack Luther, like the fly the elephant? To appease them, if I may be allowed to ask for a little quiet, I need say no more by way of preface than what is the fact, that I have never sworn allegiance to the words of Luther. So that it should not seem unbecoming to anybody if at any point I differ publicly from him, as a man surely may differ from another man, nor should it seem a criminal offence to call in question any doctrine of his, still less if one engages in a temperate disputation[4] with him for the purpose of eliciting truth.

Certainly I do not consider Luther himself would be indignant if anybody should find occasion to differ from him, since he permits himself to call in question the decrees, not only of all the doctors of the Church, but of all the schools, councils, and popes; and since he acknowledges this plainly and openly, it ought not to be counted by his friends as cheating if I take a leaf out of his book.

Furthermore, just in case anyone should mistake this for a regular gladiatorial combat, I shall confine my controversy strictly to this one doctrine, with no other object than to make the truth more plain by throwing together Scriptural texts and arguments, a method of investigation that has always been considered most proper for scholars.

So let us pursue the matter without recrimination, because this is more fitting for Christian men, and because in this way the truth, which is so often lost amid too much wrangling, may be more surely perceived.

To be sure, I know that I was not built for wrestling matches: there is surely nobody less practised in this kind of thing than I, who have always had an inner temperamental horror of fighting, and who have always preferred to sport in the wider plains of the Muses rather than to brandish a sword in a hand-to-hand fight.

His dislike of assertions

And, in fact, so far am I from delighting in 'assertions' that I would readily take refuge in the opinion of the Sceptics, wherever this is allowed by the inviolable authority of the Holy Scriptures and by the decrees of the Church, to which I everywhere willingly submit my personal feelings, whether I grasp what it prescribes or not.

Moreover, I prefer this disposition of mine to that with which I see some people endowed who are so uncontrollably attached to their own opinion that they cannot bear anything which dissents from it; but they twist whatever they read in the Scriptures into an assertion of an opinion which they have embraced once for all. They are like young men who love a girl so immoderately that they imagine they see their beloved wherever they turn, or, a much better example, like two combatants who, in the heat of a quarrel, turn whatever is at hand into a missile, whether it be a jug or a dish. I ask you, what sort of sincere judgement can there be when people behave in this way? Who will learn anything fruitful from this sort of discussion—beyond the fact that each leaves the encounter bespattered with the other's filth? There will always be many such, whom the apostle Peter describes as 'ignorant and unstable who twist the Scriptures to their own destruction'.[5]

As far as I am concerned, I admit that many different views about free choice have been handed down from the ancients about which I have, as yet, no fixed conviction, except that I think there to be a certain power of free choice. For I have read the *Assertion* of Martin Luther, and read it without prejudice, except that I have assumed a certain favour toward him, as an investigator may toward an arraigned prisoner. And yet, although he expounds his case in all its aspects with great ingenuity and fervour of spirit, I must say, quite frankly, that he has not persuaded me.

If anybody ascribes this to my slowness or inexperience, I shall not quarrel with him, provided they allow us slower ones the privilege of learning by meeting those who have received the gift of God in fuller measure, especially since Luther attributes very little importance to scholarship, and most of all to the Spirit, who is wont to instil into the more humble what he denies to the wise. So much for those who shout so loudly that Luther has more learning in his little finger than Erasmus in his whole body, a view that I shall certainly not attempt to refute here. I simply ask from such, however ill-disposed they may be, that if I grant to Luther in this Disputation that he be not weighed down by the prejudgements of doctors, councils, universities, popes, and of the emperor, they will not damage my cause by mere snap judgements.

For even though I believe myself to have mastered Luther's argument, yet I might well be mistaken, and for that reason I play the debater, not the judge; the inquirer, not the dogmatist: ready to learn from anyone if anything truer or more scholarly can be brought.[6] Yet I would willingly persuade the man in the street that in this kind of discussion it is better not to enforce contentions which may the sooner harm Christian concord than advance true religion.

The obscurity of scripture

For there are some secret places in the Holy Scriptures into which God has not wished us to penetrate more deeply and, if we try to do so, then the deeper we go, the darker and darker it becomes, by which means we are led to acknowledge the unsearchable majesty of the divine wisdom,[7] and the weakness of the human mind.

It is like that cavern near Corycos of which Pomponius Mela tells, which begins by attracting and drawing the visitor to itself by its pleasing aspect, and then as one goes deeper, a certain horror and majesty of the divine presence that inhabits the place makes one draw back.[8] So when we come to such a place, my view is that the wiser and more reverent course is to cry with St Paul: 'O the depth of the riches and wisdom and knowledge of God! How unsearchable are his judgements and how inscrutable his ways!' and with Isaiah: 'Who has heard the Spirit of the Lord, or what counsellor has instructed him?'[9] rather than to define what passes the measure of the human mind. Many things are reserved for that time when we shall no longer see through a glass darkly or in a riddle, but in which we shall contemplate the glory of the Lord when his face shall be revealed.

Therefore, in my judgement on this matter of free choice, having learned what is needful to know about this, if we are in the path of true religion, let us go on swiftly to better things, forgetful of the things which are behind, or if we are entangled in sins, let us strive with all our might and have recourse to the remedy of penitence that by all means we may entreat the mercy of the Lord without which no human will or endeavour is effective; and what is evil in us, let us impute to ourselves, and what is good let us ascribe wholly to divine benevolence, to which we owe our very being, and for the rest, whatever befalls us in this life, whether it be joyful or sad, let us believe it to be sent by him for our salvation, and that no harm can come to us from a God who is by nature just, even if some things happen that seem to us amiss, for none ought to despair of the pardon of a God who is by nature most merciful. This, I say, was in my judgement sufficient for Christian godliness, nor should we through irreverent inquisitiveness rush into those things which are hidden, not to say superfluous: whether God foreknows anything contingently; whether our will accomplishes anything in things pertaining to eternal salvation; whether it simply suffers the action of grace; whether what we do, be it of good or ill, we do by necessity or rather suffer to be done to us.

And then there are certain things of which God has willed us to be completely ignorant—such as the hour of death or the Day of Judgement: 'It is not for you to know times or seasons which the Father has fixed by his own authority', Acts 1[:7] and Mark 13[:32]: 'But of that day or that hour no one knows, not even the angels in heaven, nor the Son, but only the Father.' There are some things which God has willed that we should contemplate, as we venerate himself, in mystic silence; and, moreover, there are many passages in the sacred volumes about which many commentators have made guesses, but no one has finally cleared up their obscurity: as the distinction between the divine persons, the conjunction of the divine and human nature in Christ, the unforgivable sin; yet there are other things which God has willed to be most plainly evident, and such are the precepts for the good life. This is the Word of God, which is not to be bought in the highest heaven, nor in distant lands overseas, but it is close at hand, in our mouth and in our heart. These truths must be learned by all, but the rest are more properly committed to God, and it is more religious to worship them, being unknown, than to discuss them, being insoluble. How many questions, or rather squabbles, have arisen over the distinction of persons, the mode of generation, the distinction betweeen filiation and procession; what a fuss has been raised in the world by the wrangle about the conception of the virgin as Theotokos![10] I ask what profit has there been so far from these laborious inquiries, except that with the loss of harmony we love one another the less, while seeking to be wiser than we need.

Some truths are not for common ears

Moreover, some things there are of such a kind that, even if they were true and might be known, it would not be proper to prostitute them before common ears. Perhaps it is true, as the Sophists[11] are given to blather, that God, according to his own nature, is not less present in the hole of a beetle (I will not use the more vulgar expression that they are not ashamed to use) than in heaven, and yet this would be unprofitably discussed before the common herd. And that there are three Gods might be said truly according to the rules of dialectic, but would certainly not be spoken before the untutored multitude without great scandal. Even if I were convinced, which is not the case, that this confession which we now use was neither instituted by Christ nor could have been founded by men, and for this reason ought not to be required of any, and further that no satisfaction should be demanded for offences, yet I should fear to publish this opinion because I see so many mortals who are wonderfully prone to offences, whom the necessity of confessing either restrains altogether or at least moderates. There are some bodily diseases that are less evil to bear than their removal, as though a man were to bathe in the warm blood of murdered babes to avoid leprosy, so there are some errors that it would cause less damage to conceal than to uproot. Paul knew the difference between what things are lawful and what are expedient. It is lawful to speak the truth; it is not expedient to speak the truth to everybody at every time and in every way.[12] If I were convinced that at a certain council some wrong decision of definition had been made, I should have the right to proclaim the truth, but it would not be expedient, lest wicked men be given a handle to scorn the authority of the Fathers, even in those decisions which they have taken in a godly and devout spirit. I would rather say that they took a decision that seemed reasonable from the point of view of their own times which present needs suggest should be repealed.

The dangers inherent in Luther's teachings

Let us, therefore, suppose that there is some truth in the doctrine which Wyclif[13] taught and Luther asserted, that whatever is done by us is done not by free choice but by sheer necessity. What could be more useless than to publish this paradox to the world? Again, suppose for a moment that it were true in a certain sense, as Augustine says somewhere, that 'God works in us good and evil, and rewards his own good works in us, and punishes his evil works in us'; what a window to impiety would the public avowal of such an opinion open to countless mortals! Especially in view of the slowness of mind of mortal men, their sloth, their malice, and their incurable propensity toward all manner of evil. What weakling will be able to bear the endless and wearisome warfare against his flesh? What evildoer will take pains to correct his life? Who will be able to bring himself to love God with all his heart when He created hell seething with eternal torments in order to punish his own misdeeds in his victims as though he took delight in human torments? For that is how most people will interpret them. For the most part, men are by nature dull-witted and sensual, prone to unbelief, inclined to evil, with a bent to blasphemy, so that there is no need to add fuel to the furnace.[14] And so Paul, as a wise dispenser of the Divine Word, often brings charity to bear, and prefers to follow that which is fitting for one's neighbours rather than the letter of the law: and possesses a wisdom that he speaks among the perfect, but among the weak he reckons to know nothing, save Jesus Christ, and him crucified. Holy Scripture has its own language, adapted to our understanding. There God is angry, grieves, is indignant, rages, threatens, hates, and again has mercy, repents, changes his mind, not that such changes take place in the nature of God, but that to speak thus is suited to our infirmity and slowness. The same prudence I consider befits those who undertake the task of interpreting the Divine Word. Some things for this reason are harmful because they are not expedient, as wine for a fevered patient. Similarly, such matters might allowably have been treated in discussion by the learned world, or even in the theological schools, although I should not think even this to be expedient save with restraint; on the other hand, to debate such fables before the gaze of a mixed multitude seems to me to be not merely useless but even pernicious.

I should, therefore, prefer men to be persuaded not to waste their time and talents in labyrinths of this kind, but to refute or to affirm the views of Luther. My preface would rightly seem too verbose if it were not almost more relevant to the main issue than the disputation itself.

Epilogue: A reasonable approach to the problem

So far we have brought together those passages in the Holy Scriptures which establish free choice and those on the other side which seem to take it wholly away. Since, however, the Holy Spirit, who is their author, cannot be in conflict with himself, we are forced willy-nilly to seek some moderation of our opinion. Moreover, since different men have assumed different opinions from the same Scripture, each must have looked at it from his own point of view, and in the light of the end he is pursuing. Those who remembered how great is the apathy of mankind in seeking after godliness, and how great an evil it is to despair of salvation; these, while seeking to cure these evils, have fallen unawares into others and attributed too much to free choice. On the other hand, those who ponder how destructive it is of true godliness to trust in one's own powers and merits and how intolerable is the arrogance of some who boast their own works and sell them by measure and weight, just as oil and soap is sold; in their great diligence to avoid this evil, these either so diminish free choice that it avails nothing whatever toward a good work, or even cut its throat entirely by bringing in the absolute necessity of all things. No doubt it seems to them most desirable for the simple obedience of a Christian mind that the whole man should depend on the divine will, place all his hope and confidence in God's promises, recognize how miserable he is of himself, and love God's immense mercy, which he freely bestows on us, and submit himself wholly to God's will, whether he wills to save or destroy: to arrogate to himself no praise for good deeds, but to ascribe all the glory to God's grace, considering man to be nothing else than a living instrument of the divine Spirit, who himself purified and consecrated him with his free goodness, and who, in accordance with his inscrutable wisdom, fashions him and moulds him. Here there is nothing that a man can arrogate to his own strength and yet, with sure confidence, he may hope for the reward of eternal life from God, not because he has merited it with his good deeds, but because it seemed in accordance with God's goodness to promise it to those who trust in him. It is man's part to pray without ceasing that God will impart and increase in us his Spirit, giving thanks if anything is done well by us, that we may marvel at his power in all things, everywhere wondering at his wisdom, everywhere loving such goodness. This way of viewing the matter seems to me also compellingly plausible, for it agrees with Holy Scripture, and answers to the confession of those who, once for all dead to the world, are buried together with Christ in baptism, that the flesh having been mortified, they afterward may live and act in the Spirit of Jesus, in whose body they have been implanted by faith. Undoubtedly a godly sentiment and worthy of favour, for it takes away from us all arrogance, and transfers to Christ all the glory and confidence, which takes away from us the fear of men and demons and, though we distrust our own strength, yet makes us nonetheless strong and of good courage in the Lord. This view we praise to the point of extravagance.

For when I hear that the merit of man is so utterly worthless that all things, even the works of godly men, are sins, when I hear that our will does nothing more than clay in the hand of a potter,[15] when I hear all that we do or will referred to absolute necessity, my mind encounters many a stumbling block. First, why does one so often read that godly men, full of good works, have wrought righteousness and walked in the presence of God, turning neither to the right nor to the left, if the deeds of even the most godly men are sin, and sin of such character that, did the mercy of God not intervene, it would have plunged into hell even him for whom Christ died? How is it that we hear so much about reward if there is no such thing as merit? With what impudence is the obedience of those who obey the divine commands praised, and the disobedience of those who do not obey condemned? Why is there so frequent a mention of judgement in Holy Scriptures if there is no weighing of merits? Or are we compelled to be present at the Judgement Seat if nothing has happened through our own will, but all things have been done in us by sheer necessity? There is the further objection: What is the point of so many admonitions, so many precepts, so many threats, so many exhortations, so many expostulations, if of ourselves we do nothing, but God in accordance with his immutable will does everything in us, both to will and to perform the same? He wishes us to pray without ceasing, to watch, to fight, to contend for the prize of eternal life. Why does he wish anything to be unceasingly prayed for which he has already decreed either to give or not to give, and cannot change his decrees, since he is immutable? Why does he command us to seek with so many labours what he has decided freely to bestow? We are afflicted, we are cast out, we are reviled, we are tortured, we are killed, and thus the grace of God in us strives, conquers, and triumphs. The martyr suffers these torments and yet there is no merit given him, nay, rather, he may be said to sin in exposing his body to torments in hope of eternal life. But why has the most merciful God so willed to work in the martyrs? For a man would seem cruel, if he had decided to give something as a free gift to a friend, not to give it unless that friend were tortured to the point of despair.

But when we come to so dark a depth of the divine counsel, perhaps we shall be ordered to adore that which it is not right to pursue. The human mind will say: 'He is God, he can do what he wills, and since his nature is altogether the best, everything that he wills must also be for the best.' This, too, can be said plausibly enough, that God crowns his gifts in us, and orders his benefit to be our reward and what he has worked in us that he wills by his free goodness to be imputed to those who trust in him as though it were a debt to them, wherewith they may attain eternal life. But I know not how they are to appear consistent who so exaggerate the mercy of God to the godly that as regards others they almost make him cruel. Pious ears can admit the benevolence of one who imputes his own good to us; but it is difficult to explain how it can be a mark of his justice (for I will not speak of mercy) to hand over others to eternal torments in whom he has not deigned to work good works, when they themselves are incapable of doing good, since they have no free choice or, if they have, it can do nothing but sin. If a certain king should give a huge reward to somebody who did nothing in a war while those who behaved bravely got nothing more than their usual pay, perhaps he could reply to the murmuring soldiers: 'What wrong do you suffer if it pleases me to be freely generous to this man?' But who could seem just and clement if he crowned with highest honours a general for his good conduct, a general whom he had sent to war abundantly provided with what he needed, with machines, with men, with money, while he put another to death for failure after having sent him to battle with no equipment at all? Would not the dying man have a right to say to the king: 'Why do you punish in me what was done through your fault? If you had fitted me out like him, I would have won too.' Again, if a master were to free a slave who had merited nothing, he might have reason perhaps to say to the other servants who murmured against this, 'You are no worse off if I am kinder to this one; you have your due.' But anyone would deem a master cruel and unjust who flogged his slave to death because his body was too short or his nose too long or because of some other inelegance in his form. Would not the slave rightly cry out to his master under the blows, 'Why am I punished for what I cannot help?' and he would say this with still more justice if it were in his lord's power to alter the bodily blemish of his slave, as it is in the power of God to change our will, or if the lord had himself given the slave this deformity which had offended, as for example by cutting off his nose or making his face hideous with scars. In this same way God, in the view of some, works even evil in us. Again, as concerns the precepts, if a lord were constantly to order a slave who was bound by the feet in a treadmill, 'Go there, do that, run, come back', with frightful threats if he disobeyed and did not meanwhile release him, and even made ready the lash if he disobeyed, would not the slave rightly call the master either mad or cruel who beat a man to death for not doing what he was unable to do?

Further, when these people so immensely exaggerate faith and love in God, our ears are not offended, for we judge that the fact that the life of Christians is everywhere so corrupted by sins proceeds from no other cause than that our faith is so cold and sleepy, since it makes our belief in God a matter of words, and floats upon our lips, according to Paul: 'For man believes with his heart and so is justified' [Romans, 10:10]. I will not specially argue with those who refer all things to faith as the fountain and head of all, even though to me faith seems to be born from charity and charity in turn from faith: certainly charity nourishes faith just as oil feeds the light in a lantern; the more strongly we love him the more freely do we trust him. Nor are there lacking some who think of faith as the beginning of salvation rather than the sum, but these questions are not here in dispute.

A mediating view, and a parable of grace and free choice

But this, meanwhile, is to be avoided, that while we are wholly absorbed in extolling faith, we overthrow free choice, for if this is done away with I do not see any way in which the problem of the righteousness and the mercy of God is to be explained. Since the Early Fathers could not extricate themselves from these difficulties, some of them were driven to posit two Gods: one of the Old Testament, whom they represented as just, but not as good; another of the New Testament who was good but not just—whose wicked opinion Tertullian[16] sufficiently exploded. Manichaeus, as we have said, dreamed of two natures in man, one which could not avoid sin, and another which could not avoid doing good. Pelagius, while he feared for the justice of God, ascribed too much to free choice, and those are not so far distant from him who ascribe such power to the human will that by their own natural strength they can merit, through good works, that supreme grace by which we are justified. These seem to me, through showing man a good hope of salvation, to have wished to incite him to more endeavour, just as Cornelius[17] by his prayers and alms deserved to be taught by Peter, and the eunuch by Philip, and as the blessed Augustine when he avidly sought Christ in the letters of Paul deserved to find him. Here we can placate those who cannot bear that man can achieve any good work which he does not owe to God, when we say that it is nevertheless true that the whole work is due to God, without whom we do nothing; that the contribution of free choice is extremely small, and that this itself is part of the divine gift, that we can turn our souls to those things pertaining to salvation, or work together [*synergein*] with grace.

After his battle with Pelagius, Augustine became less just toward free choice than he had been before. Luther, on the other hand, who had previously allowed something to free choice, is now carried so far in the heat of his defense as to destroy it entirely. But I believe it was Lycurgus[18] who was rebuked by the Greeks because, in his hatred of drunkenness, he gave the order for the vines to be cut down, when he should rather, by giving access to the fountains, have excluded drunkenness without destroying the use of wine.

For in my opinion free choice could have been so

established as to avoid that confidence in our merits and the other dangers which Luther avoids, without counting those which we have mentioned already, and without losing those benefits that Luther admires. That is to my mind the advantage of the view of those who attribute entirely to grace the first impulse which stirs the soul, yet in the performance allow something to human choice which has not withdrawn itself from the grace of God. For since there are three stages in all things—beginning, progress, and end—they attribute the first and last to grace, and only in progress say that free choice achieves anything, yet in such wise that in each individual action two causes come together, the grace of God and the will of man: in such a way, however, that grace is the principal cause and the will secondary, which can do nothing apart from the principal cause, since the principal is sufficient in itself. Just as fire burns by its native force, and yet the principal cause is God who acts through the fire, and this cause would of itself be sufficient, without which the fire could do nothing if he withdrew from it.

On this more accommodating view, it is implied that a man owes all his salvation to divine grace, since the power of free choice is exceedingly trivial in this regard and this very thing which it can do is a work of the grace of God who first created free choice and then freed it and healed it. And so we can appease, if they are capable of being appeased, those who cannot bear that man should own anything good which he does not owe to God. He owes Him this indeed but otherwise and under another name, just as an inheritance which legally comes to children is not called a benevolence because this is a common right of all men; but if something is given beyond the bounds of common law, it is called a benevolence, and yet the children's debt to their parents is called inheritance.

Let us try to express our meaning in a parable. A human eye that is quite sound sees nothing in the dark, a blind one sees nothing in the light; thus the will though free can do nothing if grace withdraws from it, and yet when the light is infused, he who has sound eyes can shut off the sight of the object so as not to see, can avert his eyes, so that he ceases to see what he previously saw. When anyone has eyes that once were blinded through some defect, but can now see, he owes even more gratitude. For first he owes it to his Creator, then to the physician. Just as before sin our eye was sound, so now it is vitiated by sin; what can a man who sees boast for himself? And yet he has some merit to claim if prudently he shuts or averts his eyes. Take another illustration: a father lifts up a child who has fallen and has not yet strength to walk, however much it tries, and shows it an apple which lies over against it; the child longs to run, but on account of the weakness of its limbs it would have fallen had not its father held its hand and steadied its footsteps, so that led by its father it obtains the apple which the father willingly puts in its hand as a reward for running. The child could not have stood up if the father had not lifted it, could not have seen the apple had the father not shown it, could not advance unless the father had all the time assisted its feeble steps, could not grasp the apple had the father not put it into his hand. What, then, can the infant claim for itself? And yet it does something. But it has nothing to glory about in its own powers, for it owes its very self to its father. Let us apply this analogy to our relation with God. What, then, does the child do here? It relies with all its powers on the one who lifts it, and it accommodates as best it can its feeble steps to him who leads. No doubt the father could have drawn the child against its will, and the child could have resisted by refusing the outstretched apple; the father could have given the apple without the child's having to run to get it, but he preferred to give it in this way, as this was better for the child. I will readily allow that less is due to our industry in following after eternal life than to the boy who runs to his father's hand.

But although we see so little attributed to free choice, yet to some even this seems to be too much. For they would have grace alone to be working in us and our mind in all things to be only passive as an instrument of the divine Spirit, so that good can in no way be said to be ours save in so far as the divine benevolence freely imputes it to us; for grace does not work in us *through,* so much as *in,* free choice, in the same way as a potter works in the clay and not through the clay. But where, then, is there any room for mention of the crown and of the reward? God, they say, crowns his own gifts in us and orders his benefit to be our reward, and what he has wrought in us, he deigns to impute to us making us a partner in his Heavenly Kingdom. This I do not see, how they maintain a free choice which is quite inactive. For if they were to say that it is acted upon by grace in such a way as to co-operate with it, that would be an easier explanation; just as according to the scientists our body receives from the soul its first motion, nor can it move without the soul, and yet not only does it move itself, but it also moves other things and, as a partner in the work, is called to share in glory. But if God works in us as the potter in clay, what can be imputed to us, for good or ill? The soul of Jesus Christ we do not wish to call in question here, though that also was an instrument of the Holy Spirit. For if the infirmity of the flesh means that human merit is diminished, yet he also feared death and wished not for his own will to be done, but his Father's; and yet these people admit that he is the fountain of all merits, who yet take away from the rest of the saints all the merit of good work. Moreover, those who deny free choice entirely, but say that all things happen by absolute necessity, aver that God works in all men not only good but even evil works. Whence it would seem to follow that just as man can by no reason be said to be the author of good works, so he can in no way be said to be the author of evil works. Although this view seems plainly to ascribe cruelty and injustice to God, a sentiment offensive to pious ears (for he would not be God if there were found in him any blemish or imperfection), yet its champions can make this plea in support of their unconvincing case: 'He is God. His work must necessarily be of supreme excellence and beauty; so if you look at the order of the universe, even things evil in themselves are good seen as a whole, and show forth the glory of God, nor is it for any creature to pass judgement on the counsel of God but to submit himself entirely to it; and so, if God chooses to condemn this or that man, he ought not to complain, but embrace whatever is His good pleasure, being fully persuaded that all things are done by Him for the best, nor could they be done in any other way than the best.' Otherwise, who could endure a man who said to God, 'Why did you not make me an angel?' Could not God fairly reply, 'Impudent one, if I had made you a frog, what would you have to complain about?' And if a frog were to complain to God,'Why did you not make me a peacock bright with many-coloured plumage?' would he not rightly reply: 'Ungrateful wretch, I could have made you a mushroom or an onion. Now you can leap, drink, and sing.' Again, if a snake or a basilisk said, 'Why did you make me an animal shunned by men as deadly to all creatures, rather than a sheep?' What would God reply? Perhaps he would say: 'So it seemed good to me and in fitness with the beauty and order of the universe. There is no more injustice in it in your case than for flies and mosquitoes and other insects, each one of which I have so fashioned as a marvel to behold. The spider is not less admirable and beautiful because it is different from the elephant, nay, there is more to wonder at in the spider than in the elephant. Is it not enough for you to be an animal perfect in your species? Poison was not given to you to kill, but that you may defend with this weapon yourself and your offspring, just as the ox has horns, and lions their claws, the wolf his teeth, and the horse his hooves. Each kind of animal has his usefulness: the horse bears burdens, the ox ploughs, the ass and dog assist labour, the sheep brings to man the boon of food and clothing, and you provide material for remedies.' [19]

But let us cease from arguing from these creatures which lack reason. Our disputation was about man, whom God made in his image and likeness and for whose sake he created all things. When indeed we see some born with the most comely bodies, with outstanding qualities, as though they were born to virtue; again, others with monstrous bodies, others liable to horrible diseases, others with minds so stupid that they are but little removed from inanimate brutes and some even more brutish than the beasts, and others with minds so prone to crime that they seem almost borne onward by fate, and others openly mad and demoniac; in what ways shall we explain here the problem of the justice and mercy of God? [20] Or shall we say with Paul: 'O the depth of the riches and wisdom and knowledge of God!' [Romans, 11:33], for this I think to be better than with wicket boldness to judge the divine counsels, which are beyond the investigation of man. But it would be far more difficult to explain why God in some crowns his own benefits with immortal glory, and in others punishes his own wrongdoings with eternal punishment. To defend this paradox there is need for many more paradoxes if the line of battle is to be assured against the other side. They immeasurably exaggerate original sin, by which they would have even the most excellent powers of human nature to be so corrupt that they can do nothing of themselves except to be ignorant of God and to hate him. And they aver that, even though justified by faith, a man cannot of himself do anything but sin. And that very proneness toward sin which is left in us by the sin of our first parents, they will have it to be sin and indeed invincible sin, so that there is no precept of God which even a man justified by faith can fulfil; but so many commandments of God have no other end than to magnify the grace of God, which bestows salvation upon men without consideration of merit.

Meanwhile, these people seem to me in one place to restrict the divine mercy that in another they may widen it, as though one should provide for one's guests a very slender lunch so that the dinner may seem more sumptuous, in a way imitating those artists who, when they want to give the illusion of light in one part of their picture, darken with shadows the parts next to it. They begin, therefore, by making God almost cruel, since on account of another's sin he thus rages against the whole human race, especially when they have repented of their sins and have grievously expiated them all their days. But when they say that even those who are justified by faith do nothing but sin, nay, that in loving and trusting God we earn God's hatred, do they not here make extremely niggardly the grace of God, who so justifies man by faith that he still does nothing but sin? Furthermore, when God burdens man with so many commandments that serve for no other purpose than to make him hate God more and be more terribly damned, do not they make him worse than the tyrant Dionysius of Sicily[21] who deliberately made many laws that he suspected the majority would not keep in the absence of restraint, and at first took no notice, and then when he saw that everybody was breaking them, he began to summon them to punishment, in this way bringing everyone into his power? And yet his laws were of such a kind that they could easily be kept if anyone wished.

I will not now examine the reasons why they say that all the commandments of God are impossible to us, for that was not my intention; I simply wished to show by the way that these men, by their excess of zeal in enlarging in one place the role of grace in the plan of salvation, obscure it in other places. And I fail to see how these points of view can be consistent. Having cut the throat of free choice, they teach that a man is now led by the Spirit of Christ, whose nature will not suffer any association with sin. And yet these same people assert that even when he has received grace, a man does nothing but sin. Luther seems to delight in this kind of extravagant statement, for he seeks to put down the extravagances of others in the words of the proverb by cutting a poor knot with a blunt chopper. This boldness on the part of some goes as far as hyperbole, for they sell not only their own merits, but those of all the saints. And what works are these? Singing, the murmuring of psalms, the eating of fish, fasting, clothes, titles. This nail Luther has driven out with another when he says that all the merits of the saints are nothing but that all the deeds of men, however holy, have been sins, bringing eternal damnation, unless the mercy of God came to the rescue.

The dire results of exaggerated views

One party has made a considerable profit out of confessions and satisfactions, with which they marvelously encumbered the consciences of men, and likewise out of purgatory, concerning which they have asserted certain paradoxes. This fault the other side corrected by saying that confession is an invention of Satan; the most moderate of them say that confession is not compulsory and there is no need of satisfaction for sins, since Christ has paid the penalty for all sins; and finally that there is no purgatory. The one side go so far as to profess that the commands of petty priors are obligatory on pain of hellfire, nor do they hesitate to promise eternal life to him who shall obey. The opposite party meet this extravagance by saying that all the decrees of popes, councils, bishops, are heretical and anti-Christian. Thus one party has enlarged the power of the pontiff beyond all bounds [*panu hyperbolikos*], the other speaks openly of him in terms that I would not dare repeat. Again, one party says that the vows of monks and priests are perpetually binding on pain of hellfire, the other says that such vows are thoroughly wicked, that they are not to be undertaken, and if undertaken are not to be kept.

It is from the conflict of such exaggerated views that have

been born the thunders and lightnings which now shake the world. And if each side continues to defend bitterly its own exaggerations, I can see such a fight coming as was that between Achilles and Hector whom, since they were both equally ruthless, only death could divide. It is commonly said that the only way to make a crooked stick straight is to bend it in the opposite direction: that may be right for the correction of morals, but whether it is tolerable in the matter of doctrine I do not know. In exhorting or dissuading, I see that there *is* sometimes a place for hyperbole; thus to give confidence to a timid man you may say: 'Fear nothing, it is God who will speak and act all things in you.' And to rebuke the insolence of a wicked man it may be useful, perhaps, to say that a man is nothing but sin: and against those who wish their dogmas to be made equal with Scripture you may usefully say: 'Man is nothing but a liar.' But where axioms are put forward in the disputing of truth, I do not consider paradoxes of this kind should be used, for they are almost riddles, and in these matters it is moderation which pleases me at any rate. Pelagius has no doubt attributed too much to free choice, and Scotus[22] quite enough, but Luther first mutilated it by cutting off its right arm; then not content with this he thoroughly cut the throat of free choice and despatched it. I prefer the view of those who do attribute much to free choice, but most to grace.

Nor was it necessary, in avoiding the Scylla of arrogance, that you should be wrecked on the Charybdis of despair or indolence. Nor in mending a dislocated limb need you twist another, but rather put it back into place; nor is it necessary so to fight with an enemy in front that incautiously you receive a wound in the back. The result of this moderation will be the achievement of some good work, albeit imperfect, from which no man can arrogate anything to himself: there will be some merit, but such that the sum *is* owed to God. There is an abundance in human life of weakness, vices, crimes, so that if any man wishes to look at himself he can easily put down his conceit, although we do not assert that man however justified can do nothing but sin, especially since Christ calls him reborn, and Paul, a new creature. Why, you will say, grant anything to free choice? In order to have something to impute justly to the wicked who have voluntarily come short of the grace of God, in order that the calumny of cruelty and injustice may be excluded from God, that despair may be kept away from us, that complacency may be excluded also, and that we may be incited to endeavour. For these reasons, almost everyone admits free choice, but as inefficacious apart from the perpetual grace of God, lest we arrogate aught to ourselves. One may object, to what does free choice avail if it accomplishes nothing? I reply, to what does the whole man avail if God so works in him as a potter with clay and just as he could act on a pebble?

MARTIN LUTHER
ON THE BONDAGE OF THE WILL

from   *Review of Erasmus' Preface:*
Should divine truth be kept from common ears?

In the third section you proceed to turn us into modest and peace-loving Epicureans,[1] with a different sort of advice, though no sounder than the two already mentioned. That is to say, you tell us that some things are of such a kind that even if they were true and might be known, it would not be proper to prostitute them before common ears.

Here again you confuse and mix everything up in your usual way, putting the sacred on a level with the profane and making no distinction between them at all, so that once again you have fallen into contempt and abuse of Scripture and of God. I said above that things which are either contained in or proved by Holy Writ are not only plain, but also salutary, and can therefore safely be published, learned, and known, as indeed they ought to be. Hence your saying that they ought not to be prostituted before common ears is false if you are speaking of the things that are in Scripture: and if you are speaking of other things, what you say does not interest us and is out of place, so that you are wasting your time and paper on it. Besides, you know that there is no subject on which I agree with the Sophists,[2] so that you might well have spared me and not cast their misdoings in my teeth. For it was against me that you were to speak in that book of yours. I know where the Sophists go wrong without needing you to tell me, and they have had plenty of criticism from me. I should like this said once for all, and repeated every time you mix me up with the Sophists and make my case look as crazy as theirs, for you are being quite unfair, as you very well know.

Now, let me see the reasons for your advice. Even if it were true that 'God, according to his own nature, is no less present in the hole of a beetle' or even in a sewer than in heaven (though you are too reverent to say this yourself, and blame the Sophists for blathering so), yet you think it would be unreasonable to discuss such a subject before the common herd.

First, let them blather who will; we are not here discussing what men do, but what is right and lawful, not how we live, but how we ought to live. Which of us always lives and acts rightly? But law and precept are not condemned on that account, but they rather condemn us. Yet you go looking for irrelevancies like these, and rake a pile of them together from all sides, because this one point about the foreknowledge of God upsets you; and since you have no real argument with which to overcome it, you spend the time trying to tire out your reader with a lot of empty talk. But we will let that pass, and get back to the subject. What, then, is the point of your contention that certain matters ought not to be discussed publicly? Do you count the subject of free choice among them? In that case, all I said above about the necessity of understanding free choice will round on you again. Moreover, why did you not follow your own advice and leave your *Diatribe* unwritten? If it is right for you to discuss free choice, why do you denounce such discussion? If it is wrong, why do you do it? On the other hand, if you do not count free choice among the prohibited subjects, you are again evading the real issue, dealing like a wordy rhetorician with topics that are irrelevant and out of place.

Even so, you are wrong in the use you make of this example, and in condemning as unprofitable the public discussion of the proposition that God is in the hole or the sewer. Your thoughts about God are all too human. There are, I admit, some shallow preachers who from no motives of religion or piety, but perhaps from a desire for popularity or a thirst for some novelty or a distaste for silence, prate and trifle in the shallowest way. But these please neither God nor men, even if they assert that God is in the heaven of heavens. But where there are serious and godly preachers who teach in modest, pure, and sound words, they speak on such a subject in public without risk, and indeed with great profit. Ought we not all to teach that the Son of God was in the womb of the Virgin and came forth from her belly? But how does a human belly differ from any other unclean place? Anyone could describe it in foul and shameless terms, but we rightly condemn those who do, seeing that there are plenty of pure words with which to speak of that necessary theme even with decency and grace. Again, the body of Christ himself was human as ours is, and what is fouler than that? Are we therefore not to say that God dwelt in it bodily, as Paul has said [Colossians, 2:9]? What is fouler than death? What more horrifying than hell? Yet the prophet glories that God is present with him in death and hell [Psalm 139:8].

Therefore, a godly mind is not shocked to hear that God is present in death or hell, both of which are more horrible and foul than either a hole or a sewer. Indeed, since Scripture testifies that God is everywhere and fills all things [Jeremiah,

23:24], a godly mind not only says that He is in those places, but must needs learn and know that he is there. Or are we to suppose that if I am captured by a tyrant and thrown into a prison or a sewer—as has happened to many saints—I am not to be allowed to call upon God there or to believe that he is present with me, but must wait until I come into some finely furnished church?

If you teach us to talk such nonsense about God, and are so set against the locating of his essence, you will end by not even allowing him to remain for us in heaven; for the heaven of heavens cannot contain him, nor is it worthy of him [I Kings 8:27]. But as I have said, it is your habit to stab at us in this hateful way in order to disparage our case and make it odious, because you see that for you it is insuperable and invincible.

As for your second example, I admit that the idea that there are three Gods is a scandal if it is taught; but it is neither true, nor does Scripture teach it. The Sophists speak in this way with their newfound dialectic, but what has that to do with us?

In the remaining example, regarding confession and satisfaction, it is wonderful to see with what felicitous prudence you put your case. Everywhere you walk so delicately, as is your habit, in order to avoid giving the impression either that you do not wholeheartedly condemn our views or that you are not opposed to the tyranny of the popes, for that would be by no means safe for you. So you bid adieu meanwhile to God and to conscience—for how does it concern Erasmus what God wills in these matters and what is good for the conscience?—and launch an attack on mere externals, charging the common people[3] with abusing the preaching of free confession and satisfaction and turning it into carnal liberty to suit their own evil inclination, whereas by the necessity of confessing (you say) they were at all events restrained.

What outstandingly brilliant reasoning! Is that the way to

teach theology? To bind souls by laws and, as Ezekiel says [Ezekiel, 13:18f.], to slay them when they are not bound by God? By this token you set up for us again the whole tyranny of papal laws, as being useful and salutary because by them too the wickedness of the common people is restrained. But instead of attacking this passage in the way it deserves, let me put the point briefly. A good theologian teaches as follows: the common people are to be restrained by the external power of the sword when they behave wickedly, as Paul teaches in Romans, 13[4]; but their consciences are not to be ensnared with false laws, so that they are burdened with sins where God has not willed that there should be sins. For consciences are bound only by a commandment of God, so that the interfering tyranny of the popes, which falsely terrifies and kills souls inwardly and vainly wearies the body outwardly, has simply no place in our midst. For although it makes confession and other outward burdens compulsory, the mind is not kept in order by these means, but is rather provoked into hatred of God and men; and it is in vain that the body is tortured to death with outward observances, for this makes mere hypocrites, so that legal tyrants of this kind are nothing else but ravening wolves, thieves, and robbers of souls [Matthew, 7:15; John, 10:8]. Yet it is these that you, good spiritual counsellor that you are, commend to us again. You set before us the cruellest of soul destroyers, and want us to let them fill the world with hypocrites who blaspheme and dishonour God in their hearts, as long as outwardly they are kept in some degree of order, as if there were not another means of keeping them in order, which makes no hypocrites and is applied without any ruination of consciences, as I have said.

Here you produce analogies, of which you seek to give the impression that you have an abundant store and make very apt use. You say, for instance, that there are diseases which are less evil to bear than their removal, such as leprosy, etc. You also bring in the example of Paul, who distinguished between things lawful and things expedient [I Corinthians, 6:12; 10:23]. It is lawful, you say, to speak the truth, but it is not expedient to do so to everybody at every time in every way. What a fluent orator[4] you are! Yet you understand nothing of what you are saying. In a word, you treat this subject as if it were simply an affair between you and me about the recovery of a sum of money, or some other quite trivial matter, the loss of which (as being of much less value than your precious external peace) ought not to trouble anyone enough to prevent him from giving way, and doing or suffering as the occasion requires, so as to make it unnecessary for the world to be thrown into such an uproar. You thus plainly show that outward peace and quietness are to you far more important than faith, conscience, salvation, the Word of God, the glory of Christ, and God himself.

Let me tell you, therefore—and I beg you to let this sink deep into your mind—that what I am after in this dispute is to me something serious, necessary, and indeed eternal, something of such a kind and such importance that it ought to be asserted and defended to the death, even if the whole world had not only to be thrown into strife and confusion, but actually to return to total chaos and be reduced to nothingness. If you do not understand this or are not concerned about it, then mind your own affairs and let those understand and be concerned about it on whom God has laid the charge.

For even I, by the grace of God, am not such a fool or so mad as to have been willing to maintain and defend this cause for so long, with so much zeal and constancy (which you call obstinacy), amid so many dangers to life, so much hatred, so many treacheries, in short, amid the fury of men and demons, simply for the sake of money (which I neither possess nor desire), or popularity (which I could not obtain if I wished, in a world so incensed against me), or physical safety (of which I cannot for a moment be certain). Do you think that you alone have a heart that is moved by these tumults? Even we are not made of stone, or born of the Marpesian rocks;[5] but when nothing else can be done, we prefer to be battered by temporal tumult, rejoicing in the grace of God, for the sake of the Word of God, which must be asserted with an invincible and incorruptible mind, rather than to be shattered by eternal tumult under the wrath of God, with intolerable torment. May Christ grant, as I hope and pray, that your mind may not come to that, although your words certainly sound as if you thought, like Epicurus, that the Word of God and a future life were fables; for you seek with your magisterial advice to persuade us that, as a favour to pontiffs and princes or for the sake of peace, we ought if occasion arises, to give way and set aside the most sure Word of God. But if we do that, we set aside God, faith, salvation, and everything Christian. How much better is the admonition of Christ, that we should rather spurn the whole world [Matthew 16:26]!

You say things like these, however, because you do not read or do not observe that it is the most unvarying fate of the Word of God to have the world in a state of tumult because of it. This is plainly asserted by Christ, when he says: 'I have not come to bring peace, but a sword' [Matthew, 10:34], and in Luke: 'I came to cast fire upon the earth' [12:49]. And Paul in I [II] Corinthians 6[:5] says: 'In tumults', etc. And the prophet in the Second Psalm abundantly testifies the same, asserting that the nations are in tumult, the peoples murmur, kings rise up, princes conspire, against the Lord and against his Christ; as if he would say, numbers, rank, wealth, power, wisdom, righteousness, and whatever is exalted in the world, opposes itself to the Word of God. Look into The Acts of the Apostles and see what happens in the world on account of Paul's word alone, to say nothing of the other apostles. See how he alone sets both Gentiles and Jews by the ears, or as his enemies themselves say in the same place, he turns the world upside down [Acts, 17:6; cf. 24:5]. Under Elijah the Kingdom of Israel was troubled, as Ahab complains [I Kings, 18:17]. And what tumult there was under the other prophets!

113

They are all killed or stoned, while Israel is taken captive to Assyria and Judah to Babylon! Was this peace? The world and its god cannot and will not endure the Word of the true God, and the true God neither will nor can keep silence; so when these two Gods are at war with one another, what can there be but tumult in the whole world?

To wish to stop these tumults, therefore, is nothing else but to wish to suppress and prohibit the Word of God. For the Word of God comes, whenever it comes, to change and renew the world. Even the heathen writers testify that changes of things cannot take place without commotion and tumult, nor indeed without bloodshed. But it is the mark of a Christian to expect and endure these things with presence of mind, as Christ says: 'When you hear of wars and rumours of wars, see that you are not alarmed; for this must take place, but the end is not yet' [Matthew, 24:6]. For myself, if I did not see these tumults I should say that the Word of God was not in the world; but now, when I do see them, I heartily rejoice and have no fear, because I am quite certain that the kingdom of the pope, with all his followers, is going to collapse; for it is against this in particular that the Word of God now at large in the world, is directed.

I am aware, of course, that you, my dear Erasmus, complain in many books about these tumults and the loss of peace and concord, and with the best of intentions (as I verily believe) you try hard to find a remedy for them. But this gouty foot laughs at your doctoring hands; for here in truth you are, as you say, rowing against the stream, or rather, you are putting out a fire with straw. Stop your complaining, stop your doctoring; this tumult has arisen and is directed from above, and it will not cease till it makes all the adversaries of the Word like the mud on the streets. But it is sad to have to remind a theologian like you of these things, as if you were a pupil instead of one who ought to be teaching others.

It is here, therefore, that your aphorism (which is neat enough, though your use of it is inapposite) really belongs—I mean your aphorism about diseases that are less evil to bear than their removal. You should say that the diseases that are less evil to bear are these tumults, commotions, disturbances, seditions, sects, discords, wars, and anything else of this sort, by which the whole world is shaken and shattered on account of the Word of God. These things, I say, because they are temporal, are less evil to bear than the inveterate wickedness through which souls will inevitably be lost if they are not changed by the Word of God; and if that Word were taken away, then eternal good, God, Christ, the Spirit, would go with it. But surely it is preferable to lose the world rather than God the creator of the world, who is able to create innumerable worlds again, and who is better than infinite worlds! For what comparison is there between things temporal and things eternal? This leprosy of temporal evils ought therefore to be borne, rather than that all souls should be slaughtered and eternally damned while the world is kept in peace and preserved from these tumults by their blood and perdition, seeing that the whole world cannot pay the price of redemption for a single soul.

You have some elegant and unusual analogies and aphorisms, but when you are dealing with sacred matters your application of them is puerile and indeed perverse, for you creep on the ground and never have a thought that rises above human comprehension. For the operations of God are not childish or bourgeois or human, but divine and exceeding human grasp. But you do not seem to see that these tumults and divisions are marching through the world by the counsel and operation of God, and you are afraid lest the heavens should fall. But I, by the grace of God, see this clearly, because I see other greater troubles in time to come, by comparison with which these present seem no more than the whisper of a breeze or the murmur of a gentle stream.

But the dogma concerning the freedom of confession and satisfaction you either deny or do not know to be the Word of God. That is another question. We, however, know and are sure that it is God's Word by which Christian freedom is asserted, so that we may not allow ourselves to be trapped and brought into bondage by human traditions and laws. This we have abundantly taught elsewhere; and if you wish to go into the question, we are prepared to state our case or debate it with you as well. There are not a few books of ours[6] available on this subject.

But at the same time, you will say, the laws of the pontiffs ought in charity to be borne with and observed equally with divine laws, if by any chance it is possible in this way to maintain both eternal salvation through the Word of God and also the peace of the world. I have said above that that is not possible. The prince of this world does not allow the pope and his own pontiffs to have their laws observed freely, but his purpose is to capture and bind consciences. This the true God cannot tolerate, and so the Word of God and the traditions of men are irreconcilably opposed to one another, precisely as God himself and Satan are mutually opposed, each destroying the works and subverting the dogmas of the other like two kings laying waste each other's kingdoms. 'He who is not with me', says Christ, 'is against me' [Matthew, 12:30].

As to your fear that many who are inclined to wickedness will abuse this freedom, this should be reckoned as one of the said tumults, part of that temporal leprosy which has to be endured and that evil which has to be borne. Such people should not be considered so important that in order to prevent their abusing it the Word of God must be taken away. If all cannot be saved, yet some are saved, and it is for their sake that the Word of God comes. These love the more fervently and are the more inviolably in concord. For what evil did ungodly men not do even before, when there was no Word? Or rather, what good did they do? Was not the world always inundated with war, fraud, violence, discord, and every kind of crime? Does not Micah liken the best of the men of his day to a thorn hedge [Micah 7:4]? And what do you think he would call the rest? But now the coming of the gospel begins

116

to be blamed for the fact that the world is wicked, whereas the truth is that the good light of the gospel reveals how bad the world was when it lived in its own darkness without the gospel. In a similar way the uneducated find fault with education because their ignorance is shown up where education flourishes. That is the gratitude we show for the Word of life and salvation.

What apprehension must we not suppose there was among the Jews when the gospel set everyone free from the law of Moses? What did not so great a freedom seem likely to permit to evil men? Yet the gospel was not on that account taken away, but the ungodly were allowed to go their own way, while the godly were charged not to use their freedom as an opportunity to indulge the flesh [Galatians, 5:13].

Nor is that part of your advice or remedy of any value, where you say it is lawful to speak the truth, but not expedient to do so to everybody at every time in every way; and it is quite inappropriate for you to quote Paul's saying: 'All things are lawful for me, but not all things are expedient' [I Corinthians, 6:12]. Paul is not there speaking of doctrine or the teaching of the truth, in the way that you misinterpret him and make him mean what you want. Paul wishes the truth to be spoken everywhere at every time and in every way. He can therefore rejoice even when Christ is preached in pretence and from envy, and he declares plainly and in so many words that he rejoices in whatever way Christ is preached [Philippians, 1:15 ff.). Paul is speaking factually and about the use made of the doctrine, that is, about those who boasted of Christian freedom but were seeking their own ends and took no account of the hurt and offence given to the weak. Truth and doctrine must be preached always, openly, and constantly, and never accommodated or concealed; for there is no scandal in it, for it is the sceptre of righteousness [Psalm 45:6–7].

Who has empowered you or given you the right to bind Christian doctrine to places, persons, times, or causes when Christ wills it to be proclaimed and to reign throughout the world in entire freedom? 'The word of God is not bound,' says Paul [II Timothy, 2:9]; and will Erasmus bind the Word? God has not given us a Word that shows partiality in respect of persons, places, or times; for Christ says: 'Go into all the world' [Mark, 16:15]. He does not say, 'Go to one place and not another', as Erasmus does. And he says, 'Preach the gospel to every creature' [*ibid.*], not 'to some and not to others.' In short, you prescribe for us respect of persons, respect of places and customs, and respect of times, in the service of the Word of God, whereas it is one great part of the glory of the Word that (as Paul says)[7] there is no *prosòpolèmpsia* and God is no respecter of persons. You see again how rashly you run counter to the Word of God, as if you much prefer your own ideas and counsels.

If we now asked you to distinguish for us the times, persons, and ways in which the truth ought to be spoken, when would you be ready to do it? The world would reach the limit of time and its own end before you had established any certain rule. Meanwhile, what would become of the ministry of teaching and the souls that should be taught? But how could you be able to give us a rule when you know no means of assessing either persons or times or methods? And even if you most decidedly did, yet you do not know men's hearts. Or does 'method', 'time', and 'person' mean for you that we should teach the truth in such a way as not to offend the pope or annoy the emperor or upset the pontiffs and princes, and not to cause any commotions and tumults in the world, lest many be made to stumble and become worse? What sort of advice this is, you have seen above; but you would rather spin fine though useless phrases than say nothing at all.

How much better it would be for us miserable men to let God, who knows all men's hearts, have the glory of prescribing the manner, persons, and times for speaking the truth! For he knows what should be spoken to each, and when and how. As it is, however, he has enjoined that his gospel, which is necessary for all, should know no limit of place or time, but should be preached to all in every time and place.

NOTES

Desiderius Erasmus, *On the Freedom of the Will*

1 *Carlstadt and Eck*. In 1519, the German Catholic theologian, Johann von Eck, and the Lutheran Andreas Carlstadt, met to debate Luther's Theses of 1517.

2 *Assertion*. The allusion is to Luther's *Assertio omnium articulorum M. Lutheri per Bullam Leonis X novissimam damnatorum* (1520).

3 *The rivers run backward*: Euripides, *Medea*, 410. The use of proverbial, homely, but classically based wit to irritate the opponent is characteristic of both authors, reflecting the humanist culture in which each was or had been rooted, and the extent to which the Latin of the debate is as much colloquial as erudite.

4 *temperate disputation*. The humanist principle of the patient elucidation of truth through exchange of ideas, with the duty of mutual openness, is in the same tradition as Pico's Platonist confidence in the dialectic (see Pico, *Oration*, pp. 73–4 above), and Milton's later view of the merely partial ability of the individual to apprehend truth, with the consequent obligation of tolerance of diverse opinions: 'Truth and understanding are not such wares as to be monopolised' (*Areopagitica*, *Complete Prose Works*, II, 535). This is fundamentally a classical position, though the medieval Christian disputations were also meant to function on this principle. Sir Thomas More in his *Reply to Luther* (1523) objected to Luther's mode of argument as being an unclassical 'spew[ing] ... muck, filth, dung, shit' (*Complete Works of St Thomas More*, V, tr. S. Mandeville, ed. J. M. Headley (Yale University Press, New Haven, Conn., and London, 1969); I, 21).

5 II Peter, 3:16.

6 Compare Sir Thomas More's Utopians, who held that 'truth would eventually prevail of its own accord – as long as the matter was discussed calmly and reasonably' (*Utopia*, 1516, tr. P. Turner (Penguin Classics, Harmondsworth, 1965), p. 119). More's and Erasmus' dedication to the liberal arts and debate gave them a special awareness of the dangers of fanaticism and dogma in human relationships. It may however also be noted that Erasmus' pacific, bland expression was calculated to have an aggravating effect on opponents, and was felt by the irascible Luther to be disingenuous.

7 *divine wisdom*. This is the point where Erasmus' Christian humanism diverges from Pico's more lofty view of the godlike powers of the human intellect (*Oration*, p. 71 above). The Christian values of humility

and charity appeared to Erasmus, as they had to Petrarch, to dwarf the claims of human reason: 'It is one thing to know, another to love; one thing to understand, another to will'; 'Deep and inaccessible are the caverns where truth is hidden' (Petrarch, *On His Own Ignorance*, Cassirer, 103; 125). The impulse of this kind of humanism, therefore, is all towards unity, synthesis and harmony, stressing what may be shared by men (love) as opposed to what may separate them (dogmatic certainty). It is not difficult to see why Luther found this intolerable. Though he shared Erasmus' distrust of merely human reason, he believed in the absolute certainty of the justified soul, the separation of the elect and a God not merciful in all cases. In Erasmus, the sinning child may feel assured of automatic grace in response to a movement by the will towards sincere repentance; in Luther, the father may have rejected the child from the beginning of time, never to embrace him. He rebuked Erasmus: 'Your thoughts about God are all too human' (*On the Bondage of the Will*, 125).

8 Pomponius Mela, *De chorographia* (repr. Vienna, 1518), pp. 72–5.

9 Romans, 11:33; Isaiah, 40:13.

10 *Theotokos*: 'God-bearing', a reference to the Virgin birth. The follies of the scholastic theologians in attempting to measure the incalculable mysteries of Scripture are also satirised by Erasmus in his *Praise of Folly*: 'Could God have taken on the form of a woman, a devil, a donkey, a gourd or a flintstone? If so, how could a gourd have preached sermons, performed miracles and been nailed to the cross?' (154).

11 *Sophists*. This school of hair-splitting Greek philosophers for whom Plato showed such contempt is used by both Erasmus and Luther as a metaphor for the scholastics.

12 Erasmus here shows himself to belong to that humanist tradition which, regarding some people as more fully human than others, spreads its sympathies largely but distrusts and patronises the unlettered multitudes. (Compare Milton, *Tenure*, pp. 181–2 below). The cultural egotism implicit in this position is countered but balanced by Luther's trust in the simple clarity of the Gospel, which makes it equally available to all (p. 107 below), combined with the spiritual élitism of his doctrine of the elect, which drastically limits the number of persons to be let into Heaven.

13 *Wyclif*: John Wycliffe (*c.* 1320–1384), an English reformer who attacked the Papacy as Antichrist, and emphasised the idea of divine grace and the individual's right to interpret Scripture for himself.

14 For Erasmus, the basic depravity of human nature is rather pathetic than disgusting, and evokes a reaction of absolving charity as opposed to Luther's punishing gaze. Luther seems to feel that to sympathise with human failings and to refrain from anything that might exacerbate them is to invite contamination. The humane expression worn by Erasmus' God strikes him as a sentimental invention by Erasmus. It is, however,

interesting that Erasmus goes on to stress the purely metaphorical technique used by the Bible to make God accessible to man's finite understanding, so that his God does not share that part of our human nature which makes us subject to change (anger, jealousy, etc.). This denial of a 'human' nature in God provokes Luther (pp. 112–13 below) because it assumes that the Bible does not mean what it says. Many Protestants objected to an allegorical reading of the Bible, and to allegory in general, as impious falsification of the truth. (Even John Donne attacked 'the curious refinings of the Allegoricall Fathers'; *Essays in Divinity*, ed. E. M. Simpson (Clarendon Press, Oxford, 1952), p. 40).

15 *clay in the hand of a potter*: Isaiah, 45:9; Jeremiah, 18:6; Romans, 9:21–3. Erasmus had argued in part II of his disquisition that these texts did not exclude the possibility of the existence of free will in man, as his opponents suggested. This paragraph may be read as a précis of the arguments Erasmus has evolved in the course of the tract.

16 *Tertullian*: one of the greatest of the Latin writers amongst the earlier Christians of the second century, who wrote many treatises on the Christian life.

   Manichaeus: a third-century Persian with heretical dualistic Christian views.

   Pelagius: a fourth- to fifth-century British monk, Morgan, condemned by the Papacy, whose cult denied original sin, asserted the natural goodness of the human will and rejected the barbarous doctrine of the eternal damnation of unbaptised children.

17 *Cornelius*: See Acts, 10. Cornelius was a charitable and God-fearing Gentile of Caesarea, who was visited by a vision, and was subsequently welcomed by Peter into Christian fellowship.

   the eunuch: Acts, 8:27–39. The nameless Ethiopian eunuch showed interest and faith enough to be instructed and baptised by the Apostle Philip.

   Augustine: 'So I seized eagerly upon the venerable writings inspired by your Holy Spirit, especially those of the apostle Paul' (*Confessions*, VII.21, tr. R. S. Pine-Coffin (Penguin Classics, Harmondsworth, 1961), p. 155).

18 *Lycurgus*: the Spartan law-giver. The source of this story is not known.

19 This enthusiastic catalogue of speaking animals discussing their place in the hierarchy of being threatens to become digressive, since its function is not clarified, possibly because, rather in the spirit of Gelli and his animals in the *Circe*, Erasmus is so fascinated by the strange and various non-human beings who make up Creation; how they might be supposed to feel; and how they function in comparison with man, that he becomes imaginatively involved beyond the requirements of his discourse.

20 The obscene injustices of the universe, including those elements of nature which are most clearly wasteful or spoiled in the making – freaks, disability, madness – lead Erasmus to pitying abstention from comment on what cannot be understood. But he does not, with Luther, go so far as to make excuses for and attribute goodness to the kind of God who would carry over the world's injustices into the spiritual sphere, so as to arbitrarily bless or damn His creatures. Erasmus here is in a humanist tradition in placing the claims of human justice and reason (these being God-given faculties) above the possible accompanying dangers of unchristian presumption. The existence of the unnatural within nature was one of the most intense preoccupations of Renaissance literature, the orthodox Christian explanation being, of course, that man's fall through his ancestor, Adam, was responsible for its appearance in history, and that man's continuing fallen nature remained responsible. (See Milton, *Lycidas*, 100–2; *Paradise Lost*, XI and XII; Sir Thomas Browne, *Religio Medici*, 1643, I.37 (ed. J.-J. Denonain (Cambridge University Press, Cambridge, 1955), pp. 49–50). Erasmus does not stress this, since he wishes to emphasise human potentiality for redemption.

21 *Dionysius of Sicily*: probably Dionysius I, from 405 until 367 B.C. the tyrant of Sicily.

22 *Scotus*: Joannes Duns Scotus, known as the Doctor Subtilis, a thirteenth-century monk and scholar who attacked the idea of the harmony between faith and reason of Aquinas, supported the doctrine of the Immaculate Conception and asserted the effectiveness of free will.

Martin Luther, *On the Bondage of the Will*

1 *Epicureans*. Luther has been taunting Erasmus with the charge that his tolerance covers an amoral love of ease. Epicurus (341–270 B.C.) was not an epicure but a benevolent and austere Greek philosopher who, in his concern over men's terrors of death and the animosity of the gods, sought to alleviate human pain by teaching that happiness was man's greatest good; that all is matter; and that the gods cannot harm us or interfere with us. This anti-Providential, consolatory philosophy was abused by later (especially Roman) adherents, and came to have a bad reputation as a sordid and animalistic pleasure-philosopy. The application of the allusion to Epicurus to Erasmus' compassionate view is obvious.

2 *Sophists*. See Erasmus, *On the Freedom of the Will*, n. 11 above.

3 *the common people*. At this point, Luther shows that aspect of his Protestantism which might be classed as 'democratic': a profound belief in the fundamental equivalence of all human souls, whether they lodge in the bodies of the (unequal) poor or rich. The inner being of every man

is and must be, according to Lutheran theology, kept inviolate from the laws of every other person except God. The consequence of this respect for the equivalent integrity of all human souls is repudiation of the power of external human authority in spiritual matters (most especially, the Papacy). Where Erasmus preaches man's free will before God, Luther replies in terms of his slavery before God but his freedom with respect to his own species. But see also Luther's *Against the Robbing and Murdering Hordes of Peasants*, 1525 (*Luther's Works*, vol. 46), which drops the revolutionary stance in favour of a kind of conservatism: 'baptism does not make men free in body and property, but in soul . . . I think there is not a devil left in hell; they have all gone into the peasants' (51–2).

4   *orator.* Luther's persistently sarcastic references to his opponent's eloquence and beauty of language evidence a blend in him of admiration for the nobility of human language at its best which is an index of the greatness of the species from the point of view of the humanist (cf. Gelli, *Circe*, pp. 140–1 below), and a Puritan distrust of the aesthetically beautiful as liable to turn out to be merely specious enchantment, which should be abandoned in favour of plain-speaking.

5   *Marpesian rocks.* See Virgil, *Aeneid*, VI.471. Luther belatedly asserts his own vulnerability and capacity for pain, which makes him equal in humanity to Erasmus, by allusion to the marble quarried in Paros (Mount Marpesus) to which Virgil compares the love-tormented Dido's indifference to Aeneas in the Underworld. This confession is meant to give the sternly militant Protestantism which follows the character of a sad but necessary imperative.

6   *a few books of ours.* See, for instance, Luther's *The Babylonian Captivity* (1520) and *On Christian Liberty* (1520).

7   Romans, 2:11; Ephesians, 6:9; Colossians, 3:25.

GIOVANNI BATTISTA GELLI

Circe

1549

Translated by H. Layng in 1744

Gelli's dialogue dwells upon the theme of metamorphosis, creating an island world where the possibility of infinite choice of modes of being is opened out. Through the skill of the magician, Circe, and the artist's imagination, Being becomes a kind of fluid medium, allowing the comparison of life on different dimensions (dialogue between an oyster and a man) as if from the inside, and the opening of a route between these different states of being, along which the chooser may pass (Man becomes Elephant and eventually returns). In this remodelled world of new possibilities, Gelli has engagingly fused primitive folk-lore with an elegant humanist vision. The agent of all these magical transformations is Circe, the magician whose charms in Homer's *Odyssey* turned Odysseus' men into beasts, the incarnations of their own sensuality, and also, of course, the wicked seducer of Ovid's *Metamorphoses*.

But she is a Circe modified by the allegorising traditions of many centuries—one who in Gelli's dialogue is like an artist herself, witty, noble, and one whose magic permits the delightful liberty of free intercourse between creatures normally mute and isolated in

124

relationship to one another by their separate, established positions at intervals along the Chain of Being. She dramatises that element in human nature which Gelli's humanist predecessors had celebrated—the passion for change and exploration, the groping after elusive possibilities—and there is in fact much of Pico and Ficino in the Florentine Gelli, as he whimsically sweeps into his dialogue as many commonplaces of Renaissance thought as happen to occur to him. The form of the dialogue itself allows an inclusiveness which is characteristic of the humanist manner of thinking; yet, in doing so, it blurs and confuses any straightforward humanist message of optimism at man's happy state and superior nature, which we might expect to find in a work dealing with man's place as compared with that of the animals.

Such a blurring is a necessary consequence of the fact that this is first of all an imaginative and dramatic work, which, like the chameleon which was the humanists' favourite metaphor, keeps changing colour with the object it is imagining. For once you really imagine yourself into the nature of another being, as Gelli is doing with his impersonations of the 'thought' patterns of his hare and serpent, his deer and elephant, it follows that the world is bound to look very different. In this case, contemplation of the nature of man is less like looking into a mirror of oneself than like observing another person, perhaps critically, from various perspectives. The oysters of the dialogue really do appear to speak from an alien nature and experience, and the imaginative power of Gelli in entering that experience is so great that human life never finally emerges as a wholly desirable state by contrast. On the contrary, despite the persistence of the hero Ulysses in his bluff certainties, the pain of consciousness, the shivering, exposed human body, and all the unfairness of life, are the images that predominate. Gelli turns the dialogue form into something very like a play. His Circe figure looks forward in some ways to the figure of Shakespeare's Prospero in *The Tempest*, transforming the beings upon his enchanted island, in an intricate dance of egos which come to rest in quiet, but without any ultimate reassurance that human life can escape the ugliness and melancholy in which its roots seem buried. The vision of man's total freedom as popularised by Pico here turns back upon itself to become a frightening state of uncertainty, a homelessness envious of the steadier objects of nature which know their place. The Renaissance imagination became permeated by an awareness of this rootless condition, and Gelli's creatures are happy to escape the human experience Henry Vaughan would later regret in his poem 'Man':

> He knocks at all doors, strays and roams,
> Nay hath not so much wit as some stones have
> Which in the darkest night point to their homes,
> By some hid sense their Maker gave;
> Man is the shuttle, to whose winding quest
> And passage through these looms
> God ordained motion, but ordained no rest.
>
> (*Silex Scintillans*, 1650)

Gelli's Circe is not the evil stereotype drawn on in Spenser's *Faerie Queene* (II.xii.42–87) or Milton's *Comus* (46–77). She is respected by Ulysses at least up to the final chapter as an equal, and offers not temptation but opportunity, providing the dream which is the essential condition of perfect choice. It is ironic that Dialogue V (printed here) should, in comparing the condition of the human woman with the female animal, find Ulysses more uncouth and insulting than at any other time, at the expense of the feminine, while the same dialogue begins with a display of courtliness on his part to Circe, the feminine raised to a status of quasi–divinity. There is little doubt that this irony was apparent to the author, whose humanist imagination can give itself to understanding any predicament while Ulysses' all too human nature cannot. Therefore, Gelli reproduces every imaginable argument in favour of the emancipation of women, with some sympathy, but his protagonist occupies himself with cracking hoary jokes at the expense of women, and occasionally trying to terrify the gentle, feminist deer with 'science'. The conclusion that it is better to be free than to be a woman (even if this involves a reduction to the level of the animals) is inevitable, and this is only one in a succession of understandable refusals by various species to rejoin the human race on any terms. This is only interrupted by the elephant Aglaphemus in the final dialogue (the last part of which is also printed here). He agrees to come home from elephanthood to being a human philosopher, and concludes with a most endearing and large hymn of praise to his Creator for allowing him the option.

Although Gelli's *Circe* was translated into English during the Renaissance period (by H. Iden in 1557) and enjoyed considerable popularity, I have chosen the eighteenth-century translation by H. Layng to include here, as rendering the original more correctly and being in addition much more readable. Though his translation of Dialogue V is perhaps rather too jocose, doing less than justice to the spirited and intelligent replies of the deer, it is entirely appropriate to the manner of Ulysses.

Dialogue V
ULYSSES, CIRCE AND THE HIND

Ulysses. 'Tis said, dear *Circe*, that truth begets hatred; but surely to a noble mind nothing can be so odious as falshood; and nothing renders a person so abhorred as a discovery that his tongue holds no commerce with his heart. So that I am determined to disburthen my breast sincerely, though I hazard your favour by it.

Circe. Let not the wise *Ulysses* think me capable of being offended at the truth, which is always welcome to those that are able to bear it: So speak your thoughts securely.

Ul. Why then I must own, I labour under some suspicions, that you have not granted to these creatures so free a use of their understandings as of their tongues. If not, I must complain that I think myself abused. If otherwise, how is it to be conceived that they should be unanimous in so monstrous a proposition, that it is better to be a Beast than a Man?

Circe. Were the case as you state it, you would have reason to charge me with a breach of promise, which is ever the effect of a weak head or a bad heart. And yet I affirm to you, that when you disputed with them they had the same exercise of their intellectual faculties as when they were men.

Ul. Prodigious! that they should not be able to discern so broad a mark, when I so plainly pointed it out to them.

Circe. Who knows (which is nothing incredible) but they find some enjoyments, some pleasures, unthought of by us? But come on; boldly pursue your enterprize, all may not prove so obstinate. And be assured, that as all the animals you see have been men, what shape soever they may bear, none of them will offer you any violence. *Exit Circe.*

Ul. It was a common saying with our wise men of *Greece,*[1] that 'those whose judgement was sufficient to conduct them through life with decency and honour were justly to be esteemed in the highest rank among mortals; that those who had not sense enough to govern themselves for their own preservation, yet had enough to be advised by persons wiser than themselves, were to be placed in the second form; but those that neither had enough to direct themselves, nor to listen to those who had, were scarce worthy to be reckoned a part of human nature.' Those whom I have been discoursing with, as I take it, are of this latter sort, so that one is not to be surprized at the estimate they make of things. But as I may flatter myself that I can judge somewhat better, and am convinced how much it is the duty of man to be assistant to a distressed brother, think myself obliged to persevere till I find some worthy of the gift I have to offer.——But see, what a noble herd of stags is here! I must try if there be any of my countrymen among them.——Tell me, ye stags, if Heaven has ought in store to oblige you with, if there be any *Grecian* of your herd?

Hind. Oh! ye blessed Powers, and do I once more hear the sound of human accents! And have I myself recovered the use of speech too?

Ul. aside. Who knows but I may have less reason to suspect *Circe* here? This opens well, by thanking the Gods for the use of speech.

Hind. Are you of *Greece*, pray, who put the question?

Ul. I am, my name *Ulysses.*

Hind. I also was of *Greece*, but of a different sex: I was a Woman before *Circe* changed me into a Hind.

Ul. aside. Nay, if I have to do with a Woman, who, they say, always takes the wrong side of the question, we are not likely to gain ground.[2] However, it will be some satisfaction to have tried both sexes.

Hind. Why then does *Ulysses* give himself the trouble of wandering up and down the island in quest of his countrymen? And tell me, I adjure you by the same vows you made use of, How does it come to pass that I have the privilege of speaking with you, which I never enjoy'd since my transmutation?

Ul. If you esteem it a privilege, you may thank me for it, who by dint of intreaties, out of the love I bear my countrymen, have obtained, first, that each shall have the power of speech; after that, the blessing of being restored to their former shape; and to crown all, of being safely reconveyed to *Greece*. And as you are one, will you accept of the offer? Speak your mind freely, and I must add quickly too; for when you Ladies revolve a thing too long in your minds, either out of hurry or diffidence, you quite lose yourselves: So that your most celebrated repartees have been the most off-hand.[3]

Hind. No.——I think you could not desire an answer shorter or quicker.

Ul. I cannot say it is the wisest I ever heard, but I can safely say I never heard a shorter.

Hind. Why not the wisest?

Ul. Only because there is no sense in it.

Hind. You ought to take it for granted that I have my reasons when I say no.

Ul. That may be, but perhaps I may be better satisfied when I hear some of them.

Hind. Well then, don't you think I had some for not consenting to be restored, since you hear that I was a Woman?

Ul. I can't see any; since you must consider, that you would have been changed into a rational creature, for which you seemed to express the highest esteem, when you so devoutly thanked the Gods upon the recovery of speech, which is inseparable from rationality.

Hind. My objection was not against becoming a Rational Creature, but against becoming a Woman. For Women are held in such contempt among you, that some of the Philosophers have had the confidence to assert that we are of another species. Others have stiled us imperfect Men, and so have proceeded to philosophize upon the hypothesis of imperfection. But a little attention to their own births would have been sufficient to expose such extravagant notions.[4]

Ul. Hey! dey! Why how came you by so much philosophy?

Hind. You will be less surprized, when I tell you, that my husband was a professor of the first credit, with whom it was impossible to converse so much, without picking up a good deal of what is so easily learned.

Ul. I can tell you one thing which I perceive he could never teach you.

Hind. Pray what was that?

Ul. To overcome the itch of prattling, which is still so strong upon you, that though you could coolly reject the offer, you could not forbear being transported when you found the use of your tongue.[5]

Hind. What I have to alledge then in justification of my refusal is, that you men treat us as your slaves, or at least as your servants, not as you ought, like your equals or companions. A thing so immoral, so monstrous, that I defy you to produce a parallel to it in Nature. Cast your eyes round the Animal World, and shew me where the Female is not the partner, not the slave to the Male; sharer of his pleasures, and fellow-sufferer in his troubles? Man is the single exception. I say Man, who from being a Lord, degenerates into a Tyrant, and as he finds himself superior to us in strength and courage, is generous enough to take advantage of it.[6]

Ul. What makes you declaim thus furiously?

Hind. I tell you once more, because you use us as your servants.

Ul. Not as our servants, dear Hind; as our companions if you will.

Hind. D'ye call those companions, where the one always commands, and the other always obeys? But what aggravates our unhappiness is, that we purchase this bondage, or service, (call it what you will) with our own money. For, according to your righteous laws, when once one of us chooses to associate herself (to use your soft phrase) with one of you, her fortune must be thrown into your lap; and she that has none, is sure to be treated as a slave for life, or else her only deliverance from it, is by being shut up in some honourable prison, to become a Priestess to *Pallas* or *Diana,* or some such self-denying Goddess, but must never think to taste of any worldly pleasures more.[7]

Ul. And yet this delivery of the portion into the Husband's hands is evidently calculated for your advantage.

Hind. A very particular sort of advantage is that! Because, whereas others pay the person that serves them, we pay him whom we serve. But I desire to know how this custom was introduced for our good?

Ul. Because, when men observed your unaptness for business from irresolution or unsteadiness, it was adjudged that the safest method to preserve your fortunes, was to have them consigned to your Husbands, not as Masters of them, but as Attorneys for them, to secure them to you in bar of accidents. Accordingly you find upon their decease they revert to you: So that what you suppose is diametrically opposite to the true state of the case, and is evidently injurious to the Husband. Whereas the fairest way had been for the Husband to be obliged to deposite into some third hand just as much as he receives with his Wife; and then if there should be any defect, the loss should be in common to both. This would at least have had one good effect, that it would turn your thoughts towards improving the principal, which is not so often done, because it is looked upon to be the Husband's business to get abroad, and the Wife's to spend it at home. And yet in your widowhood you are indemnified, and all deficiencies are made good out of the man's effects.

Hind. But we that stay at home have a greater share in the getting part, than you that ramble abroad. For you never saw a vast fortune raised where there was not a Woman as notable to keep, as the Man was industrious to get.

Ul. I believe it; and always thought you had a better turn for saving money than Men;[8] for it is *timorousness* and *pusillanimity* that puts people upon hoarding. But then these very qualifications prove you to be much more fit to receive than give command; this minute care and exactness being only to be exercised in little matters. Hence the highest encomium that a Woman can merit is, they say, that she is very governable.[9]

Hind. They say! that is, you say; and it makes for your purpose to have that notion generally prevail. But ask us, or ask experience, and you will find us as fit to govern, nay preside, in affairs of the highest importance. Consider the kingdom of the *Amazons*, how long was that preserved without their being indebted to any of you, either in Politicks or in War? To relate how the bounds of the *Babylonish* empire was extended by *Semiramis*, or the *Scythian* by *Tomyris*, were to transcribe your histories, which abound with their exploits.[10]

Ul. And how many more such can you name? I fancy you may count them all upon the fingers of one hand.

Hind. For which we may thank you; who never give us an opportunity of exercising these faculties, but keep us immured within your own houses, employed in all the low offices that the care of a family brings with it; for which our sole reward is, to hear you say magisterially, that a Woman's fame and her employment should begin and end within the compass of her *own walls*. And yet even in this little way you may observe such an exactness, that the houses where there are no Women, in comparison of those where they are, put one a good deal more in mind of a den than a paradise; which some of you have had the honesty to own. As to the propriety and neatness relating to your own persons, all that I shall say is, that I don't think it difficult to distinguish which is the old Batchelor.

Ul. I grant, that you have your merit in these kind of things.

Hind. And we should distinguish ourselves as much in things of a higher nature, if we were permitted to be concerned in them.

Ul. I beg you not to go too far,[11] lest you should put me in mind of the Shoemaker, who, when they were criticising upon a statue, asserted that the shoe was cut wrong at the instep, and proved his point; upon which the fellow growing vain, was for finding fault in another place; but a stander by pulling him by the sleeve, told him, 'Friend, don't go higher than the instep, for all above that is beyond your province.'

Hind. I am glad you will allow us any thing; for, generally speaking, your worst word is too good for us.

Ul. How can that be, when we always honour you, and give you the preference?

Hind. Never, in things of any consequence; but perhaps as far as giving the upper hand at table, and a few soft appellations merely for your own sakes, whilst we have any beauty left to engage you. When that is fled, Heaven knows your behaviour towards us, both in words and deeds.

Ul. This is the height of ingratitude.

Hind. As for facts which are less generally known I shall say nothing of them; but your words are too notorious to be dissembled. Is it not a saying with you, common even to a proverb, that 'in Marriage there are but two happy days; the first when the wife is led in, the second when she is carried out?'

Ul. These are little freedoms of language that men of wit

will indulge themselves in, when they meet, to divert the cares of life: But I think their practice shews that they don't express their real sentiments, there being so very few that do not some time or other venture upon matrimony; and those that never do, are looked upon as odd creatures at best, and seldom escape censure.[12]

Hind. And yet you can all be ready enough to say, 'the Man that takes one Wife should bear the figure of Patience on his crest, but he that takes a second that of Folly.'

Ul. The moral is, that second marriages, especially where there are children, are seldom very happy; as they want that strong cement of love that joined them in the first instance. Nor do I really think patience in the case so useless a virtue, as it is so liable to be exercised by some of you; which made a man of wit say, that 'he never saw a bride going to her husband's house, but he always pictured her in his mind, carrying one hand stretched out, and in it a lighted torch, as who should say, that she was going to set on fire the family she was going into.'

Hind. Nay never be ashamed to give us the sequel: 'And the other held behind, with a hook in it, with which she had been robbing the family from which she came out.'

Ul. I cannot say that these things have not been said by men of character, and perhaps they have had their provocations too. Neither will I deny how injuriously you have been accused by some of us, men of debauched lives, or not of a capacity to consider your worth, or how much we are forced to be obliged to you. All which I am proud to allow, or should think myself unworthy the name of a Man. If Nature has given us in some things the advantage, so much the better for us: If you had been furnish'd with stronger faculties of body or mind, you had been less fit for the part Nature intended you should act, in subserviency to us. And when you behave properly in that post, we think ourselves not less obliged to you than to Nature herself for ordering it so.[13] You are not therefore to take notice of every scurrilous saying, which fools are ever ready to throw out, since we can quote you as many good things justly pronounced in your favour, such as that 'It is you alone that make life preferable to death: That you are our crown;' according to that renowned *Egyptian* King, who after having shewn his immense treasure to a Royal Brother, told him, 'he had yet a jewel to produce, of more value than all the rest,' and then presented him to his Queen.[14]

Hind. I ask, How is it then that we are used so ill by you?

Ul. And I ask, How do you mean?

Hind. I answer again, in treating us as servants, not as companions. Tell me then fairly, How came it to pass that you should, by prescription, range out to the full extent of your Will, whilst we are tied up by the short bridle of Honour? Is it that none but we can offend against Honour? You indulge every desire, and yet we must not be allowed the least slip, though we have stronger temptations to it; not from a more furious or more ungovernable will, but from your vile importunity and irresistible assiduity: And if you at length succeed in robbing a poor Lady of her honour, you are the first to repay her with a thousand reproaches.

Ul. If it be so inestimable a jewel, let them lock it up safer then.

Hind. How is that possible, when every fellow has a key to it? So that if we are drawn aside, as the fault is yours, so should the shame be also. Especially as you arrogate to yourselves a superior degree of understanding.

Ul. And yet if you would attend to the reason of this practice, you would not condemn it: But the error arises from your confounding cases, and putting yourselves, as brutes, upon the same foot with us. Now I demand, Is it right that the riches which a man has gained by his industry, or that the honours which have been the reward of his virtue, should descend to one wholly a stranger to his blood?

Hind. No, certainly.

Ul. But this must be the case, if Women were to give a

loose to unlawful desires. Now this, I say, can never happen to Brutes, who have no property to leave to their offspring, and have no concern about them, after they are able to shift for themselves.

Hind. Since we have fallen upon the subject of Children, I desire to know how that justice and equity, the want of which we have complained of, is observed by you in regard to them? For it is well known, that you cast the whole care and burthen of their infancy upon us, contrary to the usage of all other animals in the world.

Ul. And pray, don't you as dextrously shift off this incumbrance, by putting them out to nurse? which I believe is as little practised among any other animals in the world.

Hind. Who is the occasion of this but yourselves? who, during their infancy, won't give yourselves the least trouble or concern about them. But as soon as they are grown up, things take a quite different turn. Then you enter as it were into a combination together, to despise and set us at nought. Nor is this expressed in words alone, but in very deed: They are called your sons, take your name, and count themselves only of your family, without taking any farther notice of us.

Ul. Nor is this founded but on the most reasonable considerations.

Hind. I suppose the reason is grounded in this case, as in all the rest, upon your power; which can always make reason take what shape it pleases.

Ul. The reason that I intended to give was, because they derive their sensitive soul and essence of humanity from us, and us alone.

Hind. Are we then mere cyphers in the case?

Ul. You must know, the female can of herself produce nothing of a higher nature than the vegetative quality, which we enjoy in common with the plants.[15] This, I say, is the highest perfection that she can unassisted reach. Hence you see, as Nature never acts in vain, she has not distinguished plants and trees into different sexes. If there are some exceptions, as for example, in the corneile-tree, where you will find the female fruitful, and the male barren; and there can be no contact in the case, and the thing produced is of no higher a nature than the vegetative; for this, as I said before, the female is alone and of herself sufficient. This I illustrate by a familiar instance, suppose, of the hen, which of herself solely and properly can produce an egg, that has evidently the vegetative soul or nature in it, because it grows to a certain determinate size: But yet this egg, as it is unimpregnated, will ever remain unfruitful. So Physicians assure us, that you yourselves have often false conceptions, which they call *Mola*.[16] Now this, it is plain, must be endued with the vegetative power because it increases to a stated magnitude, but has no sensitive quality, because the other sex was wholly unconcerned in the production: So that as our sons derive from us alone the very animal essence and sensitive soul, they may well, as you observe, be called our sons. Hence, when they arrive at any degree of maturity, you are by universal consent, absolved from farther care, which still remains a duty upon us.

Hind. What returns are we entitled to, for all our pains and care?

Ul. To be ever honour'd, and if occasion requires, upon the decease of the father, to be always supported: Which is never refused but by wretches below the name and dignity of Men. And in truth, Nature is herself your security, who seems to have impressed stronger affections towards the mother than the father.

Hind. If you come to a comparison, we can give you such instances of our love towards our children and husbands, as would quite disgrace yours. What think you of those who, upon receiving the news of the loss of their children, have dropped down instantly dead? Of others, who upon seeing their husbands expire, have immediately dispatched themselves; as thinking it not proper to live without a husband, nor honourable to be joined to more than one?

Ul. These are glaring acts, that seem at first sight to carry a great deal of merit with them, and to claim applause, as proceeding from violence of love, or greatness of soul: Whereas in truth they arise from madness or cowardice; as distrusting that they could not survive their loss. But if Nature, who always acts for the best, had found that it were better that the Man and his Wife should drop together, she would undoubtedly have contrived that it should always be so.

But our discourse begins to be tedious, so I must put the question once more, Will you resume your former nature, and return with me to *Greece*?

Hind. By no means; and I thought I had given you sufficient reasons why, too.

Ul. If I had thought them so, I should not have troubled you with the question again.[17]

Hind. What I have to add, can be no argument to you, though they are to me, that by being a Hind, I am every way upon a par with our males, I go and come as free as they: I bring my young ones into the world with less danger, and breed them up in it with less trouble, than the best Lady of them all.

Ul. Not that I suppose the happy minute you boast of is free from pain, or that you require no care after it.

Hind. But you must consider our strength, and that we naturally are directed to a certain herb called *Ara*, the use of which immediately restores us to our health.

Ul. Is it possible that you have no concerns as we have about the education of your young ones?

Hind. Very few, I assure you, in comparison of what you suffer. Because as they have fewer wants, they must give us less trouble: and that too is so overcome by instinctive affection that it is scarce perceptible. Whereas you that are without that advantage feel it's full weight: So that not to give you the fatigue of persuading me any longer, I declare that I live much more contented as I am. But not to discourage you,

I freely own that, were I to change my shape, I would rather be a human than any other creature; as you may conclude, by our frequenting your roads more than the haunts of wild beasts. So I wish you happy in your voyage, and I will myself endeavour to be as much so as I can, for the remainder of life in these woods. And since I have recovered the use of speech, without being obliged to be a Woman again, I shall envy neither Gods nor Men.

Ul. I would not have you so obstinate, dear Hind, in your opinion, because you ought to think us better judges in the case than you are; especially as we are quite disinterested, and only recommend this to you, wholly for your own good.

Hind. That, I remember, was the old cant, when you had a mind to persuade us to any thing; and yet your chief regard was ever to yourselves.

Ul. Besides you ought to remember, that *Circe* restored you to the use of speech, for no other end but that you might be able to declare your mind to me, in relation to the proposal which was, by agreement, to be granted to those only that should desire it: So that if you still continue a Hind, I am afraid you will lose the privilege of talking, which you seem so much to enjoy

Hind. If I could suspect that, I must own it would stagger my resolution.

Ul. How can you doubt of it? Do any of your species ever speak?

Hind. Well——then e'en let it go——For as I am to converse only with Deer, and we have so many other ways of explaining our meanings and wants, (which are so few that they give us but little trouble) let who will close with your offer; for my part, I refuse, point blank.   *Exit* Hind.

from *Dialogue X*
ULYSSES AND THE ELEPHANT

Elephant. Oh! surprizing power of the human Understanding.

Ulysses. And it is the more so, by being conscious that it does understand;[18] which is above the reach of sense. For though the eye takes in the rays of light, and the ear is affected by sounds, yet the eye sees not that it sees, nor does the ear hear that it does so. For these powers being affixed to certain organs of the body, cannot reflect and reason upon themselves. Whereas the Understanding being a power spiritual and divine, may be turned in upon itself, and so discern both it's own faculties and their value, which is, let me tell you, it's peculiar privilege. Heaven itself, though of such purity and honour, is insensible of it's own worth. And the sun, the first minister of Nature, and source of light in heaven, feels not his own high station. But man, who is acquainted with his own excellency, and superiority over every other creature, whose end he seems to be (since by knowing their respective natures, he can employ them for his use) rejoices in himself, and feels a sincere contentment and self complacency. And that he might be the better qualified for this, he is furnished with a faculty that treasures up his notions, called intellectual memory, which as much excels yours, as it's objects are more noble.

Eleph. This makes a farther discovery of your happiness.

Ul. Nay, what is more, Man has this property, that it is not in the power of his Understanding, to entertain a conceit so abstruse or sublime, which, by the help of language, he cannot freely communicate. For we don't understand a voice, like you, only as a sign and expression of some common passion, such as joy, grief, fear, and the like; but by the assistance of words, whose import we have agreed upon, we can describe it just in the manner we would have it explained. It is by this canal that instruction is conveyed, and ignorance in one man is banished by the skill of another. For though the more knowing cannot always from himself impress the very thought he would communicate to the scholar, yet by this means he can put him in a method to form it in his own mind. It was from observing this, that the old *Ægyptian* sages[19] broke out into such extravagant raptures, as to call man the terrestrial God, the heavenly Animal, Resident of the Gods, Lord of all below, Favourite of all above, and in a word, the Miracle of Nature.

Eleph. Without doubt, so much perfection will require very pompous expressions to do it justice.

Ul. But there is yet another faculty, and that is not a tittle short of this in point of excellence, I mean the Will, by which we freely desire or avoid what is judged right or wrong by the Understanding: As you fly or pursue what Sense recommends or deters you from.

Eleph. Would not the appetite have been sufficient for this, without the addition of a new power?

Ul. It evidently would not; because appetite, under the influence of sense, could only desire or abhor what falls under the notice of sense. Whereas the virtues or vices which attract our love, or cause our aversion, could never come under the cognizance of sense. This then ennobles the man, by making him the free lord of all his actions; which arises from it's own freedom, not being determined by Nature more towards one extreme than the other. For though the object be good, it is no more constrained to the pursuit of it than of it's contrary. Whereas mere natural agents, being impelled towards their objects within a certain distance, must act as necessarily as the flame, which, within reach of combustible matter, cannot but set on fire. But in us the Will, though what is good and amiable be proposed to it, and it be disposed in some degree rather to pursue it, yet it is free from all force, either to choose or to reject it. Every other faculty in man, as an animal, owes it's subjection to this; for though each may be affected by it's object, without the consent of the Will, yet it must be so as always to be under it's government, whenever it pleases to exert itself. Thus, though the sight, when a visible object be presented to it, must be moved by it naturally, yet the Will can command it away, and turn it to some other; and so with the rest of the senses. And no object, nay no force on earth below, or heaven above, can constrain it to desire what it dislikes. The case is very different with the sensitive appetite; to which when an object is presented which it desires, the animal is hurried away necessarily and naturally to it, without any choice: As every observer must confess.

Eleph. Well, but after all where is the great dignity that this confers on human nature?

Ul. So great, that it was this alone made the old sages pronounce him to be the miracle of Nature.

Eleph. Give me leave to ask why?

Ul. Because every other creature being under stated laws, by which it must attain the very end which Nature has prescribed to it, and no other, it cannot supersede those directions: But man, by having his choice free, can obtain an end more or less worthy as he thinks fit, by letting himself down to creatures much below him, or by emulating those as much above. He that elevates himself no higher than the earth on which he grows, will become a mere vegetable; and he that abandons himself to sensual pleasures will degenerate into a brute. Whilst he that looks with an eye of reason on the glories of the heavens, and contemplates the stupendous regularity of Nature, will change the earthly into a celestial creature; but he that dares soar above the gross impediments of flesh, to converse with divine objects, will become little less than a God. Who therefore can look without astonishment on man, not only the most noble, and the soverign over animals, but who has this peculiar privilege indulged him by Nature, that he may make himself what he will?[20]

Eleph. How comes it to pass then, if the Will has what is good for it's object, and it be unbiassed in it's choice, that you prefer oftner what is it's contrary, and fly from virtue to follow vice?

142

Ul. The reason of this appearance is, the intimate and wonderfully strict attachment and combination it has with the senses, and from the necessity the Understanding (whose light the Will follows) is under, of taking it's information from them, who often shew him an apparent for a real good: So that the Will being diverted and misled by the one, which is imposed upon by the misrepresentations of the other, it must be granted, if it does not pursue evil, yet it does not sufficiently avoid it; nor does it exercise the sovereignity it ought over the sensitive appetite. So that in truth, all our errors proceed from the irrational part of our nature, which we have in common with you, and not from what constitutes us men.

Eleph. No more, no more, *Ulysses*, every moment of delay hinders me from the happiness I have already been too long deprived of. Let me instantly put off the Beast and resume the Man.

Ulysses changes him. Which I here grant unto thee, by the authority to me committed.

Aglaophemus. Oh miraculous effect! oh happy change! more happy, from the experience I have had of both conditions. This breaks in upon me like a flood of light, upon a wretch long pent up in darkness; or like the pleasures that a prosperous change affords one inured to misery. How I pity the wretches who refused this offer, that they might wallow on in all the sordid delights of sense! Thanks to my benefactor, who by his wisdom pointed out to me the truth, and by his eloquence warmed me in the pursuit of it. The Gods alone can render you a suitable reward, for the favours you have conferred upon me; whilst I, in obedience to strong natural impulse, make them an humble offering of my thanks, tracing up the blessings that are bestowed upon me, to the sole Original Cause of all things, from whence they are derived, especially this last, of knowing the imperfection of every other creature when compared with man. And because the only return I am capable of making is gratitude, let me indulge it, till it kindles into some rhapsody sacred to his praise. And do thou, *Ulysses*, whilst thy heart burns with the same zeal, give devout attention to this holy hymn, which I dare dictate to the world.

I

Silence ye winds, ye whisp'ring trees
    Attend; let list'ning motion cease,
Whilst the First Mover of the world's great frame
Inspires the song. Hail ever sacred name!
    Father, Maker, Source of all
    That great, or wise, or good we call,
Whether on earth, where foul corruption reigns,
Or else above, in blissful azure plains,
Where substances divine, in purer day,
Flourish unchang'd, unconscious of decay.

II

'Twas he that stretch'd the pendent earth,
    Self-poiz'd amidst the concave skies,
He gives the gushing fountains birth,
    And bids the healthful torrent rise.
        'Twas he, whose bounty stor'd
        For man, imperial lord,
    With grim inhabitants the woods,
    And peopl'd all the genial floods:
He first the soul enlighten'd from above,
And taught the heart to glow with holy love:
For him th'enlighten'd soul in rapture burns:
To him the glowing heart his love returns.

III

Ye spirits pure, ætheral train,
You that reside in mystick cells,
In secret chambers of the brain,
Where mem'ry and invention dwells,
    Pow'rs, virtues, potentates,
That round the throne of Reason stand,
    Where free volition waits,
Proud to receive her Queen's command,

> Sing the First Cause; ye pow'rs, divinities,
> Sing to your elder brothers of the skies,
> Till echoing heav'n shall catch the song divine,
> And all the world in one grand chorus join.

Ul. Let me trouble you but with this one question more; Were you not conscious of this knowledge of a First Cause in your brutal capacity?

Agla. No, but instantaneously with my change I felt this light springing up in the soul, as a property natural to it: Or rather I should express myself, that it seemed like a recovery in tthe memory of ideas it had been before acquainted with. But I have this advantage however from my experience, that by having a more perfect knowledge of the excellency of human nature, I draw this conclusion; that as man has been more beloved by the Supreme Cause, since he is more honoured than his fellow creatures, the end he ought to propose to himself, should be very different from that of other animals, who, by being without reason, must be without the knowledge of a First Cause.

Ul. Right; and to carry the thought yet higher, it cannot be but that if the knowledge of truth is the perfection of the human mind, and this cannot properly be said to be acquired here, whilst we are in this mortal frame, struggling under many obstacles, which at best must soon end in death; it must follow that when the soul is enlarged, and free from these impediments, this must be the subject of it's pursuit in some future state, unless we will suppose Nature to have acted in vain. And though man in this present life cannot, like other animals, attain the end of his nature, and acquire the sum of what he aims at, yet he may be said to enjoy it in some degree, whilst he keeps above the gross pleasures of sense, and lives in a manner agreeable to a rational creature.[21]

Agla. Let us fly then, my *Ulysses*, from this accursed shore, where this false artful woman, with her vile sorcery, makes men live like beasts, not only in manners but in shape also. Let us, I say, quit this slavery to return to *Greece*, and to the full enjoyment of all the liberty of reason. Nor do thou dare trust thyself again with the sight of the foul inchantress, lest by some new illusion she prevail with thee to remain in this unhappy land.

Ul. Come on then, it is my soul's desire. And see! how the propitious Gods, ever favourable to those who strive to imitate them, have prevented our wishes, by sending a gale inviting to our voyage.

NOTES

1 *our wise men of Greece*, e.g. Aristotle, *Politics*, I, 1–2.
2 Ulysses opens his conversation with the deer with the first of a series of comic remarks at the expense of women. Gelli seems to show a dual attitude: on the one hand, he uses the traditional insults as comic asides (and this attitude is emphasised by the present translator); on the other hand, in the original, Ulysses is consistently ironised by the failure of his definitions to describe the deer as she really is. For instance, here he doubts whether the deer, as a mere female, can be flexible enough to change her mind and make the rational choice of a return to human form; but, as it turns out, she – more than any other animal he meets except the elephant – shows positive enthusiasm for the human race.
3 The witlessness of the female was a truism universally present in Renaissance literature, providing material for comedy (*The Taming of the Shrew*, V.ii); lyric poetry (Donne, 'Loves Alchymie': 'Hope not for minde in women . . .') and epic (Milton in *Paradise Lost*, IV.297–8, defines the different mentalities of man and woman: 'For contemplation he and valour formed, / For softness she and sweet attractive grace'). Woman stood as a lower link in the Chain of Being, connecting man – the rational part of our species – with the animal kingdom.
4 This speech declares a feminist assertion of woman's rationality as a full member of the human race, whom nature, since it is by definition good, would not have created mentally deficient. The deftness of this argument proves its own point, rendering the candidly biased Ulysses nearly speechless with amazement. See Plato, *Timaeus*, 42 and 91A, for a variant on the idea quoted here that woman is a man who somehow went wrong in the making.
5 There is another ambiguity here, since it is never made clear whether the deer does indeed love talking for its own sake, as a frivolity, or, on the other hand, manifests a regard for language that is truly human in the fullest (humanist) sense. Humanists cultivated eloquence as representing the perfection of man's nature (e.g. Petrarch, *On His Own*

146

Ignorance, Cassirer, 104). Later in *Circe*, Ulysses also pontificates to the elephant on the glory of the faculty of speech (X. pp. 140–1 above).

6   Aristotle, in the *Politics*, 1259B, reacts violently against the Platonic view set out in the *Republic* and the *Laws* (804D–806C) of woman's potential equality with man, by defining the relationship between man and wife as being analagous to that between ruler and ruled. Plato had used an argument which prefigures the deer's, by saying that male and female in the animal kingdom were equals, and that one could not discriminate between, for instance, male and female watchdogs in terms of ability, so that it followed that men and women were not naturally specialised in anything except their reproductive roles (*Republic*, 452–5).

7   Gelli makes an implied analogy between the Greek priestesses devoted to Pallas (goddess of wisdom) and Diana (goddess of chastity), and the modern convents into which surplus women in the community were bundled.

8   There is a deliberate irony at the expense of Ulysses, implied in his readiness to contradict himself. Woman is, according to him, at once supremely thrifty and totally inept at managing affairs.

9   Cf. St Paul, Ephesians, 5:22, 'Wives, submit yourselves unto your own husbands, as unto your Lord'; Colossians, 3:18, 'Wives, submit yourselves unto your husbands', etc.

10 *Amazons*, a warlike race of women of Greek legend, said to have invaded at various times Thrace, Asia Minor, Greece, Syria, Arabia, Libya and Egypt. See Homer, *Iliad*, vi.186.

   Semiramis, with Ninus the founder of Nineveh; daughter of the Syrian fish-goddess, Derceto; her courage and beauty as sovereign eclipsed that of Ninus.

   Tomyris, a queen of the Massagetae, in approximately the sixth century B.C., who defeated the Persian tyrant, Cyrus, and fastened his head in a leather bag full of blood after the battle.

   It will be noticed that the *exempla* chosen by the embattled deer are all of women whose bloodthirsty strength was used to subdue men.

11 The humanist ideal of reaching beyond one's normal expectations in the direction of a higher life is explicitly denied to women here, though it is encouraged in men in Dialogue X (see p. 142). Partly it is a matter of social class: the analogy used by Ulysses of the ridiculous shoemaker is instructive here, since it illustrates the conventional view of woman as naturally belonging to an inferior class of person, whose aspiration can only appear vulgar by comparison with the aristocrat's natural dignity. (See James I, *Basilikon Doron*, pp. 172–3 below).

12 Probably homosexuality is meant.

13 Ulysses' methods of persuasion are odd. He tries to get the deer to resume her servile position in society as a woman by suggesting that (1) bountiful nature has made woman physically feeble in order that she

shall be susceptible to coercion, to perform menial tasks too disagreeable to be undertaken voluntarily by anyone, and that (2) women are not less to be congratulated on their serviceability since they were only passively manufactured to that end. There is little in this to appeal to one disinclined to return to womanhood. The core of Ulysses' argument depends on the sociological need formulated by Aristotle: 'It is absurd to argue, from the analogy of the animals, that men and women should follow the same pursuits, for animals have not to manage a household' (*Politics*, 1264B). A menial class cannot be dispensed with in a specialised society.

14   Proverbial. See *A Dictionary of The Proverbs in England in the Sixteenth and Seventeenth Centuries*, by M. P. Tilley, Michigan University Press, Ann Arbor, Michigan, 1950; W628.

15   The threefold notion of the soul is Aristotelean, deriving from *On the Soul* (II.4 – III.12). It demonstrates man's place in the hierarchy of being, including and transcending the entities beneath him: he shares the kind of life proper to the plants (growth), animals (sensation) and that which transcends them (thought). Gelli's Ulysses regards male fertilisation as a higher function than female generation, and thus with a show of science which the deer has no apparatus for refuting cleverly denies woman's full humanity (cf. *On the Soul*, 417B).

16   *Mola*: moon-calf, false conception.

17   The argument degenerates into the baffled realisation that neither can understand the other's point of view because he can never enter into his condition. Even as a human being, the deer could never share a perspective with Ulysses, being only a reduced and humiliated member of the species.

18   Ulysses claims that the distinguishing feature of man, which makes him superior in the final analysis to every other created thing, is not consciousness but self-consciousness. This makes him by implication the closest existing being to God, since, as Aristotle had riddlingly put it in the *Metaphysics*, 'it must be of itself that the divine thought thinks (since it is the most excellent of things), and its thinking is a thinking on thinking' (1074B). However, Ulysses conveniently forgets at this point the paradox which was not often ignored by Renaissance writers, and which has preoccupied the characters who have spoken in the earlier dialogues: the fact that self-consciousness, while it may under certain circumstances bring unalloyed pleasure, is also the source of all that people have found nightmarish and hard to bear about the human condition. The vision of Hamlet may be allowed to stand as a representation of the dual feeling to which the Renaissance was subject when it considered its own self-consciousness: 'there is nothing either good or bad but thinking makes it so ... O God! I could be bounded in a nutshell, and count myself a king of infinite space, were it not that I have bad dreams' (II.ii). Ulysses takes no account of the bad dreams,

because he is concentrating on an ideal of human liberty, where thought is free.

19   *some old Ægyptian sages.* There can be little doubt that Hermes Trismegistus' *Asclepius*, I, is being alluded to here. This is near paraphrase, both of Hermes and of Pico's *Oration*: see pp. 65–6 and n. 4 above.

20   Compare Pico, *Oration*, pp. 68–9 and n. 16 above. The correspondence is exact, and shows the extent to which, over the generation intervening between the writing of the *Oration* and the *Circe*, the Florentine Platonists' ideas had permeated the minds of European intellectuals and artists.

21   This doctrine owes much to Marsilio Ficino who in his *Five Questions Concerning the Mind* showed that 'man is outside the natural condition' (Cassirer, 208) in being tragically incapable of fulfilling his desires on the earth in his own lifetime, since he is composed of pure spirit sunk in gross clay; but Ficino concluded, as Gelli does, that the soul may after death escape the frustration of the body and find its fulfilment in immortality.

JAMES I

Basilikon Doron

1599

The Renaissance period witnessed, all over Europe, a concentration of power in the hereditary monarchs of individual nations, and an unprecedented excitement at the idea of the absolute sovereign, issuing in a theory of the Divine Right of Kings which was at once new in its immoderate claims and conservative in insisting on a predestined, imperishable order in the political world. James I's *Basilikon Doron* ('The Gift of the King'), written before his accession to the English throne whose stability he so damaged, and his *Trew Law of Free Monarchies* (1588), are two of the most characteristic and tactless expressions of this theory. To the fierce tides of English social and economic history James was Canute. He defined the king as a little god among men and identified (correctly) as the great adversary the Puritan sects, to whose democratic and revolutionary tendencies he responded with a frightened aggressiveness which seems to sum itself up in his famous reply to Puritanism at the Hampton Court Conference of 1604: 'If this be all your party hath to say, I will make them conform themselves, or else I will harrie them out of the land, or else do worse, only hang them, that's all.'[1] This discouraging attitude caused a great vanishing of Puritan people towards America, during his reign, and a hardening reaction in England amongst the persecuted remainder, which, following the tradition of the brave Huguenot document, *A Defence of Liberty Against Tyrants* (c. 1574–6), was to culminate in the mature republican theory of Milton and Cromwell.

James may have been influenced in his political thinking by the humanist Sir Thomas Elyot, whose *Book named The Governor* (1531) formed part of his education and rested a theory of the unlimited power of the monarchy for the good of the people on classical precedent and on the premiss that 'in everything is order, and without order may be nothing stable or permanent; and it may not be called order, except it do contain in it degrees, high and base, according to the merit or estimation of the thing that is ordered.'[2] James, splashing his pages even more liberally than Elyot with learned (but in his case often misquoted) Latin and Greek tags, rests his advice to his son, Prince Henry, on the same concept of order. He instructs his son in Book I on the King's absolute obligation to the greater King, God, but places rather less emphasis than Elyot on the common clay of which peasant and sovereign are equally composed, and on which identity Renaissance literature in England laid such emphasis. Elyot admonishes his Governor: 'nor thou hast any more of the dew of heaven, or the brightness of the sun, than any other person' (III.iii.165); Shakespeare has Perdita in *The Winter's Tale* echo the same idea for the benefit of the King of Bohemia:

> The self—same sun that shines upon his court
> Hides not his visage from our cottage, but
> Looks on all alike.
>
> (IV.iii)

In Shakespeare's *King Lear*, this awareness of mankind's essential equivalence and brotherhood is consummate, for Lear's hand 'smells of mortality' (IV.vi).

However, English literature and political thought were also dominated by the opposite image, that of the sun-king shining down upon ordinary people and made of a more perfect blend of elements than they. It is there in Marlowe's *Tamburlaine* and Shakespeare's *Henry V*; and in James' *Basilikon Doron* the Crown glows with a more than earthly brilliance. Though for James the end of government is the orthodox Aristotelean 'good of the people', the instrument of that good is seen as higher than mere flesh and blood. A kind of Tamburlaine-consciousness is much in evidence in James' political works, and he would not have found it bathetic or absurd, as we may, to hear Marlowe's Tamburlaine defining 'the ripest fruit of all' in the intellectual universe as 'the sweet fruition of an earthly crowne' (*I Tamburlaine*, 1590, II.vii). The earthly crown is valued as an exact miniature of the Heavenly one.

Yet the careful reader of *Basilikon Doron* will also catch a glimpse of a spirit less heroic, more Machiavellian, in the work, as James with a calculating and rather anxious expression seeks to indoctrinate his son in the politic art of keeping each social class in its proper place. While he rejects tyranny, James outlines for his son a programme for inhibiting other peoples' liberty and for protecting his own security which would not have disgraced Machiavelli's Prince (in his own eyes). The text reproduced here represents the greater part of the second Book of *Basilikon Doron*, taken from *The Workes of the Most High and Mighty Prince, James, By the Grace of God Kinge of Great Brittaine France & Ireland Defendor of ye Faith etc*:, London, 1616. I omit the topical notes in the margins, as well as the classical references, which are general, often highly inaccurate, and of dubious authorship.

OF A KINGS DVETIE IN HIS OFFICE
The second booke

But as ye are clothed with two callings, so must ye be alike careful for the discharge of them both: that as yee are a good Christian, so yee may be a good King, discharging your Office (as I shewed before) in the points of Iustice and Equitie: which in two sundrie waies ye must doe: the one, in establishing and executing, (which is the life of the Law) good Lawes among your people: the other, by your behauiour in your owne person, and with your seruants, to teach your people by your example: for people are naturally inclined to counterfaite (like apes) their Princes maners, according to the notable saying of *Plato*, expressed by the Poet—

Componitur orbis
Regis ad exemplum, nec sic inflectere sensus
Humanos edicta valent, quàm vita regentis.

For the part of making, and executing of Lawes, consider first the trew difference betwixt a lawfull good King, and an vsurping Tyran, and yee shall the more easily vnderstand your duetie herein: for *contraria iuxta se posita magis elucescunt.*[3] The one acknowledgeth himselfe ordained for his people, hauing receiued from God a burthen of gouernment, whereof he must be countable: the other thinketh his people ordeined for him, a prey to his passions and inordinate appetites, as the fruites of his magnanimitie: And therefore, as their ends are directly contrarie, so are their whole actions, as meanes, whereby they preasse to attaine to their endes. A good King, thinking his highest honour to consist in the due discharge of his calling, emploieth all his studie and paines, to procure and maintaine, by the making and execution of good Lawes, the well-fare and peace of his people; and as their naturall father[4] and kindly Master, thinketh his greatest contentment standeth in their prosperitie, and his greatest suretie in hauing their hearts, subiecting his owne priuate affections and appetites to the weale and standing of his Subiects, euer thinking common interesse his chiefest particular: where by the contrarie, an vsurping Tyran, thinking his greatest honour and felicitie to consist in attaining *per fas, vel nefas*[5] to his ambitious pretences, thinketh neuer himselfe sure, but by the dissention and factions among his people, and counterfaiting the Saint while he once creepe in credite, will then (by inuerting all good Lawes to serve onely for his vnrulie priuate affections) frame the common-weale euer to aduance his particular: building his suretie vpon his peoples miserie: and in the end (as a stepfather and an vncouth hireling) make vp his owne hand vpon the ruines of the Republicke. And according to their actions, so receiue they their reward: For a good King (after a happie and famous reigne)[6] dieth in peace, lamented by his subiects, and admired by his neighbours; and leauing a reuerent renowne behinde him in earth, obtaineth the Crowne of eternall felicitie in heauen. And although some of them (which falleth out very rarelie) may be cut off by the treason of some vnnaturall subiects, yet liueth their fame after them, and some notable plague faileth neuer to ouertake the committers in this life, besides their infamie to all posterities hereafter: Where by the contrarie, a Tyrannes miserable and infamous life, armeth in end his owne Subiects to become his burreaux: and although that rebellion be euer vnlawfull on their part, yet is the world so wearied of him, that his fall is little meaned by the rest of his Subjects, and but smiled at by his neighbours. And besides the infamous memorie he leaueth behind him here, and the endlesse paine hee sustaineth hereafter, it oft falleth out, that the committers not onely escape vnpunished, but farther, the fact will remaine as allowed by the Law in diuers aages thereafter. It is easie then for you (my Sonne) to make a choise of one of these two sorts of rulers, by following the way of vertue to establish your standing; yea, in case ye fell in the high way, yet should it be with the honourable report, and iust regrate of all honest men.

And therefore to returne to my purpose anent the gouernement of your Subiects, by making and putting good Lawes to execution; I remit the making of them to your owne discretion, as ye shall finde the necessitie of new-rising corruptions to require them: for, *ex malis moribus bonæ leges natæ sunt:*[7] besides, that in this country, wee haue alreadie moe good Lawes then are well execute, and am onely to insist in your forme of gouernment anent their execution. Onely remember, that as Parliaments haue bene ordained for making of Lawes, so ye abuse not their institution, in holding them for any mens particulars: For as a Parliament is the honourablest and highest iudgement in the land (as being the Kings head Court) if it be well vsed, which is by making of good Lawes in it; so is it the in-iustest Iudgement-seat that may be, being abused to mens particulars: irreuocable decreits against particular parties, being giuen therin vnder colour of generall Lawes, and oft-times th'Estates not knowing themselues whom thereby they hurt. And therefore hold no Parliaments, but for necessitie of new Lawes, which would be but seldome: for few Lawes and well put in execution, are best in a well ruled common-weale. As for the matter of fore-faltures,[8] which also are done in Parliament, it is not good tigging with these things; but my aduice is, ye fore-fault none but for such odious crimes as may make them vnworthie euer to be restored againe: And for smaller offences, ye haue other penalties sharpe enough to be vsed against theo.

And as for the execution of good Lawes, whereat I left, remember that among the differences that I put betwixt the formes of the gouernment of a good King, and an vsurping Tyran; I shew how a Tyran would enter like a Saint while he found himselfe fast vnder-foot, and then would suffer his vnrulie affections to burst foorth. Therefore be yee contrare at your first entrie to your Kingdome, to the *Quinquennium Neronis*,[9] with his tender hearted wish, *Vellem nescirem literas*, in giuing the Law full execution against all breakers thereof but exception. For since ye come not to your reigne *precariò*, nor by conquest, but by right and due discent; feare no vproares for doing of iustice, since ye may assure your selfe, the most part of your people will euer naturally fauour Iustice: prouiding alwaies, that ye doe it onely for loue to Iustice, and not for satisfying any particular passions of yours, vnder colour thereof: otherwise, how iustly that euer the offender deserue it, ye are guiltie of murther before God: For ye must consider, that God euer looketh to your inward intention in all your actions.

And when yee haue by the seueritie of Iustice once setled

your countries, and made them know that ye can strike, then may ye thereafter all the daies of your life mixe Iustice with Mercie, punishing or sparing, as ye shall finde the crime to haue bene wilfully or rashly committed, and according to the by-past behauiour of the committer. For if otherwise ye kyth your clemencie at the first, the offences would soone come to such heapes, and the contempt of you grow so great, that when ye would fall to punish, the number of them to be punished, would exceed the innocent; and yee would be troubled to resolue whom-at to begin: and against your nature would be compelled then to wracke many, whom the chastisement of few in the beginning might haue preserued. But in this, my ouerdeare bought experience may serue you for a sufficient lesson; For I confesse, where I thought (by being gracious at the beginning) to win all mens hearts to a louing and willing obedience, I by the contrary found, the disorder of the countrie, and the losse of my thankes to be all my reward.

But as this seuere Iustice of yours vpon all offences would bee but for a time, (as I haue alreadie said) so is there some horrible crimes that yee are bound in conscience neuer to forgiue: such as Witch-craft,[10] wilfull murther, Incest, (especially within the degrees of consanguinitie) Sodomie, poisoning, and false coine. As for offences against your owne person and authoritie, since the fault concerneth your selfe, I remit to your owne choise to punish or pardon therein, as your heart serueth you, and according to the circumstances of the turne, and the qualitie of the committer.

Here would I also eike another crime to bee vnpardonable, if I should not be thought partiall: but the fatherly loue I beare you, will make mee breake the bounds of shame in opening it vnto you. It is then, the false and vnreuerent writing or speaking of malicious men against your Parents and Predecessors: ye know the command in Gods lawe, *Honour your Father and Mother*: and consequently, sen ye are the lawful magistrate, suffer not both your Princes and your Parents to be dishonoured by any; especially, sith the example also toucheth your selfe, in leauing thereby to your successors, the measure of that which they shal mete out againe to you in your like behalfe. I graunt wee haue all our faults, which, priuately betwixt you and God, should serue you for examples to meditate vpon, and mend in your person; but should not be a matter of discourse to others whatsoeuer. And sith ye are come of as honourable Predecessours as any Prince liuing, represse the insolence of such, as vnder pretence to taxe a vice in the person, seeke craftily to staine the race, and to steale the affection of the people from their posteritie: For how can they loue you, that hated them whom-of ye are come? Wherefore destroy men innocent young sucking Wolues and Foxes, but for the hatred they beare to their race? and why wil a coult of a Courser of Naples, giue a greater price in a market, then an Asse-colt, but for loue of the race? It is therefore a thing monstrous, to see a man loue the childe, and hate the Parents: as on the other part, the infaming and making odious of the parents, is the readiest way to bring the sonne in contempt. And for conclusion of this point, I may also alledge my owne experience: For besides the iudgments of God, that with my eyes I haue seene fall vpon all them that were chiefe traitours to my parents, I may iustly affirme, I neuer found yet a constant biding by me in all my straites, by any that were of perfite aage in my parents dayes, but onely by such as constantly bode by them; I meane specially by them that serued the Queene my mother: for so that I discharge my conscience to you, my Sonne, in reuealing to you the trewth, I care not, what any traitour or treason-allower thinke of it.[11]

And although the crime of oppression be not in this ranke of vnpardonable crimes, yet the ouer-common vse of it in this nation, as if it were a vertue, especially by the greatest ranke of subjects in the land, requireth the King to be a sharpe censurer thereof. Be diligent therefore to trie, and awfull to beate downe the hornes of proud oppressours: embrace the quarrell of the poore and distressed, as your owne particular, thinking it your greatest honour to represse the oppressours: care for the pleasure of none, neither spare ye anie paines in your owne person, to see their wrongs redressed: and remember of the honourable stile giuen to my grand-father of worthie memorie, in being called *the poore mans King*.[12] And as the most part of a Kings Office, standeth in deciding that question of *Meum* and *Tuum*, among his subjects; so remember when ye sit in iudgement, that the Throne ye sit on is Gods, as *Moyses* saith, and sway neither to the right hand nor to the left; either louing the rich, or pittying the poore. Iustice should be blinde and friendlesse: it is not there ye should reward your friends, or seeke to crosse your enemies.

Here now speaking of oppressours and of iustice, the purpose leadeth me to speake of Hie-land and Border oppressions. As for the Hie-lands, I shortly comprehend them all in two sorts of people: the one, that dwelleth in our maine land, that are barbarous for the most part, and yet mixed with some shewe of ciuilitie: the other, that dwelleth in the Iles, and are alluterly barbares, without any sort or shew of ciuilitie. For the first sort, put straitly to execution the Lawes made alreadie by me against their Ouer-lords, and the chiefes of their Clannes, and it will be no difficultie to danton them. As for the other sort, follow forth the course that I haue intended, in planting Colonies among them of answerable In-lands subiects, that within short time may reforme and ciuilize the best inclined among them; rooting out or transporting the barbarous and stubborne sort, and planting ciuilitie in their roomes.

But as for the Borders, because I know, if ye enjoy not this whole Ile, according to Gods right and your lineall discent, yee will neuer get leaue to brooke this North and barrennest part thereof; no, not your owne head whereon the Crowne should stand; I neede not in that case trouble you with them: for then they will be the middest of the Ile, and so as easily ruled as any part thereof.

And that yee may the readier with wisedome and Iustice gouerne your subiects, by knowing what vices they are naturallie most inclined to, as a good Physician, who must first know what peccant humours his Patient naturallie is most subject vnto, before he can begin his cure: I shall therefore shortly note vnto you, the principall faults that euery ranke of the people of this countrey is most affected vnto. And as for *England*, I will not speake be-gesse of them, neuer hauing been among them, although I hope in that God, who euer fauoureth the right, before I die, to be as well acquainted with their fashions.[13]

As the whole Subiects of our countrey (by the ancient and fundamentall policie of our Kingdome) are diuided into three estates, so is euerie estate hereof generally subject to some speciall vices; which in a maner by long habitude, are thought rather vertue then vice among them; not that euerie particular man in any of these rankes of men, is subiect vnto them, for there is good and euill of all sorts; but that I meane, I haue found by experience, these vices to haue taken greatest holde with these rankes of men.

And first, that I prejudge not the Church of her ancient priuiledges, reason would shee should haue the first place for orders sake, in this catalogue.

The naturall sickenesse that hath euer troubled, and beene the decay of all the Churches, since the beginning of the world, changing the candlesticke from one to another, as *Iohn* saith, hath beene Pride, Ambition, and Auarice: and now last, these same infirmities wrought the ouerthrow of the Popish Church, in this countrey and diuers others. But the reformation of Religion in *Scotland*, being extraordinarily wrought by God, wherin many things were inordinately done by a popular tumult and rebellion, of such as blindly were doing the worke of God, but clogged with their owne passions and particular respects, as well appeared by the destruction of our policie, and not proceeding from the Princes order, as it did in our neighbour countrey of *England*, as likewise in

159

Denmarke, and sundry parts of *Germanie*;[14] some fierie spirited men in the ministerie, got such a guiding of the people at that time of confusion, as finding the gust of gouernment sweete, they begouth to fantasie to themselues a Democraticke forme of gouernment: and hauing (by the inquitie of time) beene ouerwell baited vpon the wracke, first of my Grandmother, and next of mine owne mother, and after vsurping the libertie of the time in my long minoritie, setled themselues so fast vpon that imagined Democracie, as they fed themselues with the hope to become *Tribuni plebis*:[15] and so in a popular gouernment by leading the people by the nose, to beare the sway of all the rule. And for this cause, there neuer rose faction in the time of my minoritie, nor trouble sensyne, but they that were vpon that factious part, were euer carefull to perswade and allure these vnruly spirits among the ministerie, to spouse that quarrell as their owne: wherethrough I was ofttimes calumniated in their populare Sermons, not for any euill or vice in me, but because I was a King, which they thought the highest euill. And because they were ashamed to professe this quarrel, they were busie to look narrowly in all my actions; and I warrant you a mote in my eye, yea a false report, was matter enough for them to worke vpon: and yet for all their cunning, whereby they pretended to distinguish the lawfulnesse of the office, from the vice of the person, some of them would sometimes snapper out well grossely with the trewth of their intentions, informing the people, that all Kings and Princes were naturally enemies to the libertie of the Church, and could neuer patiently beare the yoke of Christ: with such sound doctrine fed they their flockes. And because the learned, graue, and honest men of the ministerie, were euer ashamed and offended with their temeritie and presumption, preassing by all good meanes by their authoritie and example, to reduce them to a greater moderation; there could be no way found out so meete in their conceit, that were turbulent spirits among them, for maintaining their plots, as paritie in the Church: whereby the ignorants were emboldened (as bairdes) to crie the learned, godly, and modest out of it: partie the mother of confusion, and enemie to Vnitie, which is the mother of order: For if by the example thereof, once established in the Ecclesiasticall gouernment, the Politicke and ciuill estate should be drawen to the like, the great confusion that thereupon would arise may easily be discerned. Take heede therefore (my Sonne) to such Puritanes, verie pestes in the Church and Common-weale, whom no deserts can oblige, neither oathes or promises binde, breathing nothing but sedition and calumnies, aspiring without measure, railing without reason, and making their owne imaginations (without any warrant of the word) the square of their conscience. I protest before the great God, and since I am here as vpon my Testament, it is no place for me to lie in, that ye shall neuer find with any Hie-land or Border-theeues greater ingratitude, and moe lies and vile periuries, then with these phanaticke spirits: And suffer not the principals of them to brooke your land, if ye like to sit at rest; except yee would keepe them for trying your patience, as *Socrates* did an euill wife.[16]

And for preseruatiue against their poison, entertaine and aduance the godly, learned and modest men of the ministerie, whom-of (God be praised) there lacketh not a sufficient number: and by their prouision to Bishoprickes and Benefices (annulling that vile acte of Annexation,[17] if ye finde it not done to your hand) yee shall not onely banish their conceited paritie, whereof I haue spoken, and their other imaginarie grounds; which can neither stand with the order of the Church, nor the peace of a commonweale and well ruled Monarchie: but shall also re-establish the olde institution of three Estates in Parliament, which can no otherwise be done: But in this I hope (if God spare me dayes) to make you a faire entrie, alwayes where I leaue, follow ye my steps.

And to end my aduice anent the Church estate, cherish no man more then a good Pastor, hate no man more then a proude Puritane; thinking it one of your fairest styles, to be called a louing nourish-father to the Church, seeing all the Churches within your dominions planted with good Pastors, the Schooles (the seminarie of the Church) maintained, the doctrine and discipline preserued in puritie, according to Gods word, a sufficient prouision for their sustentation, a comely order in their policie, pride punished, humilitie aduanced, and they so to reuerence their superiours, and their flockes them, as the flourishing of your Church in pietie, peace, and learning, may be one of the chiefe points of your earthly glory, being euer alike ware with both the extremities; as well as yee represse the vaine Puritane, so not to suffer proude Papall Bishops; but as some for their qualities will deserue to bee preferred before others, so chaine them with such bondes as may preserue that estate from creeping to corruption.

The next estate now that by order commeth in purpose, according to their rankes in Parliament, is the Nobilitie, although second in ranke, yet ouer farre first in greatnesse and power, either to doe good or euill, as they are inclined.

The naturall sickenesse that I haue perceiued this estate subiect to in my time, hath beene, a fectlesse arrogant conceit of their greatnes and power; drinking in with their very nourish-milke, that their honor stood in committing three points of iniquitie: to thrall by oppression, the meaner sort that dwelleth neere them, to their seruice and following, although they holde nothing of them: to maintaine their seruants and dependers in any wrong, although they be not answerable to the lawes (for any body will maintaine his man in a right cause) and for anie displeasure, that they apprehend to be done vnto them by their neighbour, to take vp a plaine feide[18] against him; and (without respect to God, King, or common-weale) to bang it out brauely, hee and all his kinne against him and all his: yea they will thinke the King farre in their common, in-case they agree to grant an assurance to a short day, for keeping of the peace: where, by their naturall dewtie, they are oblished to obey the lawe, and keepe the peace all the daies of their life, vpon the perill of their verie craigges.

For remeid to these euils in their estate, teach your Nobilitie to keepe your lawes as precisely as the meanest; feare not their orping or beeing discontented, as long as yee rule well; for their pretended reformation of Princes taketh neuer effect, but where euill gouernement precedeth. Acquaint your selfe so with all the honest men of your Barrons and Gentlemen, and be in your giuing accesse so open and affable to euery ranke of honest persons, as may make them peart without scarring at you, to make their owne suites to you themselues, and not to employ the great Lordes their intercessours; for intercession to Saints is Papistrie: so shall ye bring to a measure their monstrous backes. And for their barbarous feides, put the lawes to due execution made by mee there-anent; beginning euer rathest at him that yee loue best, and is most oblished vnto you; to make him an example to the rest. For yee shall make all your reformations to beginne at your elbow, and so by degrees to flow to the extremities of the land. And rest not, vntill yee roote out these barbarous feides; that their effects may bee as well smoared downe, as their barbarous name is vnknowen to anie other nation: For if this Treatise were written either in French or Latine, I could not get them named vnto you but by circumlocution.[19] And for your easier abolishing of them, put sharpelie to execution my lawes made against Gunnes and traiterous Pistolets; thinking in your heart, tearming in your speech, and vsing by your punishments, all such as weare and vse them, as brigands and cut-throates.

On the other part, eschew the other extremitie, in lightlying and contemning your Nobilitie. Remember howe that errour brake the King my grand-fathers heart.[20] But consider that vertue followeth oftest noble blood: the worthinesse of their antecessors craueth a reuerent regard to be had vnto them: honour them therefore that are obedient to the law among them, as Peeres and Fathers of your land: the more frequently that your Court can bee garnished with them; thinke it the more your honour; acquainting and employing them in all your greatest affaires; sen it is, they must be your armes and executers of your lawes: and so vse your selfe louinglie to the obedient, and rigorously to the stubborne, as may make the greatest of them to thinke, that the chiefest point of their honour, standeth in striuing with the meanest of the land in humilitie towards you, and obedience to your Lawes: beating euer in their eares, that one of the principall points of seruice that ye craue of them, is, in their persons to practise, and by their power to procure due obedience to the Law; without the which, no seruice they can make, can be agreeable vnto you.[21]

But the greatest hinderance to the execution of our Lawes in this countrie, are these heritable Shirefdomes and Regalities, which being in the hands of the great men, do wracke the whole countrie: For which I know no present remedie, but by taking the sharper account of them in their Offices; vsing all punishment against the slouthfull, that the Law will permit: and euer as they vaike, for any offences committed by them, dispone them neuer heritably againe: preassing, with time, to draw it to the laudable custome of England: which ye may the easilier doe, being King of both, as I hope in God ye shall.

And as to the third and last estate, which is our Burghes (for the small Barrones are but an inferiour part of the Nobilitie and of their estate) they are composed of two sorts of men; Merchants and Craftes-men: either of these sorts being subiect to their owne infirmities.[22]

The Merchants thinke the whole common-weale ordeined for making them vp; and accounting it their lawfull gaine and trade, to enrich themselues vpon the losse of all the rest of the people, they transport from vs things necessarie; bringing backe sometimes vnnecessary things, and at other times nothing at all. They buy for vs the worst wares, and sell them at the dearest prices: and albeit the victuals fall or rise of their prices, according to the aboundance or skantnesse thereof;

yet the prices of their wares euer rise, but neuer fall: being as constant in that their euill custome, as if it were a setled Law for them. They are also the speciall cause of the corruption of the coyne, transporting all our owne, and bringing in forraine, vpon what price they please to set on it: For order putting to them, put the good Lawes in execution that are already made anent these abuses; but especially doe three things: Establish honest, diligent, but few Searchers, for many hands make slight worke; and haue an honest and diligent Thesaurer to take count of them: Permit and allure forraine Merchants to trade here: so shall ye haue best and best cheape wares, not buying them at the third hand: And set euery yeere downe a certaine price of all things; considering first, how it is in other countries: and the price set reasonably downe, if the Merchants will not bring them home on the price, cry forrainers free to bring them.

And because I haue made mention here of the coyne, make your money of fine Gold and Siluer; causing the people be payed with substance, and not abused with number: so shall ye enrich the common-weale, and haue a great treasure laid vp in store, if ye fall in warres or in any straites: For the making it baser, will breed your commoditie; but it is not to bee vsed, but at a great necessitie.

And the Craftes-men thinke, we should be content with their worke, how bad and deare soeuer it be; and if they in any thing be controlled, vp goeth the blew-blanket: But for their part, take example by England, how it hath flourished both in wealth and policie, since the strangers Craftes-men came in among them: Therefore not onely permit, but allure strangers to come heere also; taking as strait order for repressing the mutining of ours at them, as was done in England, at their first in-bringing there.

But vnto one fault is all the common people of this Kingdome subiect, as well burgh as land; which is, to iudge and speake rashly of their Prince, setting the Common-weale vpon foure props, as wee call it; euer wearying of the present estate, and desirous of nouelties. For remedie whereof (besides the execution of Lawes that are to be used against vnreuerent speakers) I know no better meane, then so to rule, as may iustly stop their mouthes from all such idle and vnreuerent speaches; and so to prop the weale of your people, with prouident care for their good gouernment, that iustly, *Momus*[23] himselfe may haue no ground to grudge at: and yet so to temper and mixe your seueritie with mildnes, that as the vniust railers may be restrained with a reuerent awe; so the good and louing Subjects, may not onely liue in suretie and wealth, but be stirred vp and inuited by your benigne courtesies, to open their mouthes in the iust praise of your so well moderated regiment. In respect whereof, and therewith also the more to allure them to a common amitie among themselues, certaine dayes in the yeere would be appointed, for delighting the people with publicke spectacles of all honest games, and exercise of armes: as also for conueening of neighbours, for entertaining friendship and heartlinesse, by honest feasting and merrinesse:[24] For I cannot see what greater superstition can be in making playes and lawfull games in Maie, and good cheere at Christmas, then in eating fish in Lent, and vpon Fridayes, the Papists as well vsing the one as the other: so that alwayes the Sabboths be kept holy, and no vnlawfull pastime be vsed: And as this forme of contenting the peoples mindes, hath beene vsed in all well gouerned Republicks: so will it make you to performe in your gouernment that olde good sentence,

Omne tulit punctum, qui miscuit vtile dulci.[25]

Ye see now (my Sonne) how for the zeale I beare to acquaint you with the plaine and single veritie of all things, I haue not spared to be something Satyricke, in touching well quickly the faults in all the estates of my kingdome: But I protest before God, I doe it with the fatherly loue that I owe to them all; onely hating their vices, whereof there is a good number of honest men free in euery estate . . .

But specially take good heed to the choice of your seruants, that ye preferre to the offices of the Crowne and estate: for in other offices yee haue onely to take heede to your owne weale; but these concerne likewise the weale of your people; for the which yee must bee answerable to God. Choose then for all these Offices, men of knowen wisedome, honestie, and good conscience; well practised in the points of the craft, that yee ordaine them for, and free of all factions and partialities; but specially free of that filthie vice of Flatterie, the pest of all Princes, and wracke of Republicks: For since in the first part of this Treatise, I fore-warned you to be at warre with your owne inward flatterer *philautia*, [26] how much more should ye be at war with outward flatterers,[27] who are nothing so sib to you, as your selfe is; by the selling of such counterfeit wares, onely preassing to ground their greatnesse vpon your ruines? And therefore bee carefull to preferre none, as yee will bee answerable to God but onely for their worthinesse: But specially choose honest, diligent, meane, but responsall men, to bee your receiuers in money matters: meane I say, that ye may when yee please, take a sharpe account of their intromission, without perill of their breeding any trouble to your estate: for this ouersight hath beene the greatest cause of my mis-thriuing in money matters. Especially, put neuer a forrainer, in any principall office of estate: for that will neuer faile to stirre vp sedition and enuie in the countreymens hearts, both against you and him: But (as I saide before) if God prouide you with moe countries then this; choose the borne-men of euery countrey, to bee your chief counsellers therein.

And for conclusion of my aduice anent the choice of your seruants, delight to be serued with men of the noblest blood that may bee had: for besides that their seruice shall breed you great good-will and least enuie, contrarie to that of start-vps; ye shall oft finde vertue follow noble races, as I haue said before speaking of the Nobilitie.

Now, as to the other point, anent your gouerning of your

seruants when yee haue chosen them; make your Court and companie to bee a patterne of godlinesse and all honest vertues, to all the rest of the people. Bee a daily watch-man ouer your seruants, that they obey your lawes precisely: For how can your lawes bee kept in the countrey, if they be broken at your eare? Punishing the breach thereof in a Courteour, more seuerely, then in the person of any other of your subiects: and aboue all, suffer none of them (by abusing their credite with you to oppresse or wrong any of your subiects. Be homely or strange with them, as ye thinke their behauiour deserueth, and their nature may beare with. Thinke a quarrellous man a pest in your companie. Bee carefull euer to preferre the gentilest natured and trustiest, to the inwardest Offices about you, especially in your chamber. Suffer none about you to meddle in any mens particulars, but like the Turkes Ianisares,[28] let them know no father but you, nor particular but yours. And if any will medde in their kinne or friends quarrels, giue them their leaue: for since ye must be of no surname nor kinne, but equall to all honest men; it becommeth you not to bee followed with partiall or factious seruants. Teach obedience to your seruants, and not to thinke themselues ouer-wise: and, as when any of them deserueth it, ye must not spare to put them away, so, without a seene cause, change none of them. Pay them, as all others your subiects, with *præmium* or *pœna*[29] as they deserue, which is the very ground-stone of good gouernement. Employ euery man as ye thinke him qualified, but vse not one in all things, lest he waxe proude, and be enuied of his fellowes. Loue them best, that are plainnest with you, and disguise not the trewth for all their kinne: suffer none to be euill tongued, nor backbiters of them they hate: command a hartly and brotherly loue among all them that serue you. And shortly, maintaine peace in your Court, bannish enuie, cherish modestie, bannish deboshed insolence, foster humilitie, and represse pride: setting downe such a comely and honourable order in all the points of your seruice; that when strangers shall visite your Court, they may with the Queene of *Sheba*, admire your wisedome in the glorie of your house, and comely order among your seruants.

But the principall blessing that yee can get of good companie, will stand in your marrying of a godly and vertuous wife: for shee must bee nearer vnto you, than any other companie, being *Flesh of your flesh, and bone of your bone*, as *Adam* saide of *Heuah*. And because I know not but God may call me, before ye be readie for Mariage; I will shortly set downe to you heere my aduice therein.

First of all consider, that Mariage is the greatest earthly felicitie or miserie, that can come to a man, according as it pleaseth God to blesse or curse the same. Since then without the blessing of GOD, yee cannot looke for a happie successe in Mariage, yee must bee carefull both in your preparation for it, and in the choice and vsage of your wife, to procure the same. By your preparation, I meane, that yee must keepe your bodie cleane and vnpolluted, till yee giue it to your wife, whom-to onely it belongeth. For how can ye iustly craue to bee ioyned with a pure virgine, if your bodie be polluted? why should the one halfe bee cleane, and the other defiled?[30] And although I know, fornication is thought but a light and a veniall sinne, by the most part of the world, yet remember well what I said to you in my first Booke anent conscience, and count euery sinne and breach of Gods law, not according as the vaine world esteemeth of it, but as God the Iudge and maker of the lawe accounteth of the same. Heare God commanding by the mouth of *Paul*, to *abstaine from fornication*, declaring that the *fornicator shall not inherite the Kingdome of heauen*: and by the mouth of *Iohn* reckoning our fornication amongst other grieuous sinnes, that debarre the committers amongst *dogs and swine, from entry in that spirituall and heauenly Ierusalem.* And consider, if a man shall once take vpon him, to count that light, which God calleth heauie; and veniall that, which God calleth grieuous; beginning first to measure any one sinne by the rule of his lust and appetites, and not of his conscience; what shall let him doe so with the next, that his affections shall stirre him to, the like reason seruing for all: and so to goe forward till he place his whole corrupted affections in Gods roome? And then what shall come of him; but, as a man giuen ouer to his owne filthy affections, shall perish into them? And because wee are all of that nature, that sibbest examples touch vs neerest, consider the difference of successe that God granted in the Mariages of the King my grand-father, and me your owne father: the reward of his incontinencie, (proceeding from his euill education) being the suddaine death at one time of two pleasant yong Princes; and a daughter onely borne to succeed to him, whom hee had neuer the hap, so much as once to see or blesse before his death: leauing a double curse behinde him to the land, both a Woman of sexe, and a new borne babe of aage to reigne ouer them.[31] And as for the blessing God hath bestowed on mee, in granting me both a greater continencie, and the fruits following there-upon, your selfe, and sib folkes to you, are (praise be to God) sufficient witnesses: which, I hope the same God of his infinite mercie, shall continue and increase, without repentance to me and my posteritie. Be not ashamed then, to keepe cleane your body, which is the Temple of the holy Spirit, notwithstanding all vaine allurements to the contrary, discerning trewly and wisely of euery vertue and vice, according to the trew qualities thereof, and not according to the vaine conceits of men.

As for your choise in Mariage, respect chiefly the three causes, wherefore Mariage was first ordeined by God; and then ioyne three accessories, so farre as they may be obtained, not derogating to the principalles.

The three causes it was ordeined for, are, for staying of lust, for procreation of children, and that man should by his Wife, get a helper like himselfe. Deferre not then to Marie till your aage: for it is ordeined for quenching the lust of your youth: Especially a King must tymouslie Marie for the weale of his people. Neither Marie yee, for any accessory cause or worldly respects, a woman vnable, either through aage, nature, or accident, for procreation of children: for in a King that were a double fault, as well against his owne weale, as against the weale of his people. Neither also Marie one of knowne euill conditions, or vicious education: for the woman is ordeined to be a helper, and not a hinderer to man.

The three accessories, which as I haue said, ought also to be respected, without derogating to the principall causes, are beautie, riches, and friendship by alliance, which are all blessings of God. For beautie increaseth your loue to your Wife, contenting you the better with her, without caring for others: and riches and great alliance, doe both make her the abler to be a helper vnto you. But if ouer great respect being had to these accessories, the principall causes bee ouerseene (which is ouer oft practised in the world) as of themselues they are a blessing being well vsed; so the abuse of them will turne them in a curse. For what can all these worldly respects auaile, when a man shall finde himselfe coupled with a diuel, to be one flesh with him and the halfe marrow in his bed? Then (though too late) shall he finde that beautie without bountie, wealth without wisdome, and great friendship without grace and honestie; are but faire shewes, and the deceitfull masques of infinite miseries.

But haue ye respect, my Sonne, to these three speciall causes in your Mariage, which flow from the first institution therof, & *cætera omnia adjicientur vobis*.[32] And therefore I would rather haue you to Marie one that were fully of your owne Religion; her ranke and other qualities being agreeable to your estate. For although that to my great regrate, the number of any Princes of power and account, professing our Religion, bee but very small; and that therefore this aduice seemes to be the more strait and difficile: yet ye haue deeply to weigh, and consider vpon these doubts, how ye and your wife can been of one flesh, and keepe vnitie betwixt you, being members of two opposite Churches: disagreement in Religion bringeth euer with it, disagreement in maners; and the dissention betwixt your Preachers and hers, wil breed and foster a dissention among your subiects, taking their example from your family; besides the perill of the euill education of your children. Neither pride you that ye wil be able to frame and make her as ye please: that deceiued *Salomon* the wisest King that euer was; the grace of Perseuerance, not being a flower that groweth in our garden.[33]

Remember also that Mariage is one of the greatest actions that a man doeth in all his time, especially in taking of his first Wife: and if hee Marie first basely beneath his ranke, he will euer be the lesse accounted of thereafter. And lastly, remember to choose your Wife as I aduised you to choose your seruants: that she be of a whole and cleane race, not subiect to the hereditary sicknesses, either of the soule or the body: For if a man wil be careful to breed horses and dogs of good kinds, how much more careful should he be, for the breed of his owne loines? So shal ye in your Mariage haue respect to your conscience, honour, and naturall weale in your successours.

When yee are Maried, keepe inuiolably your promise made to God in your Mariage; which standeth all in doing of one thing, and abstayning from another: to treat her in all things as your wife, and the halfe of your selfe; and to make your body (which then is no more yours, but properly hers) common with none other. I trust I need not to insist here to disswade you from the filthy vice of adulterie: remember onely what solemne promise yee make to God at your Mariage: and since it is onely by the force of that promise that your children succeed to you, which otherwayes they could not doe; æquitie and reason would, ye should keepe your part thereof. God is euer a seuere auenger of all periuries; and it is no oath made in iest, that giueth power to children to succeed to great kingdomes. Haue the King my grand-fathers example before your eyes, who by his adulterie, bred the wracke of his lawfull daughter and heire; in begetting that bastard, who vnnaturally rebelled, and procured the ruine of his owne Souerane and sister. And what good her posteritie hath gotten sensyne, of some of that vnlawfull generation, *Bothuell* his treacherous attempts can beare witnesse. Keepe praecisely then your promise made at Mariage, as ye would wish to be partaker of the blessing therein.

And for your behauiour to your Wife, the Scripture can best giue you counsell therein: Treat her as your owne flesh, command her as her Lord, cherish her as your helper, rule her as your pupill, and please her in all things reasonable; but teach her not to be curious in things that belong her not: Ye are the head, shee is your body; It is your office to command, and hers to obey; but yet with such a sweet harmonie, as shee should be as ready to obey, as ye to command; as willing to follow, as ye to go before; your loue being wholly knit vnto her, and all her affections louingly bent to follow your will.

And to conclude, keepe specially three rules with your Wife: first, suffer her neuer to meddle with the Politicke gouernment of the Commonweale, but holde her at the Oeconomicke rule of the house; and yet all to be subiect to your direction: keepe carefully good and chaste company about her, for women are the frailest sexe; and be neuer both angry at once, but when ye see her in passion, ye should with reason danton yours: for both when yee are setled, ye are meetest to iudge of her errours; and when she is come to her selfe, she may be best made to apprehend her offence, and reuerence your rebuke.[34]

If God send you succession, be carefull for their vertuous education: loue them as ye ought, but let them know as much of it, as the gentlenesse of their nature will deserue; contayning them euer in a reuerent loue and feare of you. And in case it please God to prouide you to all these three Kingdomes, make your eldest sonne *Isaac*, leauing him all your kingdomes; and prouide the rest with priuate possessions: Otherwayes by deuiding your kingdomes, yee shall leaue the seed of diuision and discord among your posteritie; as befell to this Ile, by the diuision and assignement therof, to the three sonnes of *Brutus*, *Locrine*, *Albanact*, and *Camber*.[35] But if God giue you not succession, defraud neuer the nearest by right, what-soeuer conceit yee haue of the person: For Kingdomes are euer at Gods disposition, and in that case we are but liue-rentars, lying no more in the Kings, nor peoples hands to dispossesse the righteous heire.

And as your company should be a paterne to the rest of the people, so should your person be a lampe and mirrour to your company: giuing light to your seruants to walke in the path of vertue, and representing vnto them such worthie qualities, as they should preasse to imitate.

NOTES

1 As quoted by D. M. Wolfe in *Milton in the Puritan Revolution* (T. Nelson, New York, 1941), p. 17.

2 *The Book named The Governor*, I.i.3–4; ed. S. E. Lehmberg (Everyman's Library, London, 1962).

3 *Componitur orbis*: The world shapes itself after its ruler's pattern, nor can edicts sway men's minds so much as their monarch's life (Claudian, *Panegyric on the fourth Consulship of the Emperor Honorius*, 299–301; Loeb *Claudian*, tr. M. Platnauer (New York and London, 1922), I).

  contraria iuxta: juxtaposed opposites are mutually illuminating.

4 The fatherhood of the king was an emotive commonplace of Royalist thinking. It suggested an indissoluble family tie between king and people, demanding the most absolute allegiance on the part of the 'sons' and the stigma of 'parricide' for the rebel. Aristotle (*Politics*, 1252B) had seen the State as an overflow of the family system, and the son as bearing an obligation to the father too massive ever to be discharged, since the debt was the gift of life itself. Hooker (*Laws of Ecclesiastical Polity*, I.viii.191) also attributed the origin of kingship to the sovereignty of the father within the household by natural law. Later, Milton and the revolutionaries fought the seductive claims of this idea by stressing the brotherhood of all men as opposed to the fatherhood of one (*The Readie and the Easie Way to Establish a Commonwealth*, 1660; *Complete Prose Works*, VII, 429), and by maintaining that the son's debt to his father is not in any case inalienable: 'We do not endure even a father who is tyrannical' (*Defence of the English People*, 1651;

Complete Prose Works, IV, 327). See Du Moulin's *Cry of the King's Blood to Heaven Against the English Parricides* (1652), printed in Milton's *Complete Prose Works*, IV, which hurls invective against 'that Foul Rascal John Milton, the Advocate of Parricide and Parricides' (1078), and defines the killing of Charles I, the father of the people, as a crime compared to which 'the crime of the Jews in killing Christ was nothing' (1049).

5 *Per fas, vel nefas*: by fair means or foul.

6 The contrast between the good king's happy life and the bad king's miserable one was again commonplace. See *The Mirror for Magistrates*, 1559, ed. L. B. Campbell (Barnes and Noble, New York, 1960), pp. 111, 160, 385, etc. See also Milton's *Tenure*, p. 181 and n. 3 below.

7 *ex malis*: from corrupt customs good laws are born.

8 *fore-falture* (forfeiture), the confiscation of property by Parliament as punishment for an offence.

9 *Quinquennium Neronis*: games instituted by Nero in A.D. 60. James refers here to Seneca's essay, *To the Emperor Nero, On Mercy*, in which he attempts to beguile the young Emperor away from his cruel pastimes by mingling advice with flattery. The occasion was provided, he says, by the Emperor, on being reluctant to sign a death-warrant, crying out, 'Would that I had not learned to write!' (*On Mercy*, II; *Moral Essays*, I, tr. J. W. Basore (Loeb, London and New York, 1928), p. 431). James' association of the Stuarts with Nero is scarcely a happy one. His advice to his son to execute the law rigorously is, further, not dissimilar in feeling to Machiavelli's suggestion in *The Prince* (XVII) that a little preliminary bloodshed acts as a preventive medicine when getting control of a people.

10 James was scared of witches, ever since he was persecuted by the witches of Berwick. See his *Daemonologie* (Edinburgh, 1597). On his accession to the English throne, he instituted the death penalty for witchcraft.

11 James here shows a touchiness about a king's ancestry which is at least as much a matter of personal hurt at the insults shown to his Roman Catholic mother, Mary Queen of Scots, as it is to do with the theory of hereditary right.

12 *the poore mans King*. James V (1512–42) used fatuously to wander round the countryside dressed as a humble farmer, the Goodman of Ballengiech. Nobody was taken in. He ruthlessly imposed law and order, suppressing the powerful barons.

13 James here makes the first of a series of not very oblique references to the succession.

14 James approves of the more conservative reformations which had taken place in countries whose rulers had themselves guided the reformation – Denmark, Sweden, the north German principalities,

England. Religious revolution, however, entailed political revolution in France, the Netherlands and Scotland, where Protestantism tended more towards Calvinism as advocating a dangerous separation between Church and State. In Scotland, John Knox, the austere and zealous disciple of Calvin, had established the Reformation *against* the Crown.

15 *Tribuni plebis*: Roman tribunes of the people, who were in origin a protecting magistracy of the plebeian class against the patricians. Their power grew until, in the latter part of the Republic, they became tyrants.

16 James has outlined the growth of the Presbyterian doctrine and polity in Scotland. His grandmother, Mary of Guise, as Queen Regent, died in 1560 at the height of the war against the Protestant 'Army of the Congregation of Christ' and the English, to the joy of Knox. The Kirk of Scotland cut all ties with Rome, and a Book of Discipline on Calvinist lines was instituted. The religious struggle continued in Scotland throughout the reign of Mary Stuart and the minority of James, who was kidnapped in 1582 with the approval of the Protestant General Assembly. Later, James slyly attempted to impose episcopacy on the Kirk.

17 *Act of Annexation*. James, with an empty treasury, had annexed to himself in 1587 all the lands and revenues still held by the episcopal benefices. However, these were, in practice, worthless.

18 *feide*: the feuding of the clans.

19 James points to the extreme cultural gap between the civilised Ancient world (embodied in the Latin language) with the courtly modern world (the French language of law), and the barbarous Scots habits and tongue.

20 See n. 12.

21 James' equation of the hereditary nobility with moral nobility stems politically from the need to reconcile his aggressive barons to himself, and intellectually from a conservative view of social hierarchy. Whereas republican thinkers saw the aristocracy either as the descendants of an earlier elected migistracy (see Milton, *Tenure*, p. 189 below) or as in line from the original gang of Norman thugs who accompanied William the Conqueror across the Channel in 1066 (e.g. Nathaniel Bacon, *Historicall Discourse of the Uniformity of the Government of England*, 1647), Royalists saw the aristocracy as the embodiment of intrinsic merit. This view flourished in the courtesy books: 'where virtue is in a gentleman it is commonly mixed with more sufferance, more affability, and mildness, than for the more part it is in a person rural or of a very base lineage' (*The Book named The Governor*, III.14); Nature makes nobleness hereditary, in men as in trees, 'whose slippes and graftes alwaies for the most part are like unto the stocke of the tree they came from' (Baldassare Castiglione, *The Book of the Courtier*, 1528, tr. T. Hoby, 1561 (Dent, London, 1959), I.32). This view of the natural

goodness of the aristocracy is dramatised by Shakespeare in the persons of Marina (*Pericles*), Guiderius and Arviragus (*Cymbeline*), Perdita (*The Winter's Tale*) and Miranda (*The Tempest*); by Spenser in *The Faerie Queene*, VI.v.1–2.

22 The irony of James' attack on the abuses occasioned by the merchant classes lies in the fact that his own reign as King of England would show an unprecedented blossoming of the vices of speculation, profiteering, monopoly, adulteration of goods and the ruining of the ancient families, partly as a result of his own feckless economic policies. Jacobean dramatic literature has capitalism as one of its main objects of satire: 'The usurer hangs the cozener' (*King Lear*, IV.vi); 'What need hath nature / Of silver dishes, or gold chamber-pots?' (Ben Jonson, *The Staple of News*, 1625; III.ii); 'honesty / Is like a stock of money laid to sleep, / Which ne'er so little broke, does never keep' (*The Revenger's Tragedy*, I.iii), etc.

23 *Momus*: a Greek personification of mockery and censure.

24 For the Puritan objection to holiday revels, see Phillip Stubbes, *Anatomie of Abuses ... in the Country of Ailgna*, 1583, ed. F. V. Furnival (London, 1877–82).

25 Horace, *Art of Poetry*, 343: He who mingles the useful with the sweet always carries his point.

26 *philautia*: self-love.

27 *flatterers*. All the authors of courtesy-books warn against flatterers. Ascham (*The Scholemaster*, I, 78) thinks they came creeping over from Italy with 'the belie of a Swyne, the hed of an Asse, the brayne of a Foxe, the wombe of a wolfe'. See also Bolingbroke in *Richard II* on 'the caterpillars of the commonwealth' (II.iii); Webster's Bosola in *The Duchess of Malfi* on flatterers (I.i); the obsequious Nobles of *The Revenger's Tragedy* (V.iii), etc.

28 *Turkes Ianisares*: military officials of the Turkish emperors.

29 *praemium or poena*: reward or punishment.

30 What Milton called 'the sage / And serious doctrine of Virginity' (*Comus*, 786–7) and Shakespeare's Isabella thought worth the life of her brother (*Measure for Measure*, III.i), James applauds for motives which gradually reveal themselves as political and historical. Scottish kings had provided plentiful bastards but few true heirs. This is why James insists on the virginity of the male as strongly as that of the female – in order that the king may not waste his efforts where they will yield no political fruit. At the same time, he also draws on the larger tradition of thinking of chastity as an embodiment of the ethic of Temperance, the preservation of perfect and inviolable balance in the self. This ethic had been exemplified by Guyon in Spenser's *Faerie Queene* (II.xii. 69), and would be celebrated in Milton's *Comus* as indicating the 'sober laws' of Nature (766). In this sense, Chastity becomes a much greater thing than a purely sexual continence: it

represents the temperate, natural and reasonable soul. Compare Plato, *Republic*, 430E; Aristotle, *Nicomachean Ethics*, I–II; VII. Later in the *Basilikon Doron*, Temperance emerges as James' most cherished virtue.

31 James V's two legitimate sons by Mary of Guise died in infancy, and he himself died leaving the baby Mary Stuart to succeed. Mary of Guise became Regent. Subsequently to the escape of Mary Queen of Scots to England, James V's bastard, the Earl of Moray, became Regent.

32 *& coetera omnia adjicientur vobis*: all these things shall be added unto you (Matthew, 6:33).

33 Solomon was a type of the man deluded by female wiles. See II Chronicles, 9.

34 James takes the orthodox view of woman's frailty, inferiority and stupidity. Compare Gelli, *Circe*, pp. 129–39 and n. 3 above. This is not calculated to endear James to the still reigning Elizabeth I.

35 For the story of the wars between the three sons of Brutus, the mythical conqueror of Britain, see Geoffrey of Monmouth's twelfth-century *History of the Kings of Britain*, and Spenser's *Faerie Queene*, II.x.13–16. Locrine, the rightful heir, triumphed. Renaissance thinkers viewed the idea of the division with horror: King Lear's division of Britain between his daughters (*Faerie Queene*, II.x.27–32; *King Lear*, I.ii) was seen as folly amounting to criminality, and an object lesson on the need for unity in the body politic. See also Thomas Norton and Thomas Sackville's *Gorboduc*, 1565, I.ii, for the same theme.

JOHN MILTON

The Tenure of Kings and Magistrates

1649

The Tenure of Kings and Magistrates reveals Milton the Puritan and humanist thinker at a painful crisis in both his and the nation's life. To read it is like watching a final rift open out between the old humanist idealisms about 'natural law', 'human dignity' and 'freedom', and a depressed political realism, which found its most absolute expression a couple of years later in the publication of Hobbes' *Leviathan* (1651). Milton felt that there had been a Golden Age; that we still retained the vestiges of our early perfection – but for Hobbes, there was only a dark age at the beginning, out of which we had scarcely yet crawled, nor could we ever reasonably expect to, motivated as the human race universally was by cringing fear and the wish to survive. There is a great sadness at the heart of Milton's tract as though he suspected that the Hobbesian view was in fact the truer one, against which the Ciceronian eloquence and the magic phrases about liberty could only falteringly strive. The tract begins with a sigh: the tone is for a moment the colloquial one of a father whose children have been a disappointment, but who has learned to understand their motives and to accept that the general condition of the human soul is not a very noble one. This tone is very close to Aristotle's early admission in his *Politics* (1276B) that 'it is of the nature of desire not to be satisfied, and most men live only for the gratification of it', and, like the *Politics*, Milton's *Tenure* is so structured as to attempt to cope with that disagreeable fact at the same time as it tries to offer a remedy.

The tract is a call to hesitant Parliamentarians to put the son of James I to death, as a punishment for his tyrannies, and in the name of freedom. It is therefore inspired by the blood and mess of the real political world during the English Revolution. But its intellectual basis is ancient and Aristotelean, so that Milton's version of the real and counterfeit freedoms is really a restatement of Aristotle's original formulation of them in the *Politics*, and his disqualification of the majority from the right to enjoy true liberty also has a source here. Politically, this is conditioned by the bitterness of watching his contemporaries waste the possibilities which had almost brought the Golden Age back into being. In an earlier tract, *Of Reformation in England* (*Complete Prose Works*, I.566) written in 1641, his opinion of the human race as a whole, down to its poorest and simplest members – 'not only the *wise*, and *learned*, but the *simple*, the *poor*, the *babes*' – was hopeful, and much more in accord with the Christian democratic spirit of the left-wing Puritans, and the optimistic convictions of humanism. However, over the years, the number of people for whom Milton felt able to entertain hope suffered continuous diminution, and 'the *poor*' and 'the *babes*' were no longer welcome in his vision. Milton's liberty, like that of his classical authorities, is based on the need for the good and intelligent man to have his freedom, in order to govern himself, with a view to yet greater perfection in himself and society: it remains, therefore, humanist in its allowance for the perfectibility of individuals. This is the 'ancient liberty' defended in his sonnet XII (1646), and regretted in *Paradise Lost*:

> Since thy original lapse, true liberty
> Is lost, which always with right reason dwells
> Twinned, and from her hath no dividual being.

(XII.83–5)

Such liberty is harsh, rigorous in its demands on the conscience, and merciless in its adherence to the ideal of a meritocracy: it was willing to splinter apart the old order without remorse and, finally,

to bear the Restoration and its own defeat with heroic fortitude
rather than any sense of failure. With the passing of the spirit which
informed the *Tenure*, the Renaissance in England was finally over.

The text printed here is from the second edition, dated 1650, and
constitutes approximately the first third of the document. Although
The Tenure of Kings and Magistrates is a complex response to the
particular events of English history at a crucial point (when the
Presbyterian party in the Commons was attempting to block the
Army in its desire to try and execute Charles I), I have provided
only fairly minimal notes on allusions to contemporary politics, out
of a desire to concentrate on Milton's political theory itself. Anyone
wishing to follow up the fascinating references to contemporary
events might consult the notes to the excellent Yale edition of
Milton's *Complete Prose Works*.

JOHN MILTON
THE TENURE OF KINGS AND MAGISTRATES

If men within themselves would be govern'd by reason, and
not generally give up thir understanding to a double tyrannie,
of Custom from without, and blind affections within, they
would discerne better, what it is to favour and uphold the
Tyrant of a Nation.[1] But being slaves within doors, no wonder
that they strive so much to have the public State conformably
govern'd to the inward vitious rule, by which they govern
themselves. For indeed none can love freedom heartilie, but
good men; the rest love not freedom, but licence; which never
hath more scope or more indulgence then under Tyrants.[2]
Hence is it that Tyrants are not oft offended, nor stand much
in doubt of bad men, as being all naturally servile; but in
whom vertue and true worth most is eminent, them they feare
in earnest, as by right thir Maisters, against them lies all thir
hatred and suspicion.[3] Consequentlie neither doe bad men
hate Tyrants, but have been alwayes readiest with the falsifi'd
names of *Loyalty*, and *Obedience*, to cover over thir base
compliances. And although somtimes for shame, and when it

comes to thir owne grievances, of purse especially, they would seeme good Patriots, and side with the better cause, yet when others for the deliverance of thir Countrie, endu'd with fortitude and Heroick vertue to feare nothing but the curse writt'n against those *That doe the worke of the Lord negligently*,[4] woulde goe on to remove, not only the calamities and thraldoms of a People, but the roots and causes whence they spring, streight these men,[5] and sure helpers at need, as if they hated only the miseries but not the mischiefs, after they have juggl'd and palter'd with the world, bandied and born armes against thir King, devested him, disannointed him, nay curs'd him all over in thir Pulpits and thir Pamphlets, to the ingaging of sincere and real men, beyond what is possible or honest to retreat from, not only turne revolters from those principles, which only could at first move them, but lay the staine of disloyaltie, and worse, on those proceedings, which are the necessary consequences of thir own former actions; nor dislik'd by themselves, were they manag'd to the intire advantages of thir own Faction; not considering the while that he toward whom they boasted thir new fidelitie, counted them accessory; and by those Statutes and Lawes which they so impotently brandish against others, would have doom'd them to a Traytors death, for what they have don alreadie. 'Tis true, that most men are apt anough to civill Wars and commotions as a noveltie, and for a flash hot and active; but through sloth or inconstancie, and weakness of spirit either fainting, ere thir own pretences, though never so just, be half attain'd, or through an inbred falshood and wickednes, betray oft times to destruction with themselves, men of noblest temper joyn'd with them for causes, whereof they in their rash undertakings were not capable.

If God and a good cause give them Victory,[6] the prosecution whereof for the most part, inevitably draws after it the alteration of Lawes, change of Goverment, downfal of Princes with thir families; then comes the task to those Worthies which are the soule of that enterprize, to be swett and labour'd out amidst the throng and noises of Vulgar and irrational men. Some contesting for privileges, customs, forms, and that old entanglement of Iniquity, thir gibrish Lawes, though the badge of thir ancient slavery. Others who have beene fiercest against thir Prince, under the notion of a Tyrant, and no mean incendiaries of the Warr against him, when God out of his providence and high disposal hath deliver'd him into the hand of thir brethren, on a suddain and in a new garbe of Allegiance, which thir doings have long since cancell'd; they plead for him, pity him, extoll him, protest against those that talk of bringing him to the tryal of Justice, which is the Sword of God, superior to all mortal things, in whose hand soever by apparent signes his testified will is to put it.[7] But certainly if we consider who and what they are, on a suddain grown so pitifull, wee may conclude, thir pitty can be no true, and Christian commiseration, but either levitie and shallowness of minde, or else a carnal admiring of that worldly pomp and greatness, from whence they see him fall'n; or rather lastly a dissembl'd and seditious pity, fain'd of industry to begett new discord. As for mercy, if it be to a Tyrant, under which Name they themselves have cited him so oft in the hearing of God, of Angels, and the holy Church assembl'd, and there charg'd him with the spilling of more innocent blood by farr, then ever *Nero*[8] did, undoubtedly the mercy they pretend, is the mercy of wicked men; and their mercies, wee read are cruelties; hazarding the welfare of a whole Nation, to have sav'd one, whom so oft they have tearm'd *Agag*;[9] and vilifying the blood of many *Jonathans*,[10] that have sav'd *Israel*; insisting with much niceness on the unnecessariest clause of thir Covnant, wherein the feare of change, and the absurd contradiction of a flattering hostilitie had hamperd them, but not scrupling to give away for complements, to an implacable revenge, the heads of many thousand Christians more.

Another sort there is, who comming in the cours of these affaires, to have thir share in great actions, above the form of

Lawe or Custom, at least to give thir voice and approbation, begin to swerve, and almost shiver at the Majesty and grandeur of som noble deed, as if they were newly enter'd into a great sin; disputing presidents, forms, and circumstances, when the Common-wealth nigh perishes for want of deeds in substance, don with just and faithfull expedition. To these I wish better instruction, and vertue equal to thir calling; the former of which, that is to say Instruction, I shall indeavour, as my dutie is, to bestow on them; and exhort them not to startle from the just and pious resolution of adhering with all thir assistance to the present Parlament & Army, in the glorious way wherin Justice and Victory hath set them; the only warrants[11] through all ages, next under immediat Revelation, to exercise supream power, in those proceedings which hitherto appeare equal to what hath been don in any age or Nation heretofore, justly or magnanimouslie. Nor let them be discourag'd or deterr'd by any new Apostate Scarcrowes, who under show of giving counsel, send out their barking monitories and *memento's*, empty of ought else but the spleene of a frustrated Faction.[12] For how can that pretended counsel bee either sound or faithfull, when they that give it, see not for madness and vexation of thir ends lost, that those Statutes and Scriptures which both falsly and scandalously, they wrest against thir Friends and Associates, would by sentence of the common adversarie, fall first and heaviest upon thir own heads. Neither let milde and tender dispositions be foolishly softn'd from thir duty and perseverance, with the unmaskuline Rhetorick of any puling Priest or Chaplain,[13] sent as a friendly Letter of advice, for fashion sake in privat, and forthwith publisht by the Sender himself, that wee may know how much of friend there was in it, to cast an odious envie upon them, to whom it was pretended to be sent in charitie. Nor let any man be deluded by either the ignorance or the notorious hypocrisie and self-repugnance of our dancing Divines, who have the conscience and the boldness, to come with Scripture in thir mouthes, gloss'd and fitted for thir turnes with a double contradictory sense, transforming the sacred verity of God, to an Idol with two Faces, looking at once two several ways; and with the same quotations to charge others, which in the same case they made serve to justifie themselves. For while the hope to bee made Classic and Provincial Lords led them on, while pluralities[14] greas'd them thick and deep, to the shame and scandal of Religion, more then all the Sects and Heresies they exclaim against, then to fight against the Kings person, and no less a Party of his Lords and Commons, or to put force upon both the Houses, was good, was lawfull, was no resisting of Superior powers; they onely were powers not to be resisted, who countenanc'd the good, and punish't the evil. But now that thir censorious domineering is not suffer'd to be universal, truth and conscience to be freed, Tithes[15] and Pluralities to be no more, though competent allowance provided, and the warme experience of large gifts, and they so good at taking them; yet now to exclude & seize upon impeach't Members, to bring Deliquents without exemption to a faire Tribunal by the common National Law against murder, is now to be no less then *Corah*, *Dathan*, and *Abiram*.[16] He who but erewhile in the Pulpits was a cursed Tyrant, and enemie to God and Saints, lad'n with all the innocent blood spilt in three Kingdoms, and so to be fought against, is now, though nothing penitent or alter'd from his first principles, a lawfull Magistrate, a Sovran Lord, the Lords anointed,[17] not to be touch'd, though by themselves imprison'd. As if this onely were obedience, to preserve the meere useless bulke of his person, and that onely in prison, not in the field, and to disobey his commands, deny him his dignity and office, evry where to resist his power but where they thinke it onely surviving in thir own faction.

But who in particular is a Tyrant cannot be determin'd in a general discours, otherwise then by supposition; his particular charge, and the sufficient proof of it must determin that: which I leave to Magistrates, at least to the uprighter sort of them, and of the people, though in number less by many, in whom faction least hath prevaild above the Law of nature and right reason, to judge as they find cause.[18] But this I dare owne as part of my faith, that if such a one there be, by whose Commission, whole massachers have been committed on his faithfull Subjects, his Provinces offerd to pawn or alienation, as the hire of those whom he had sollicited to come in and destroy whole Citties and Countries; be he King, or Tyrant, or Emperour, the Sword of Justice is above him; in whose hand soever is found sufficient power to avenge the effusion, and so great a deluge of innocent blood. For if all human power to execute, not accidentally but intendedly, the wrath of God upon evil doers without exception, be of God; then that power, whether ordinary, or if that faile, extraordinary so executing that intent of God, is lawfull, and not to be resisted. But to unfold more at large this whole Question, though with all expedient brevity, I shall here set downe from first beginning, the original of Kings; how and wherfore exalted to that dignitie above thir Brethren; and from thence shall prove, that turning to Tyranny they may bee as lawfully depos'd and punish'd, as they were at first elected: This I shall doe by autorities and reasons, not learnt in corners among Scisms and Heresies, as our doubling Divines are ready to calumniat, but fetch't out of the midst of choicest and most authentic learning, and no prohibited Authors, nor many Heathen,[19] but Mosaical, Christian, Orthodoxal, and which must needs be more convincing to our Adversaries, Presbyterial.

No man who knows ought, can be so stupid to deny that all men naturally were borne free,[20] being the image and resemblance of God himself, and were by privilege above all the creatures, born to command and not to obey: and that they liv'd so. Till from the root of *Adams* transgression, falling among themselves to doe wrong and violence, and foreseeing that such courses must needs tend to the destruction of them all, they agreed by common league to bind each other from mutual injury, and joyntly to defend

186

themselves against any that gave disturbance or opposition to such agreement. Hence came Citties, Townes and Commonwealths. And because no faith in all was found sufficiently binding, they saw it needfull to ordaine som authoritie, that might restrain by force and punishment what was violated against peace and common right. This autoritie and power of self-defence and preservation being originally and naturally in every one of them, and unitedly in them all, for ease, for order, and least each man should be his own partial Judge, they communicated and deriv'd either to one, whom for the eminence of his wisdom and integritie they chose above the rest, or to more then one whom they thought of equal deserving: the first was call'd a King; the other Magistrates. Not to be thir Lords and Maisters (though afterward those names in som places were giv'n voluntarily to such as had been Authors of inestimable good to the people) but, to be thir Deputies and Commissioners,[21] to execute, by vertue of thir intrusted power, that justice which else every man by the bond of nature and of Cov'nant must have executed for himself, and for one another. And to him that shall consider well why among free Persons, one man by civil right should beare autority and jurisdiction over another, no other end or reason can be imaginable. These for a while govern'd well, and with much equity decided all things at thir own arbitrement: till the temptation of such a power left absolute in thir hands, perverted them at length to injustice and partialitie. Then did they who now by tryal had found the danger and inconveniences of committing arbitrary power to any, invent Laws either fram'd, or consented to by all, that should confine and limit the autority of whom they chose to govern them: that so man, of whose failing they had proof, might no more rule over them, but law and reason abstracted as much as might be from personal errors and frailties.[22] When this would not serve, but that the Law was either not executed, or misapply'd they were constrain'd from that time, the onely remedy left them, to put conditions and take Oaths from all Kings and Magistrates at thir first instalment to doe impartial justice by Law: who upon those termes and no other, receav'd Allegeance from the people, that is to say, bond or Covnant to obey them in execution of those Lawes which they the people had themselves made, or assented to. And this ofttimes with express warning, that if the King or Magistrate prov'd unfaithfull to his trust, the people would be disingag'd. They added also Counselors and Parlaments, nor to be onely at his beck, but with him or without him, at set times, or at all times, when any danger threatn'd to have care of the public safety. Therefore saith *Claudius Sesell* a French Statesman, *The Parlament was set as a bridle to the King*;[23] which I instance rather, because that Monarchy is granted by all to be a farr more absolute then ours. That this and the rest of what hath hitherto been spok'n is most true, might be copiously made appeare throughout all Stories Heathen and Christian; ev'n of those Nations where Kings and Emperours have sought meanes to abolish all ancient memory of the Peoples right by thir encroachments and usurpations. But I spare long insertions, appealing to the German, French, Italian, Arragonian, English, and not least the Scottish Histories: not forgetting this onely by the way, that *William* the Norman though a Conqueror, and not unsworn at his Coronation, was compell'd the second time to take oath at *S. Albanes*, ere the people would be brought to yeild obedience.[24]

It being thus manifest that the power of Kings and Magistrates is nothing else, but what is only derivative, transferr'd and committed to them in trust from the People, to the Common good of them all, in whom the power yet remaines fundamentally, and cannot be tak'n from them, without a violation of thir natural birthright, and seeing that from hence *Aristotle* and the best of Political writers have defin'd a King, him who governs to the good and profit of his People, and not for his own ends,[25] it follows from necessary causes, that the Titles of Sov'ran Lord, natural Lord, and the like, are either arrogancies, or flatteries, not admitted by

Emperours and Kings of best note, and dislikt by the Church both of Jews, *Isai.* 26.13. and ancient Christians, as appears by *Tertullian*[26] and others. Although generally the people of Asia, and with them the Jews also, especially since the time they chose a King against the advice and counsel of God, are noted by wise Authors much inclinable to slavery.

Secondly, that to say, as is usual, the King hath as good right to his Crown and dignitie, as any man to his inheritance, is to make the Subject no better then the Kings slave, his chattell, or his possession that may be bought and sould. And doubtless if hereditary title were sufficiently inquir'd, the best foundation of it would be found either but in courtesie or convenience. But suppose[27] it to be of right hereditarie, what can be more just and legal, if a subject for certain crimes be to forfet by Law from himself, and posterity, all his inheritance to the King, then that a King for crimes proportional, should forfet all his title and inheritance to the people: unless the people must be thought created all for him, he not for them, and they all in one body inferior to him single, which were a kinde of treason against the dignitie of mankind to affirm.

Thirdly it follows, that to say Kings are accountable to none but God, is the overturning of all Law and government. For if they may refuse to give account, then all cov'nants made with them at Coronation; all Oathes are in vaine, and meer mockeries, all Lawes which they sweare to keep, made to no purpose; for if the King feare not God, as how many of them doe not? we hold then our lives and estates, by the tenure of his meer grace and mercy, as from a God, not a mortal Magistrate, a position that none but Court Parasites or men besotted would maintain. And no Christian Prince, not drunk with high mind, and prouder then those Pagan *Caesars* that deifi'd[28] themselves, would arrogate so unreasonably above human condition, or derogate so basely from a whole Nation of men his Brethren, as if for him only subsisting, and to serve his glory; valuing them in comparison of his owne brute will and pleasure, no more then so many beasts, or vermin under his Feet, not to be reasoned with, but to be trod on; among whom there might be found so many thousand Men for wisdom, vertue, nobleness of mind, and all other respects, but the fortune of his dignity, farr above him. Yet some would perswade us, that this absurd opinion was King *Davids*; because in the 51 *Psalm* he cries out to God, *Against thee onely have I sinn'd*;[29] as if *David* had imagin'd that to murder *Uriah* and adulterate his Wife, had bin no sinn against his Neighbour, when as that Law of *Moses* was to the King expresly, *Deut*. 17. not to think so highly of himself above his Brethren. David therfore by those words could mean no other, then either that the depth of his guiltiness was known to God onely, or to so few as had not the will or power to question him, or that the sin against God was greater beyond compare then against *Uriah*. What ever his meaning were, any wise man will see that the pathetical words of a Psalme can be no certaine decision to a poynt that hath abundantly more certain rules to go by. How much more rationally spake the Heathen King *Demophoon* in a Tragedy of *Euripides* then these Interpreters would put upon King *David*, *I rule not my people by Tyranny, as if they were Barbarians, but am my self liable, if I doe unjustly, to suffer justly*.[30] Not unlike was the speech of *Trajan* the worthy Emperor, to one whom he made General of his Praetorian Forces. Take this drawn sword, saith he, to use for me, if I reigne well, if not, to use against me. Thus *Dion* relates. And not *Trajan* onely, but *Theodosius* the yonger, a Christian Emperor and one of the best, causd it to be enacted as a rule undenyable and fit to be acknowledg'd by all Kings and Emperors, that a Prince is bound to the Laws; that on the autority of Law the autority of a Prince depends, and to the Laws ought submitt.[31] Which Edict of his remains yet in the *Code* of *Justinian 1. 1. tit*. 24. as a sacred constitution to all the succeeding Emperors. How then can any King in Europe maintain and write himself accountable to none but God, when Emperors in thir own imperial Statutes have writt'n and decreed themselves accountable to Law. And indeed where such account is not fear'd, he that bids a man reigne over him above Law, may bid as well a savage Beast.[32]

It follows lastly, that since the King or Magistrate holds his autoritie of the people, both originaly and naturally for their good in the first place, and not his own, then may the people as oft as they shall judge it for the best, either choose him or reject him, retaine him or depose him though no Tyrant, meerly by the liberty and right of free born Men, to be govern'd as seems to them best. This, though it cannot but stand with plain reason, shall be made good also by Scripture. *Deut.* 17.14. *When thou art come into the Land which the Lord thy God giveth thee, and shalt say I will set a King over mee, like as all the Nations about mee.* These words confirme us that the right of choosing, yea of changing thir own Goverment is by the grant of God himself in the People.[33]

NOTES

1 The Platonic and Aristotelean wish that the individual and the State might be governed by sovereign 'reason' and the recognition of the close relationship between (1) the tyranny over the self exerted by habit and whim, and (2) that of the tyrant over the nation, is characteristic of Milton's classicism applied to political theory. (See Plato, *Republic*, 434D–445B; Aristotle, *Politics*, 1287A).

2 Aristotle, defining democrats, says that they reason falsely that liberty and equality consist in 'the doing what a man likes' (*Politics*, 1310A). See also Plato, *Republic*, 558C, who identifies democratic liberty with 'an agreeable form of anarchy'. It is worth noting that Royalist theorists were in perfect agreement with Milton on this definition of freedom, though not in application or consequences. See for instance the formulation by the author of *Eikon Basilike* (1648) (supposed to be Charles I himself just prior to his execution; probably Dr Gauden) which accuses men of being seduced into a desire for liberty misunderstood as meaning 'to do what every man liketh best', whereas 'divinest liberty' is 'to will what every man should' (ed. C. M. Phillimore (Oxford and London, 1879) V, 126). This is in itself not particularly Aristotelean, just a commonplace: it is in the total context of Milton's ideal meritocracy that he shows the depth of the effect made on him by

the *Politics*. But, see also the anti-Aristotelean Hobbes' *Leviathan* (1651), on 'the specious name of Libertie' (I.21.267).

3 *by right thir Maisters*. The despot's natural fear of the power inherent in goodness and now forfeit by him (which had been dramatised for instance in Shakespeare's *Macbeth* in Macbeth's fear of the dead Duncan and Banquo) is a well-known psychological phenomenon attributed here to more than the mere remnant of conscience in the usurper. Plato had described the tyrant's dreadful loneliness, 'always in need' (*Republic*, 578A); conversely, Aristotle called the virtuous person 'like a god among men' (*Politics*, 1284A). This natural divinity and God-ordained status in the natural hierarchy accounts for the feeling in Milton's tyrant of having challenged a right which, having the supernatural sanction, will have to be atoned for at some time.

4 *Jeremiah*, 48:10 (Milton's own note).

5 'These men' are the Presbyterian group in Parliament, who had fought against the king but were against his execution. Milton attempts to show that to renege would be to compromise their entire part in the war against tyranny, whose logical and moral consequence can only be tyrannicide.

6 *Victory*. As a Puritan, Milton naturally took a strictly providential view of historical events, which could all be interpreted by the devout observer as signs of whether the Almighty was pleased or otherwise with one's activities. (See in this connection *Paradise Lost*, XI and XII, with Michael's horrific account of the punishment and rewards dispensed to man since Adam's fall.) But Milton was not so stupid as to imagine even at the moment of writing *The Tenure*, with the Roundhead Army the indisputable victor of the Civil War, that victory was *always* synonymous with God's sanctioning of the winning cause. Milton only stressed the theory which logically ends in a 'Might is Right' ethic at this point because of the importance to him of establishing the new regime on a firm basis. In the slightly later *Eikonoklastes* he was more hesitant in emphasising this notion ('Most men are too apt, and commonly the worst of men, so to interpret and expound the judgements of God, and all other events of providence or chance, as makes most to the justifying of their own cause, though never so evill ...' (*Complete Prose Works*, III, 428–9)); and after the failure of the Commonwealth in 1660, his theory of God's providential arrangements of earthly events shifts to cope with the humiliation of the English Republicans. Now, according to *Paradise Lost*, XII, 95–6, 'tyranny must be, / Though to the tyrant thereby no excuse'.

7 *the Sword of God*. This symbol towers over Milton's regicide tracts: it is meant to stand against the sensations of charity and pity which the Royalists were busily and successfully arousing for the lonely king in his imprisonment and death. See also *Eikonoklastes*, 346; 391; 432 – 'Shall the Justice of God give place, and serv to glorifie the mercies of a

man?' The mere man he thus vilifies is bound to appear, to ordinary seventeenth-century people as to us, emotionally preferable to the embattled God of Justice of Milton's tracts, a figure based rather on Old Testament and Revelation doctrines than on the kind Christ of the Gospels (cf. St Peter's speech in *Lycidas*, where the Sword of Justice at the Last Judgement 'Stands ready to smite once, and smite no more' (131)). In the regicide literature, Milton tries to assimilate the trial of Charles I to the image of the Last Judgement, so that his execution shall appear as a kind of necessary damnation.

8   *Nero*: a type of the merciless tyrant for the Renaissance, whose fascinating perversions, mingling sensuality with blood-lust, were noted for their indiscriminateness. See Suetonius, *The Twelve Caesars*, with which bizarre account Milton would have been familiar; also Milton's *A Defence of the English People* (*Complete Prose Works*, IV, 335); Fulke Greville's poem, *A Treatise of Monarchy*, II, 74, which also uses the tradition of Nero as the tyrant who sooner or later engineers his own downfall.

9   *Agag*: I Samuel, 15:33. Samuel cut this Amalekite king to pieces 'before the Lord in Gilgal'.

10   *Jonathans*: I Samuel, 14: 1–45. The reference here is to the determination of Jonathan's father, Saul, to despatch him after he had dealt with the Philistines.

11   *the only warrants*: see n. 6. It is characteristic of the Puritan revolutionary mind that, while it is often as scrupulous as any conservative in burrowing through history, civil law, and Scripture for precedents (and, failing these, inventing them) it can also dispense with them as the undesirable paraphernalia of man's fallen past, and a positive burden to those seeking renewal. This Puritan contempt for mere tradition may be seen satirised in, for instance, Jonsonian comedy (Ananias: 'I hate Traditions; / I do not trust them —', *The Alchemist*, III.ii.106–7). Milton, on the other hand, was humanist enough to love them but to forsake them when new action seemed called for.

12   *Apostate Scarcrowes*, the Presbyterian counter-revolutionaries, especially the influential William Prynne and his *A Briefe Memento* (1649).

13   Probably Charles I's chaplain, Dr Gauden, and his *Religious and Loyal Protestation*, is meant. The whole thrust of this passage, with its disgust for 'our dancing divines' is in the true old Protestant and humanist spirit of acrimony against a lying, worldly clergy. See Introduction, p. 15 above; also Luther's pamphlet of 1520, *On the Babylonian Captivity of the Church*, with its hatred of 'the wicked tyrannies of these brazen men, who with their farcical and childish fancies mock and overthrow the liberty and glory of the Christian religion' (tr. A. T. W. Steinhäuser in *Luther's Works*, XXXVI, ed. A. R. Wentz and H. T. Lehmann (Muhlenberg Press, Philadelphia, 1959),

p. 116); Erasmus, *Praise of Folly*, Penguin edn., 164–72. Milton's objection to priests lording it over ordinary people belongs to both traditions, but also includes a very personal animus and relish. Compare his *Of Reformation in England*, for the most spectacular display of violence against a priesthood variously abused in terms of imagery of disease, animals, excrement and the less dignified portions of the human anatomy, e.g. *Complete Prose Works*, I.537, 583–5, etc.

14 *Pluralities*: the remunerative holding of several clerical offices in the Church, none of which could possibly be fulfilled adequately.

15 *Tithes*: much resented obligatory taxes to enrich the established Church.

16 *Corah, Dathan, Abiram* mutinied against God's chosen leaders, Moses and Aaron (Numbers, 16) and so became emblematic figures signifying sedition, and treason against both God and man.

17 *the Lords anointed.* Upon this phrase rests the entire structure of Christian justification of monarchy by 'Divine Right'. David in I Samuel 24:10 and 26:11 had twice forborne to punish King Saul on the grounds that he was God's anointed: Royalist writers extended this to mean that a king's person was inviolate since it had been sanctified by God, and the sovereign's sole responsibility was therefore to God. This was official Tudor theory, echoed in Shakespearean history plays. Shakespeare, while recognising the fallibility and humanity of kings, dramatises official doctrine in asserting, even with the feeble, arbitrary and self-deceiving Richard II: 'Not all the water in the rough rude sea / Can wash the balm from an anointed king' (III.ii). Milton treats such notions as pure jargon, given the modern (fallen) context, and the anointing ceremony in the Coronation service as mere show, not meaningful symbolism.

18 *the Law of nature and right reason.* If, as everybody knew, God had created Nature, then Nature must be good: goodness always reveals itself in order: therefore, to find what is good, you have only to discover the order (laws) inherent in what is natural. The way to do this is to exercise the natural faculty of 'right reason' (roughly equivalent to a kind of divine common sense) which everybody has by virtue of being human. By using it, one is enabled to read correctly God's handwriting in the Book of Nature. These are roughly the common assumptions which Milton is calling upon here. See for the moral law, deducible by right reason, Cicero, *The Republic*, III.xxii.33; Hooker, *Laws of Ecclesiastical Polity*, I.3. A poetical statement of the limited but real virtue of the 'natural man' is to be found in the allegory of the salvage nation in Spenser's *Faerie Queene*, I.vi. A challenge to the whole idea is found in Hobbes' *Leviathan*, I.13–15. Compare James I, *Basilikon Doron*, pp. 163–4 and n. 21 above.

19 *nor many Heathen*: a lingering regret at having to sacrifice the pleasure of dwelling on the Ancients, as being pagans and therefore

questionable ethically as propaganda, here. This renunciation marks the split between Milton's humanist dedication to learning and his Puritan ethical rigour, which is felt throughout his career.

20 This assertion of blended Christian and classical mythology (Eden and the Golden Age) is traditional, though most authors (e.g. Fulke Greville, *A Treatise of Monarchy*, I; Spenser, *Faerie Queene*, II.vii.16) do not assume that the Golden Age was a republic. Interestingly, Milton is here contradicting his greatest political authority, Aristotle, who attacks the idea of the Golden Age, saying that the first human beings 'may be supposed to have been no better than ordinary or even foolish people among ourselves . . .' (*Politics*, 1269A). Aristotle regards monarchy as the most 'natural' form of government, whereas Milton (and Hobbes) see it as the result of an artificial social contract entered into rationally by the whole people in order to cope with the anarchy resulting from the Fall.

21 *Deputies and Commissioners*. The radical difference between the Miltonic and the Hobbesian view of social contract becomes evident here. In *Leviathan* (I.xxiv.106) the 'mutual transferring of right' by the whole people to the care of one man, the king, is, once made, inalienable; for Milton, the covenant was provisional upon the people's continuing will to be ruled by one man, and the monarch remained permanently accountable to his people, who remained free. See also Aristotle, *Politics*, 1287A, on the limitations of kingly power.

22 Milton has here envisaged a kind of second Fall, this time a political one on the part of the ruler, located at some deliberately vague era in human history, during which the Aristotelean maxim of the necessary coincidence of the interest of the sovereign with that of the people ceased to be applied (*Politics*, 1279A). This part of Milton's argument is faithful to Aristotle.

23 Claude de Seissel, *La Grande Monarchie de France* (1519). See also for a fine anonymous and also French statement of the principles Milton is elucidating, the Huguenot *Defence of Liberty Against Tyrants*.

24 Milton is referring to the traditional forcing by the Anglo-Saxon people of the Norman Conqueror, William, to take a second oath after he had broken the first, promising the English their ancient laws and liberties.

25 See n. 22.

26 Tertullian, in *On the Crown* (A.D. 201), inveighs against the showy glories of earthly kingship.

27 A notable instance of Milton's slippery ability to argue contradictory cases simultaneously, which constituted almost a requirement or a decorum of itself in seventeenth-century political writing, where the quantity of arguments seems to have been almost as important as their quality. The first argument (that people cannot be property) is a

humanist one, relying on a respect for human dignity which proudly refuses to be qualified. The second is a crafty application of the erroneous metaphor to confound its protagonist and prove the first argument. It should be noticed that all Milton's arguments at this point are tending in a democratic direction, though they never actually get there as analogous logic does in the Leveller tracts, for Milton uses the term 'the people' with a quite cynical neglect for its expected meaning. He really only means by it the Independents and the Army, but as his aim is to attract the maximum sympathy he allows it to *appear* to represent the normal 'all men'.

28 *pagan Caesars.* See Suetonius' entertaining account of the Roman emperors creating themselves gods in *The Twelve Caesars.* Augustus was deified only after his death but, after this, deification became official policy; the ludicrous and offensive Caligula, for example, 'established a shrine to himself as God, with priests, the costliest possible victims, and a life-sized golden image, which was dressed every day in clothes identical to those that he happened to be wearing'. Milton's comparison was not as far-fetched as it appears: witness James I's solemn interpretation of his role as that of a 'little GOD to sit on his Throne' (*Basilikon Doron*, I; *Political Works of James I*, ed. C. H. McIlwain (Cambridge, 1918), pp. 54–5).

29 Psalm 51:4. The story of the killing of Uriah was universally explained by Royalist apologists as signifying that the monarch is exempt from human responsibilities, however disgustingly he behaves. The private and public functions of the sovereign were often distinguished; for example Milton's enemy, Salmasius, in *The Defence of the Kingdom*, 1649 (as translated by K. A. McEuen in *Complete Prose Works of John Milton*, IV, 1014) says: 'The king though an adulterer and homicide can rule well'.

30 Milton is on dubious ground here in (1) seeming to prefer the pagan king Demophoon in Euripides' *Heraclidae* (418–21) to the authority of Scripture, and (2) regarding the psalms as holding the authority only of a kind of poetry.

31 See George Buchanan, *Rerum Scoticarum Historia*, XX, for the stories of Trajan and Theodosius.

32 *a savage Beast.* Milton here touches on the classic theme both of classical and Christian philosophy – the paradox of the degradation of the man who tries to climb up the ladder of being at the expense of the rest into a sub-human condition. There was scarcely a respected author of the Ancient world who had not defined the tyrant as the most bestial of men. In Plato's *Republic*, X, the despots were the incurably wicked who could never escape from the closed, bellowing mouth of the Underworld; see also Aristotle, *Politics*, 1287A; and especially Cicero, *On Duties*, III.vi.32, describing tyrants as 'fierce and savage monsters in human form'. See Pico's *Oration*, pp. 63–4. The figure of Satan in

Paradise Lost is itself a representation of the animal status of the aspirant to divinity (e.g. X, 504–77). Finally, see Sir Walter Raleigh's *Preface to The History of the World* (1614): 'the greatest and most glorious kings have gnawn the grass of the earth with beasts, for pride and ambition towards God' (*Selected Prose and Poetry*, ed. A. M. C. Latham (London, 1965), p. 183).

33   There follow a detailed account of Biblical authorities, rather tedious to the modern taste; a justification of tyrannicide; and plentiful examples of Protestant justifications of revolution, aimed at edifying or refuting unwilling Presbyterians.

Select bibliography

PRIMARY SOURCES

ARISTOTLE. *The Works of Aristotle*. Ed. J. A. Smith and W. D. Ross. 12 vols. Oxford: 1908–55.

ASCHAM, Roger. *The Scholemaster: or plaine and perfite way of teachyng children the Latin tong*, 1570. Ed. J. E. B. Mayor. London, 1863.

AUGUSTINE. *Confessions*. Tr. R. S. Pine-Coffin. Penguin Classics: Harmondsworth, 1961.

BACON, Sir Francis. *The Advancement of Learning*. Ed. G. W. Kitchin. Everyman's Library. Dent: London and New York, 1915.

BROWNE, Sir Thomas. *Religio Medici*. Ed. J.-J. Denonain. Cambridge University Press: Cambridge, 1955.

BRUNO, Giordano. *Opere italiene*. Ed. G. Gentile and V. Spampanato. 3 vols. Bari, Gius. Laterza & Figli, 1925–7.

——*The Expulsion of the Triumphant Beast*, 1584. Tr. A. D. Imerti. Rutgers University Press: New Brunswick, 1964.

BRUTUS, Junius. *A Defence of Liberty Against Tyrants*: a translation of the *Vindiciae Contra Tyrannos*. Reprint of 1689 edn. Introd. H. Laski. G. Bell and Sons: London, 1924.

CHARLES I (King). *Eikon Basilike. The Portraiture of His Majesty King Charles I*, 1649. Ed. C. M. Phillimore. Oxford, 1879.

CICERO. *De Natura Deorum*. Tr. H. Rackham. Loeb Classical Library. Heinemann: London, 1951.

——*De Officiis*. Tr. W. Miller. Loeb Classical Library. Heinemann: London, 1913.

——*De Re Publica, De Legibus*. Tr. C. W. Keyes. Loeb Classical Library. Heinemann: London, 1928.

COPERNICUS, Nicolas. *Complete Works*. Sponsored by the Polish Academy of Science. Macmillan: London, 1972.

DANIEL, Samuel. *The Civile Wares*, 1609. Ed. L. Michel. Yale University Press: New Haven, Conn., 1958.

DAVIES, Sir John. *Orchestra or a Poem of Dancing*, 1596. Ed. E. M. W. Tillyard. Chatto and Windus: London, 1947.

DIONYSIUS, the Areopagite. *'On the Divine Names' and 'The Mystical Theology'*. Tr. C. E. Rolt. Macmillan: London and New York, 1966.

DONNE, John. *The Divine Poems*. Ed. H. Gardner. Clarendon Press: Oxford, 1952.

——*Selected Prose*. Chosen by E. Simpson. Ed. H. Gardner and T. Healy. Clarendon Press: Oxford, 1967.

DRUMMOND, William (of Hawthornden). *Poems and Prose*. Ed. R. H. MacDonald. Scottish Academic Press: Edinburgh, 1976.

ELIZABETH I (Queen). *The Public Speaking of Queen Elizabeth*. Ed. G. P. Rice. Columbia University Press: New York, 1951.

ELYOT, Sir Thomas. *The Book named The Governor*, 1531. Ed. S. E. Lehmberg. Everyman's Library. Dent: London, 1962.

ERASMUS, Desiderius. *Twenty Select Colloquies of Erasmus*. Tr. R. L'Estrange, 1680. Abbey Classics Reprint: London, 1923.

——*The Praise of Folly*. Tr. B. Radice. Penguin Classics: Harmondsworth, 1971.

——*De Pueris Instituendis*, 1529. *Opera Omnia*, I. North-Holland Publishing Company: Amsterdam, 1969–74.

FICINO, Marsilio. *Opera Omnia*. 2 vols. Monumenta Politica et Philosophica Rariora. Series I. Bottega d'Erasmo: Turin, 1962.

——*Marsilio Ficino: The Philebus Commentary. A Critical Edition and Translation* by M. J. B. Allen. University of California Press: Berkeley, Los Angeles and London, 1975.

GALILEI, Galileo. *Discoveries and Opinions*. Tr. S. Drake. Doubleday and Co.: New York, 1957.

GREVILLE, Fulke (Lord Brooke). *The Remains, being Poems of Monarchy and Religion*. Ed. G. A. Wilkes. Oxford University Press: London, 1965.

HERMES TRISMEGISTUS. *Hermetica*. Ed. W. Scott. 4 vols. Clarendon Press: Oxford, 1924–36.

HERBERT, George. *The English Poems of George Herbert*. Ed. C. A. Patrides. Everyman's University Library. Dent: London, 1974.

HOBBES, Thomas. *Leviathan*, 1651. Ed. C. B. Macpherson. Pelican Books: Harmondsworth, 1968.

HOOKER, Richard. *Of the Laws of Ecclesiastical Polity*, I–V. 2 vols. Everyman's Library. Dent: London and New York, 1907.

JAMES I (King). *The Workes of the Most High and Mighty Prince, James, By the Grace of God Kinge of Great Brittaine France & Ireland Defendor of ye Faith* &c. London, 1616.

JONSON, Ben. *Works*. Ed. C. H. Herford and P. Simpson. Clarendon Press: Oxford, 1937.

LUTHER, Martin. *Luther's Works*. General ed. J. Pelikan and H. T. Lehmann. 54 vols. Concordia Publishing Ho. & Muhlenberg Press: Philadelphia, Pn., 1955–76.

MACHIAVELLI, Niccolò. *The Prince*. Tr. G. Bull. Penguin Classics: Harmondsworth, 1961.

MARLOWE, Christopher. *The Complete Works*. Ed. F. Bowers. 2 vols. Cambridge University Press: Cambridge, 1973.

MILTON, John. *The Complete Poems*. Ed. J. Carey and A. Fowler.

Longmans' Annotated English Poets: London and Harlow, 1968.

——*Complete Prose Works of John Milton*. General ed. A. S. P. Woodhouse. 7 out of 8 vols. Yale University Press: New Haven, Conn. and London, 1953– .

MIRANDOLA, Pico della. *Opera Omnia*. Basel, 1572. Facsimile, introd. E. Garin. 2 vols. Monumenta Politica Philosophica Humanista Rariora. Series I. Bottega d'Erasmo: Turin, 1971.

MIRROR FOR MAGISTRATES, The. Ed. L. B. Campbell. Barnes and Noble: New York, 1960.

MORE, Sir Thomas. *Utopia*. Tr. P. Turner. Penguin Classics: Harmondsworth, 1965.

——*Responsio ad Lutherum*, 1523. *The Complete Works of St. Thomas More*, V. Ed. J. M. Headley, 2 pt. Yale University Press: New Haven, Conn., 1969.

OVID. *The Metamorphoses of Ovid*. Tr. M. M. Innes. Penguin Classics: Harmondsworth, 1971.

——*Tristia, Ex Ponto*. Tr. A. L. Wheeler. Loeb Classical Library. Heinemann: London, 1924.

PETRARCH, Francesco. *On His Own Ignorance And That Of Many Others*. Tr. H Nachod in *The Renaissance Philosophy of Man*. Ed. E. Cassirer et al. University of Chicago Press: Chicago, Ill., 1948.

PLATO. *Gorgias*. Tr. W. Hamilton. Penguin Classics: Harmondsworth, 1960.

——*Parmenides*. Tr. A. E. Taylor. Clarendon Press: Oxford, 1934.

——*Protagoras and Meno*. Tr. W. K. C. Guthrie. Penguin Classics: Harmondsworth, 1956.

——*Phaedrus and Letters VII and VIII*. Tr. W. Hamilton. Penguin Classics: Harmondsworth, 1973.

——*Republic*. Tr. F. M. Cornford. Oxford University Press: London, 1945.

——*Symposium*. Tr. W. Hamilton. Penguin Classics: Harmondsworth, 1951.

——*Timaeus and Critias*. Tr. H. D. P. Lee. Penguin Classics: Harmondsworth, 1971.

PLOTINUS. *Enneads*. Tr. A. H. Armstrong. 3 vols. Loeb Classical Library. Heinemann: London, 1966–7.

POMPONAZZI, Pietro. *On the Immortality of the Soul*. Tr. W. H. Hay etc. in E. Cassirer, *The Renaissance Philosophy of Man* (see PETRARCH, Francesco).

RALEIGH, Sir Walter. *Selected Prose and Poetry*. Ed. A. M. C. Latham. University of London, Athlone Press: London, 1965.

SENECA. *Moral Essays*. Tr. J. W. Basore. 3 vols. Loeb Classical Library. Heinemann: London, 1928–35.

SHAKESPEARE, William. *The Complete Works*. Ed. W. J. Craig. Oxford University Press: London, 1943.

SPENSER, Edmund. *Poetical Works.* Ed. J. C. Smith and E. de Selincourt. Oxford University Press, London, 1912.

SUETONIUS. *The Twelve Caesars.* Tr. R. Graves. Penguin Books: Harmondsworth, 1957.

VAUGHAN, Henry. *The Complete Poems.* Ed. A. Rudrum. Penguin English Poets: Harmondsworth, 1976.

WILSON, Thomas. *Arte of Rhetorique,* 1553. 1560 edn. Ed. G. H. Mair. Tudor and Stuart Library: Oxford, 1909.

SECONDARY SOURCES AND FURTHER READING

BARKAN, L. *Nature's Work of Art. The Human Body as Image of the World.* Yale University Press: New Haven, Conn., and London, 1975.

BLUNT, Sir A. *Artistic Theory in Italy, 1450–1600,* 1940. Clarendon Press: Oxford, 1962.

BUSH, D. *The Renaissance and English Humanism,* 1939. University of Toronto Press: Toronto and London, 1962.

CHADWICK, O. *The Reformation.* The Pelican History of the Church, Vol. 3. Penguin Books: Harmondsworth, 1972.

CROMBIE, A. C. *Augustine to Galileo. Science in the Later Middle Ages and Early Modern Times. XIII–XVII Centuries.* 2 vols. Mercury Books: London, 1961.

DIJKSTERHUIS, E. J. *The Mechanization of the World Picture,* 1950. Tr. C. Dikshoorn. Oxford University Press: London, Oxford and New York, 1969.

HAY, D. (ed.) *The Age of the Renaissance.* McGraw-Hill Book Co.: New York and London, 1967.

HILL, C. *Puritanism and Revolution,* 1958. Panther Books: London, 1969.

——Society and Puritanism in Pre-Revolutionary England. Panther Books: London, 1969.

JAYNE, S. Introduction to translation of Marsilio Ficino's *Commentary on Plato's Symposium.* University of Missouri Press: Columbia, 1944.

KLIBANSKY, R; PANOFSKY, E; SAXL, F. *Saturn and Melancholy.* Nelson: London, 1964.

KRISTELLER, P. O. *Renaissance Thought. The Classic, Scholastic, and Humanist Strains.* Harper Torchbooks: New York, 1961.

——Renaissance Thought, II. Papers on Humanism and the Arts. Harper Torchbooks: New York, Evanston, Ill., and London, 1965.

LEVIN, H., *The Myth of the Golden Age in the Renaissance,* 1969. Oxford University Press: New York, 1972.

LEWIS, C. S. *The Discarded Image. An Introduction to Medieval and Renaissance Literature.* Cambridge University Press: Cambridge, 1964.

LOVEJOY, A. O. *The Great Chain of Being. A Study of the History of an Idea*, 1936. Harper Torchbooks: New York, 1960.

PANOFSKY, E. *Studies in Iconology. Humanistic Themes in the Art of the Renaissance*, 1939. Harper Torchbooks: New York and Evanston, Ill., 1962.

——*Renaissance and Renascences in Western Art*, 1965. Paladin Books: London, 1970.

PATTISON, B. *Music and Poetry of the English Renaissance*, 1948. 2nd edn. Methuen: London, 1970.

PENROSE, B. *Travel and Discovery in the Renaissance, 1420–1620*. Harvard University Press: Cambridge, Mass., 1952.

SEZNEC, J. *The Survival of the Pagan Gods. The Mythological Tradition and its Place in Renaissance Humanism and Art*, 1940. Tr. B. F. Sessions. Harper Torchbooks: New York, 1961.

WALKER, D. P. *The Ancient Theology. Studies in Christian Platonism from the Fifteenth to the Eighteenth Century*. Duckworth: London, 1972.

WENDEL, F. *Calvin. The Origins and Development of his Religious Thought*. Tr. P. Mairet. Fontana Library. Collins: London, 1965.

WILLEY, B. *The English Moralists*, 1964. Methuen University Paperbacks: London, 1965.

WIND, E. *Pagan Mysteries in the Renaissance*, 1958. Revised edn. Peregrine Books: Harmondsworth, 1967.

YATES, F. A. *The Art of Memory*. Routledge and Kegan Paul: London, 1966.

——*Theatre of the World*. Routledge and Kegan Paul: London, 1969.

——*Astraea. The Imperial Theme in the Sixteenth Century*. Routledge and Kegan Paul: London and Boston, 1975.